Government vs. Environment

Edited by Donald R. Leal
and Roger E. Meiners

ROWMAN & LITTLEFIELD PUBLISHERS, INC.
Lanham • *Boulder* • *New York* • *Oxford*

ROWMAN & LITTLEFIELD PUBLISHERS, INC.

Published in the United States of America
by Rowman & Littlefield Publishers, Inc.
4720 Boston Way, Lanham, Maryland 20706
www.rowmanlittlefield.com

12 Hid's Copse Road
Cumnor Hill, Oxford OX2 9JJ, England

Copyright © 2002 by PERC (Political Economy Research Center).

British Library Cataloguing in Publication Information Available

Library of Congress Cataloging-in-Publication Data

Government versus environment / edited by Donald R. Leal and Roger E. Meiners
    p. cm. – (Political economy forum)
  Includes bibliographical references and index.
  ISBN 0-7425-2180-X (alk. paper) – ISBN 0-7425-2181-8 (pbk : alk. paper)
    1. Environmental policy–United States. 2. Environmental protection–United States. I.
Leal, Donald. II. Meiners, Roger E. III. Series.

GE180 G69 2002
363.7'056'0973–dc21

2001057858

Printed in the United States of America

♾️™ The paper used in this publication meets the minimum requirements of
American National Standard for Information Sciences—Permanence of Paper
for Printed Library Materials, ANSI/NISO Z39.48-1992.

Contents

Tables and Figures

Prologue

Donald R. Leal and Roger E. Meiners

For the most part, economists and other analysts have characterized environmental problems as "externalities" that emerge from the market and require corrective government action. Rather than identifying the cause as institutional failures, such as ill-defined or poorly enforced property rights or perverse political incentives that cause or exacerbate environmental problems, markets alone are often blamed. Politicians have been more than willing to respond either with more regulation or more federal control of resources, but they have been far less willing to look at government's track record in the environment.

In the political economy literature there has been too little attention paid to the impacts of "government failures" on the environment. One exception is a 1981 PERC volume titled *Bureaucracy vs. Environment*, edited by John Baden and Richard L. Stroup. That volume focused on the environmental and economic costs of bureaucratic management of timber, range, water, and energy resources by federal resource agencies in the United States. In their introduction, Baden and Stroup identify the problem as one of authority without accountability. Bureaucratic resource managers, unlike their counterparts in the private sector, have no bottom line demarcating revenues and costs, and rational ignorance on the part of voters allows public-sector managers to avoid the same scrutiny that many private-sector managers face from stockholders. As a result, bureaucratic managers may ignore the economic and environmental costs of their actions and instead focus on improving their own well-being through such things as increased budgets and larger staffs.

This book expands that scope and helps dispel the myth that the government is the savior of the environment. The reader will find in case after case, across time and levels of government, major stories that can be classified as the government acting against the interests of the environment. But in the two decades since publication of the earlier volume, our understanding of why certain problems persist in the public sector has improved.

Government employees often have incentives that cause them to be involved in environmentally destructive results, but it is not correct to blame the employees for most problems that emerge from a host of public programs. Government employees work for agencies that are funded and given their marching orders by their bosses: politicians in Congress and the administration. Political bosses are more than happy to have complaints directed at bureaucrats, who must take the heat for carrying out policies under the supervision of those bosses. As employees know, if the boss does not wish to take the blame for a bad decision, employees may be forced to bear the blame—and better do so or face the wrath of the boss.

In all the episodes reported in these original case studies we see environmental problems—often correctly identified by environmental organizations—that tend to be misunderstood as the fault of bureaucrats who are attacked for not understanding the problems or for being uncaring. But government employees tend to know quite well some of the shortcomings of the policies they have an obligation to enforce. Most are dedicated to the mission of their agency and want to do an effective job, but are often hamstrung by political decision makers.

These decision makers know very well what they are doing. They are well informed and highly motivated to get and keep their office. They have been successful by doing what they do, so instincts tell them to keep doing what has worked. Whereas that is understandable, it should give great pause to those who have real concerns about environmental problems to seek further solutions via the political process.

In chapter 1, we provide an analytical framework for examining cases of government versus the environment, arguing that special interests working with political entrepreneurs are the reasons behind the creation of policies that lead to perverse results for the environment. There are many parallels between military and environmental policy making so that dedicated environmentalists should not be sanguine with "government solutions" for real problems. In chapter 2, Roger E. Meiners and Andrew P. Morriss examine the perverse political incentives behind overuse of DDT in the United States that led to its being banned. Our policy against DDT is being exported around the world, resulting in a return of malaria in the Third World that has produced a tragedy little discussed.

It is easy to blame big factory trawlers for overfishing in the oceans, as some environmental groups do. But in chapter 3, Donald R. Leal argues that the lack of property rights and ineffective regulations lead to overfishing as well as wasteful investments by fishers. This problem is exacerbated by government policies that subsidized the expansion of fishing in already depleted fisheries.

Government has had a hand in creating problems with too much water or too little water, as well as too much beachside development. In chapter 4, David E. Gerard tackles federal flood policies and argues that these policies create perverse incentives to overbuild in natural floodplain areas of the United States. The problem is exacerbated because when flooding occurs, the federal government is there to disguise the true risks of living in floodplains with such things as federal flood insurance. Clay J. Landry's historical look at the Everglades in chapter 5 is timely. Landry describes the federal and state policies that led to the draining and pollution of natural water flows in the Everglades. Now Congress is embarking on a very expensive course to fix the problems. Later, in chapter 10, Landry examines how the U.S. Army Corps of Engineers promotes beachside development while engaging in dubious environmental practices.

Entrusting government to care for wildlife and other natural resources was the hallmark of Teddy Roosevelt's progressives. Unfortunately the government's track record in managing natural resources has been far less than sterling. In chapter 6, J. Bishop Grewell examines government's persecution of various wildlife species over the past century. For some species, such as coyotes and prairie dogs, persecution continues. In chapter 7, Holly Lippke Fretwell examines the federal government's record of husbanding our national forests. Fiscal performance is abysmal. The Forest Service continues to lose the federal treasury millions annually while managing forest assets worth billions. Moreover, decades of fire suppression have created a tinderbox in environmentally unhealthy forests. The "government solution" is to set aside more lands from active forest management. In chapter 9, Grewell examines how the government promotes crowding and resource degradation in the crown jewels of the national park system by subsidizing recreationists at taxpayer expense.

In chapter 8, Matthew Brown examines the policies of the World Bank. Focusing on dam building in India, Brown finds the same perverse incentives that lead to environmental destruction and government waste at the national level at work at the international level. This does not bode well for global environmentalists putting faith in international government instruments such as the Kyoto Protocol.

In concluding, we would like to thank those who have supported the completion of this book, including the research behind the chapters. William Dunn provided inspiration as well as financial support for the bulk of the research and book publication. In addition, the Jaquelin Hume Foundation provided additional financial support of the research end of the project. We owe a special thanks to Dianna Rienhart, Durrae Johanek, and Sheila Spain for taking the material from our word processors to the final form suitable for publishing. We also thank Monica Lane Guenther for keeping us in line when it came to deadlines and budgets.

1

Greener Pastures? The Defective Attraction of Federal Environmental Policy

Donald R. Leal and Roger E. Meiners

Environmental policy at the national level has been championed by revered and reviled politicians alike. At the turn of the century, Theodore Roosevelt used the power of his bully pulpit to usher in the progressive movement in which federal government control of land and water resources, and scientific management were preferred over private ownership and markets (Nelson 1995). In the 1970s, Pres. Richard Nixon played a major role in the shift of responsibility for air and water pollution control and endangered species from the states and private entities to the federal government. Nixon created the Environmental Protection Agency (EPA) by executive order, and his administration spearheaded passage of the Clean Air Act, the Clean Water Act, and the Endangered Species Act.

Environmentalists are quick to praise Roosevelt as one of the great leaders of the early conservation movement for his role in creating the federal estate. They are not so quick to point to Nixon's accomplishments in extending the powers of the federal government in the name of environmental protection. It must be more than a little curious to environmentalists that Richard Nixon, who is widely portrayed as nearly evil incarnate, should approach the same stature as Theodore Roosevelt on the environmental front. Did he suffer from a bipolar disorder? Good on the environment, bad on other things? No, he was the same man, acting as politician and president, in all areas. He did what he perceived to be in his political self-interest with respect to environmental matters, Vietnam, and other issues of the day.

Environmental policy, when personal or sentimental, produces results that cannot be explained on the basis of rational evidence. If we subject environmental politics to the analytical frameworks of economic theory and public choice theory, and sometimes simply common sense, clear-eyed reality,

1

the puzzle of wasteful, destructive government policies toward the environment begins to unfold. In this chapter we review some findings about environmental policies that recent research has helped us to understand, and provide some background and analytical tools relevant to understanding the purpose of this book and the research it presents—that there is little reason to think of environmental politics as more benevolent than special interest politics in any other policy area.

ENVIRONMENTAL HOBGOBLINS: THE POLITICS OF ALARMISM

Accurate information is costly to obtain and absorb, so we are all ignorant of many things and we all think certain things are true that are not. Ignorance and misinformation do not matter much in most instances, unless they are the basis for public policy. For example, some ignorant and misinformed people in the 1950s believed that there were Communists hiding under their beds, or at least infiltrating the military and the highest levels of government. Sen. Joseph McCarthy exploited ignorance and helped to provide misinformation to mislead the public. He may have believed everything he said was true, but he learned it was in his political interest to say what he did. It garnered an unknown junior senator significant political power (for a while) and public attention, but it also led to policies that cost the nation dear sums and produced gross violations of the rights of some Americans.

Alarmism has left its mark on federal environmental policy as well. During the nineteenth century, few questioned the wisdom of privatization that put more than 1 billion acres of public land into private ownership. But at the start of the twentieth century a new political theme had emerged that led to the creation of a growing federal estate that today accounts for one-third of the nation's land and a public domain totaling more than 40 percent (Fretwell 2000). Part of the dramatic transformation in public land policy had surfaced because Theodore Roosevelt and other politically powerful conservationists at the time were convinced that private ownership was promoting the rape and ruin of timberlands and, ultimately, would produce a timber shortage. Roosevelt warned that "if the present rate of forest destruction is allowed to continue, with nothing to offset it, a timber famine in the future is inevitable" (Roosevelt 1905, 9). The idea that only federal management could promote good resource stewardship came to dominate land policy. Roosevelt's rhetoric aside, there is little evidence of a timber famine in the United States at the time (Johnson and Libecap 1980, 376–79). Moreover, data from private preservation efforts at the turn of the last century indicate that markets did account for nonmarket, noncommodity values (Anderson and Leal 1997, 21–42).

Since Rachel Carson's *Silent Spring* was published four decades ago, a new theme has dominated environmental policy—the environment versus economic growth theme. Polling data indicate that a majority of Americans think that the government and business are "not worried enough" about the environment, and that we should sacrifice economic growth to protect the environment (Gallup Organization 2000). Such a concern is not surprising given the persistent "doomsday" theme issued by influential political leaders and government agencies. In 1980, the Carter administration issued *Global 2000*, a massive report predicting environmental and economic collapse worldwide by 2000. "If present trends continue," the report claimed, "the world in 2000 will be more crowded, more polluted, less stable ecologically, and more vulnerable to disruption than the world we live in now" (U.S. Council on Environmental Quality and Department of State 1980, 1). Beating the same drum, Al Gore's book, *Earth in the Balance*, claims that unless political leaders are given additional powers to regulate critical aspects of economic activity (e.g., energy, housing, and transportation), the earth will wither and die from global warming and other environmental problems allegedly spurred on by economic growth (Gore 1992). These writings should be classified as producing issues for scientific debate, but instead they serve as powerful tools for ambitious politicians and the administrators who work for them.

Let us review some of today's fears under this theme and explore the facts. For example, in 2000, EPA administrator Carol Browner, announcing new water-control regulations that give the EPA significantly expanded control powers, asserted that this is needed because "more than 90 percent of all Americans live within ten miles of a polluted body of water" (Browner 2000). At the same time, the EPA announced that although "significant progress in improving our air quality" has occurred, the threat from air pollution remains grave because it causes "birth defects, brain and nerve damage," and other health horrors (EPA 2000). What else should the public think but that more federal controls are justified if our water and air pose such serious threats? Of course there are serious environmental issues, but they have little relationship to these scare tactics.

Contrary to such statements by the EPA that the air is dangerous to breathe, the quality of air in the United States (and the rest of the developed world) has been rising for the better part of a century. Indeed, most key measures of air quality were improving long before the federal government took control of air quality in the early 1970s. The data on air pollutants show that the rate of improvement has not increased since the federal takeover in the early 1970s (Goklany 1999).

Federal control of air quality does not appear to have been a major contributor to already improving air quality, but it has produced some incredibly costly federal policy in air pollution control. A classic case is the amendment of the Clean Air Act in 1977. In an effort to reduce sulfur dioxide emissions, Congress required "best available technology" standards for new coal-fired generating plants. Instead of setting specific emissions standards and allowing plants to meet them by using cleaner, low-sulfur western coal, the new standards forced owners of generation facilities to install stack-gas scrubbers, which cost more to buy and operate than the more environmentally friendly alternative (Ackerman and Hassler 1981).

Sulfur dioxide reductions could have been accomplished at a much lower cost by burning low-sulfur coal, but a "clean air–dirty coal" coalition made up of eastern coal producers and environmentalists lobbied for the technology-based standards. Robert Crandall described the motivation for the coalition:

> Eastern coal producers feared that sensible environmental policy would lead electric utilities to buy increasing amounts of low-sulphur Western coal. Since much of the Appalachian and Midwestern coal is high in sulphur content, it would eventually lose market share to the cleaner Western coal. Requiring stack-gas scrubbers for all new plants, regardless of the sulphur content of the coal burned, would eliminate the incentive for Eastern and Midwestern utilities to import low-sulphur Western coal. Environmentalists, for some reason, have had a burning desire to require utilities to install scrubbers, even though alternative technologies may be substantially less costly in most cases. (Crandall 1981, 678)

Because the EPA could not monitor scrubber efficiency, the result was high new-plant compliance costs and a reduced rate of replacement of older, dirty utility boilers. Moreover, the clean air–dirty coal policy distributed wealth from electricity consumers who paid higher rates, to eastern coal miners, who feared losing their jobs.

Love Canal, the granddaddy of toxic waste sites, was used to spur political support for another bit of costly federal environmental legislation—the Comprehensive Environmental Response and Liability Act, better known as Superfund. When Superfund legislation was passed in 1980 (along with a tax hike), it was supposed to expedite the cleansing of the nation's hazardous waste sites such as Love Canal. It was projected to cost several billion dollars and to be paid for mainly by those whose pollution poses serious risks. But it has been "the shortcut that failed" (Stroup 1996, 116). A General Accounting Office (GAO) study reports that between 1980 and June 30, 1999, only 176 sites out of 1,231 had been cleaned up and removed from the National Priority List (GAO 1999a, 5).

Moreover, Superfund was supposed to reduce the health risk, especially from cancer from hazardous waste sites, but the EPA does not necessarily focus on the most risky sites. A study by the AEI-Brookings Joint Center for Regulatory Studies shows that sites chosen by regulators for cleanup were largely a function of "risk politics" and "risk-protection biases" (Viscusi and Hamilton 1999, 1025). Another GAO study reports that the average length of time for cleanup of the Superfund sites finalized by 1996 was 10.6 years, several times longer than cleanup under state laws (GAO 1999b). Superfund has drained billions of dollars and may, in net, produce negative outcomes for the environment, but it remains with us today.

Ironically, Love Canal did not pose the dangers that were alleged at the time. It was asserted that Love Canal caused a "high incidence of miscarriages, birth defects, liver cancer, [and] seizure-inducing childhood diseases in a residential subdivision" built over the canal (Valenta and Valenta 1995, 195). Ironically none of these assertions were uncovered in the lawsuit filed by Love Canal residents against the chemical company that dumped toxic wastes in the ditch in question. A federal judge ruled that the company that owned Love Canal should have been more forthcoming about toxic wastes but found evidence of only "relatively minor noticeable injury" to residents, not deadly diseases (*U.S. v. Hooker* 1994, 1039).

Deforestation is another area plagued by misinformation. In parts of the world, such as the Amazon and Indonesia, there is certainly more timber harvesting than is economically rational, but this is because policies by national governments encourage land clearing not because the market demands wasteful destruction. For example, in Malaysia, the Philippines, and the Brazilian Amazon the only way to establish private ownership of land in the government's eyes is to clear the land of trees. Dennis J. Mahar, an economic adviser for the World Bank, identified some other policies that encouraged deforestation in Brazil, including providing settlers who clear land for agriculture with subsidies and carrying out massive road-building programs with financial loans from the World Bank (Mahar 1989, 11, 22). In Indonesia forest loss took place because the national government gave companies generous tax benefits to encourage logging (Repetto 1988, 13, 16). Even so, as was the case in the United States at the beginning of the twentieth century, there is no evidence that we are running out of forests worldwide and need government to stockpile trees (Stott 1999). Tree inventories in America today are not being depleted. In fact, the percent of land in the United States that is covered with trees today is not much different than it was before the followers of Columbus arrived in the New World (Sedjo 1991).

Water quality is another area in which confusion reigns. Contaminated water in undeveloped nations is a major health problem. Only 50 to 60 percent of the people in developing nations have access to safe water and sanitation compared with 90-plus in market-oriented, developed nations (Goklany 2000, 156). With the exception of a few isolated cases reported over the past decade, water is so clean in the United States that it poses trivial health problems (Goklany 1996). To say that 90 percent of the U.S. population lives near polluted water creates the impression that we face the kinds of dangers known mostly by peoples living in the Third World.

It is true that water, besides being important for human health, supports aquatic life and provides other environmental functions, so we have good reason to be concerned about water quality. Unfortunately, the EPA cannot give us a good inventory of water quality in the United States. After three decades of federal command and control of water quality, the federal government still cannot tell us much about the majority of America's waters. It has examined only 23 percent of the rivers, 42 percent of the lakes, and 32 percent of the estuaries in the country (Freshwater Forum 2000, 9–10). Despite lacking such basic knowledge, the EPA has engaged in a massive power grab by issuing new regulations that assert control over everything that remotely affects water (EPA 2000).

In sum, any area of the environment that has been entrusted to the government tends to produce, at best, a mixed bag in terms of environmental quality if we look at the record of physical evidence and ignore the economic consequences and impact on individual freedom. Assertions that economic progress must be sacrificed for the environment to be protected are completely at odds with the record. In the United States and around the world, economic wealth means a cleaner environment—richer people can afford to pay for it (Goklany 2000). Further, the common belief that the government is the best protector of the environment is also at odds with the record. At worst, as happens on public lands in the United States and across entire nations in some instances, the environment is far worse than if it were in the hands of ordinary citizens. At best, governmental control of environmental resources may entrench the status quo, as if prevailing beliefs of the day were the wisdom of the ages.

Most stories of environmental horrors have, at root, government action or government policies. The persistent belief that if the "right people" get in control of government they will solve the problems of the world is like hoping that Santa Claus or Harry Potter will magically fix things. The world is more mundane than that; there are no magical solutions. We must focus on incentives that lead humans to protect the environment. We next consider some essential points about incentives created by economic conditions and legal rules. But first we address a shortcoming of traditional analysis of economics applied to environmental issues.

LIMITATIONS OF ECONOMIC ANALYSIS OF THE ENVIRONMENT

Standard economic analysis about environmental problems traditionally goes as follows: When there is pollution we call it an externality, which is a broad class of costs we bear that other people impose on us without permission (pollution is the most common example). That is, if there is no control on who can use a river, it may turn into an open sewer, and many will suffer from the loss of the river and the threat the pollution may pose. To solve the problem, a tax should be imposed on pollution dumped into the river until the amount dumped is low enough that it causes no harm to others.

Ponder the theoretical and real-world issues related to this. First, where do you draw the line on what is an externality? If many people think the color of your shirt is hideous and offensive, should a tax be imposed on that color of shirt so that you, and other people of bad taste, will quit wearing it? Economic theory provides no instruction on where to draw the line on externalities. In such cases, we must appeal to all-knowing legislators, via their expert economists, for proper taxes to solve the problems.

As simplistic as this sounds, it is a cornerstone of standard economic analysis about environmental problems. Second, is there any reason to think that legislators and regulators will really make the best decisions to solve real problems? Traditional rules of property law have long had solutions to many of these problems (see later). The evidence is that real-world politicians, who know a lot about taxes and are happy to have revenues under their control and have heard economists preach about the benefits of taxing pollution for many years, show no interest in this theoretically sound way to address real pollution problems. We do not have pollution taxes. Real politicians prefer political solutions that maximize the benefits they receive. Traditional economic analysis of externalities is an interesting abstract proposition, but is devoid of practicality and predicts nothing. Politicians prefer to maintain active control of things, including the environment, as a Nobel laureate in economics pointed out to the profession years ago (Buchanan and Tullock 1975). Getting the environment out of the hands of the political decision makers and into the hands of responsible owners is critical to getting the incentives right. That is the essence of the studies reported in this volume and in other works that have expanded economics beyond the traditional narrow view.

WHO OWNS THE ENVIRONMENT?

Allowing people to have the legal ability to protect environmental amenities and have legal responsibilities for damages they cause to the environment is central to protecting and improving the environment (Hill and Meiners 1998; Meiners and Morriss 2000). In the legal and economic literature this is referred to as property rights. When individuals, or a group of individuals acting voluntarily through an organization, own assets, including environmental assets, they protect the asset from abuse by others, work to enhance the asset, and can be held liable for abuse of the asset that imposes costs on others. Environmental assets controlled collectively through the government do not have property rights that lend themselves to effective economic, biological, or aesthetic use of the asset. Just as privately owned houses tend to be the best kept, and government-run housing projects the worst kept, the same is true of the environment, but the issues can be more complex because of the fact that many environmental amenities are shared by so many.

The tragedy of the commons has been widely understood for some time. If no one owns, or has responsibility for protection of, an environmental asset, it will be overutilized and degraded. If everyone has the "right" to kill bison, salmon, or whales because no one owns them, they will be slaughtered because people can profit from exploiting the "free" resource. If everyone owns an asset, no one can protect it from others, so it will be ruined. Fortunately, self-interest tends to rear its beautiful head and people will lay claim to valuable assets. If such claims are effective, and someone is recognized as the legal owner of an asset, they have incentives to protect and nourish it for future benefits.

The world is filled with examples of ingenious solutions that individuals and communities have devised, under traditional property rules, to solve environmental problems (Anderson 1998; Anderson and Leal 1997). In a legal system that respects property rights, most property is owned by individuals, or groups of individuals, who have the rights to exclude others from the use of their property, to protect it and enhance it for the future, and to transfer ownership, in part or in whole, to others of their choosing. They also have a legal obligation to others not to abuse their property in such a way that it inflicts legally recognized injury on their neighbors. This is the essence of the common law of this nation and others with an English legal base, and is similar to the rules of property in most traditional code-law nations. Under traditional legal rules, property owners have strong rights over the use of their property so long as they do not inflict injury on others. This has been essential to the unprecedented growth of widespread wealth in the modern world. In societies in which property is not strongly protected, in the past or today, less wealth is generated and the environment is not protected as much (Norton 1998).

Traditional common law rules, which have been pushed aside in part by the modern command and control of the environment by the national government, served as the bedrock of legal protection for the environment (Meiners and Yandle 1999). People, empowered by law to protect their property and their health from invasion by others, provide strong protection for the world in which they live. Thousands upon thousands of cases over the years show how the courts, protecting property rights, punish those who damage the environment of others. Everyone has a far stronger interest in their property and their environment than can well-meaning politicians or regulators, who live far away and must respond to a host of special interests.

Ordinary people, bringing small lawsuits against polluters, do not get the national attention that dramatic enviro-political announcements covered by the media do, but they can be more effective. For instance, in England, for decades people who like to fish (anglers) have chipped in to cover the cost of suits against polluters who injure fish. The record of this small, quiet effort has been astonishingly successful (Bate 2000), as are many other efforts by people who come together to support a common environmental interest. The environment is protected by millions of property owners vigilant to protect their rights. This attracts little attention because just as when competition works and prices fall and product quality rises, we just accept that as the state of the world. It is generally only when major media events happen that we ponder certain problems and possible solutions.

PUBLIC CHOICE AND THE ENVIRONMENT

The theory of public choice helps us understand why inefficient and environmentally destructive policies for the environment emerge from the political process. The process is no different whether the problem is highway construction, military weapons, or an environmental issue (Buchanan, Tullock, and Tollison 1980). In most instances, well-organized and highly motivated interest groups are immediately involved in policy construction. On the other side is the large mass of unorganized, rationally ignorant citizens who know little about what transpires.

We can think of the political arena as a large market in which favors are bought and sold. Politicians act as brokers in the process. Special interest groups that have the most at stake—either to gain from a new policy or to prevent a loss from being imposed by a change in policy—will "outbid" the unorganized larger mass that bears or will bear much of the cost of the policy (McChesney 1997). The benefits of obtaining the policy are great to those who press for the policy. The cost of the policy is small to each citizen who contributes taxes or incurs costs through the regulatory process. The citizens remain rationally ignorant about most such policies because the benefit of becoming informed about the policies is small and the cost of obtaining accurate information is high. When applied to the area of pollution control, public choice explains why federal environmental regulations focus on inputs and command-and-control rules, not environmental outcomes.

It's Just Politics

When Dwight Eisenhower left the presidency, he warned of the "military-industrial complex." He knew that military bureaucrats would overstate how much money they needed to provide an adequate defense, and they would be joined in this by support from the makers of weaponry, who would ply Congress with promises of rich weapons contracts for their states. Politicians would favor a strong national defense so long as weapons contracts brought money home and if they got to build military bases in their states, bringing further goodies home.

We now know that scare stories about the USSR led to what can be criticized as overspending on the military for several decades. Military leaders had strong incentives to overstate the Russian threat. Larger budgets are preferred by heads of bureaucracies, such as the generals, and, that aside, they would prefer overinvestment so that in the event of a conflict they could not be blamed for underestimating the enemy. Citizens are in a difficult position. Unlike private sellers, who compete with each other to sell us their goods or services, thereby allowing us the benefit of multiple sources of information, governments are often monopoly providers. Not only is the U.S. military the only supplier of national defense to U.S. citizens, Congress also has the power to force us to buy certain levels of military provisions. Even if we are sure we have all the military we need, we cannot refuse the order of Congress to pay for even more. Popular support for the military, which was especially strong in the 1950s, allowed politicians to exploit the sentiment by having us buy unneeded, overpriced weapons systems and supplies (Finegan 2000). We are still stuck with numerous military bases that have no strategic value and may impair national defense because resources are drained into ineffective military weapons and bases dictated by Congress.

The key elements of environmental politics is no different than it is for the military. Political interests dominate the structure of statutes that affect the environment, just as politics determines most legislative outcomes (Anderson 2000). Special interests seek to enhance their well-being by imposing restrictions on the property of others. The property becomes less valuable because of the restrictions, meanwhile, special interests obtain the benefits without compensating the property owners. Or under the guise of environmentalism, special interests frequently avoid bearing costs that are imposed by new rules by being grandfathered in so the new rules impose higher costs on their would-be competitors. The special interest nature of the statutory process cannot be avoided, so those who seek to have a politically controlled environment via the regulatory process have a massive hurdle to overcome—get legislators to ignore the interests that are a part of the legislative process. We think this is a utopian dream, but it poses a serious challenge that advocates of government control of the environment must address.

Those who believe there can be a world in which legislators are immune to special interest pressures have the so-far impossible chore of showing that central planners can make effective use of and provide quality protection for property. One of the great lessons of the past century was that socialist planning of resources produces ecological and economic disasters. Central planning could not produce something as simple as wheat efficiently. The notion that Washington planners, under the watchful eyes of Congress and the administration, can design and execute scientifically correct environmental protection, better than people can provide for themselves as they interact with each other freely, or through the state and local legislative process, is farfetched. Further, unless one believes that the ruling elite deserves to exploit the masses, there is nothing fair, efficient, or environmentally pure about the results of central control.

CONCLUSION

Under national command and control of the environment for three decades, the central government has assumed astonishing power over environmental assets—land, water, air—so that not much of our world is left out of current or potential control of politicians and the bureaucrats who work under their control. We have become much like serfs in medieval England (Morriss and Meiners 2000). We are allowed to occupy land and pay taxes on it at the whim of our lords. They can impose so many restrictions on our land that it can become more sensible to abandon it than to try to retain possession. This entails a huge loss of personal freedom, the destruction of economic value, and, of course, dreadful consequences for the environment.

The rest of the chapters in this book are slices of the many ways in which governments have adopted policies that are environmentally destructive and economically wasteful. These are not aberrations that can be set aside as unfortunate mistakes in an otherwise successful move to central planning of the environment. Politics is pervasive. The more control Congress, the administration, and bureaus in Washington have over the environment, the worse the impact can be expected to be over time.

REFERENCES

Ackerman, Bruce, and William T. Hassler. 1981. *Clean Coal, Dirty Air, or How the Clean Air Act Became a Multibillion-Dollar Bail-out for High Sulphur Coal Producers and What Should Be Done about It.* New Haven, CT: Yale University Press.

Anderson, Terry L. 1998. Viewing Wildlife through Coase Colored Glasses. In *Who Owns the Environment?* ed. Peter J. Hill and Roger E. Meiners. Lanham, MD: Rowman & Littlefield, 259–82.

Anderson, Terry L., and Donald R. Leal. 1997. *Enviro-Capitalists: Doing Good While Doing Well.* Lanham, MD: Rowman & Littlefield.

Anderson, Terry L., ed. 2000. *Political Environmentalism: Going behind the Green Curtain.* Stanford, CA: Hoover Institution Press.

Bate, Roger. 2000. Protecting English and Welsh Rivers: The Role of the Anglers' Conservation Association. In *The Common Law and the Environment: Rethinking the Statutory Basis for Modern Environmental Law,* ed. Roger E. Meiners and Andrew P. Morriss. Lanham, MD: Rowman & Littlefield, 86–108.

Browner, Carol M. 2000. TMDL Announcement. Remarks of Administrator Carol M. Browner, U.S. Environmental Protection Agency, July 11. Online: www.epa.gov/epahome/speeches_0713.htm (cited: May 15, 2001).

Buchanan, James M., and Gordon Tullock. 1975. Polluters' Profits and Political Response: Direct Control Versus Taxes. *American Economic Review* 65 (March): 139–47.

Buchanan, James M., Gordon Tullock, and Robert D. Tollison, eds. 1980. *Toward a Theory of Rent-Seeking Society.* College Station: Texas A&M University Press.

Crandall, Robert. 1981. Ackerman and Hassler's Clean Coal/Dirty Air. *Bell Journal of Economics* 1 (Autumn): 678.

Environmental Protection Agency. 2000. EPA Report Stresses Need for Continued Air Quality Improvement. Online: yosemite.epa.gov (cited: August 7, 2000).

Finegan, Brian J. 2000. *The Federal Subsidy Beast.* Sun Valley, ID: Alary Press.

Freshwater Forum. 2000. Water Quality Conditions in U.S. after 30 Years of Clean Water Act. *U.S. Water News,* August.

Fretwell, Holly Lippke. 2000. Federal Estate: Is Bigger Better? In *Public Lands III.* Bozeman, MT: PERC, May.

Gallup Organization. 2000. Environment. November 21. Online: www.gallup.com/poll/indicators/indenvironment.asp (cited: December 2000).

General Accounting Office. 1999a. *Superfund: Half the Sites Have All Cleanup Remedies in Place or Completed.* GAO/RCED-99-245. Washington, DC, July.

———. 1999b. *Superfund: Progress, Problems, and Future Outlook.* GAO/T-RCED-99-128. Washington, DC, March.

Goklany, Indur M. 1996. Factors Affecting Environmental Impacts: The Effects of Technology on Long-Term Trends in Cropland, Air Pollution and Water-Related Diseases. *Ambio* 25: 497–503.

———. 1999. *Clearing the Air: The Real Story of the War on Air Pollution.* Washington, DC: Cato Institute.

———. 2000. Richer Is More Resilient: Dealing with Climate Change and More Urgent Environmental Problems. In *Earth Report 2000,* ed. Ronald Bailey. New York: McGraw-Hill, 155–88.

Gore, Albert. 1992. *Earth in the Balance: Ecology and the Human Spirit.* New York: Houghton-Mifflin.

Hill, Peter J., and Roger E. Meiners, eds. 1998. *Who Owns the Environment?* Lanham, MD: Rowman & Littlefield.

Johnson, Ronald N., and Gary D. Libecap. 1980. Efficient Markets and Great Lakes Timber: A Conservation Issue Reexamined. *Explorations in Economic History* 17: 376–85.

Mahar, Dennis J. 1989. *Government Policies and Deforestation in Brazil's Amazon Region.* Washington, DC: World Bank.

McChesney, Fred S. 1997. *Money for Nothing: Politicians, Rent Extraction, and Political Extortion.* Cambridge, MA: Harvard University Press.

Meiners, Roger E., and Andrew P. Morriss, eds. 2000. *The Common Law and the Environment: Rethinking the Statutory Basis of Modern Environmental Law.* Lanham, MD: Rowman & Littlefield.

Meiners, Roger E., and Bruce Yandle. 1999. Common Law and the Conceit of Modern Environmental Policy. *George Mason Law Review* 7(4): 923–63.

Morriss, Andrew P., and Roger E. Meiners. 2000. The Destructive Role of Land-Use Planning. *Tulane Environmental Law Journal* 14: 1–43.

Nelson, Robert H. 1995. *Public Lands and Private Rights: The Failure of Scientific Management*. Lanham, MD: Rowman & Littlefield.

Norton, Seth W. 1998. Property Rights, the Environment, and Economic Well-Being. In *Who Owns the Environment?* ed. Peter J. Hill and Roger E. Meiners. Lanham, MD: Rowman & Littlefield, 37–54.

Repetto, Robert. 1988. *The Forest for the Trees? Government Policies and the Misuse of Forest Resources*. Washington, DC: World Resources Institute.

Roosevelt, Theodore. 1905. The Forest and the Life of a Nation. In *Proceedings of the American Forest Congress*. Washington, DC: American Forestry Association, 3–12.

Sedjo, Roger A. 1991. Forest Resources: Resilient and Serviceable. In *America's Renewable Resources: Past Trends and Present Challenges*, ed. Kenneth Frederick and Roger Sedjo. Washington, DC: Resources for the Future, 81–123.

Stott, Philip. 1999. *Tropical Rain Forest: A Political Economy of Hegemonic Mythmaking*. London: Coronet Books.

Stroup, Richard L. 1996. Superfund: The Shortcut that Failed. *PERC Policy Series*, PS-5. Bozeman, MT: PERC, May.

U.S. Council on Environmental Quality and Department of State 1980. *Global 2000 Report to the President*. Vol. 1. Washington, DC: Government Printing Office.

Valenta, Christina, and William Valenta. 1995. *Introduction to Environmental Law and Policy*. St. Paul, MN: West Publishing Co.

Viscusi, W. Kip, and James T. Hamilton. 1999. Are Risk Regulators Rational? Evidence from Hazardous Waste Cleanup Decisions. *American Economic Review* 89(4): 1010–27.

CASE CITED

United States v. Hooker Chemical & Plastics Corp., 850 F.Supp. 993 (W.D.N.Y., 1994).

2

Silent Springs and Silent Villages: Pesticides and the Trampling of Property Rights

Roger E. Meiners and Andrew P. Morriss

The bald eagle has made a comeback. The estimate of nesting pairs in the lower forty-eight states has risen fifteenfold since its low point in the 1960s, and the eagle has been seen over cities from Seattle to Tampa. In 1999 President Clinton announced that the bird no longer needed protection under the Endangered Species Act (Carlton 1999, A23). One reason cited for the decline of the eagle, and many other birds, was the use of DDT. The ban imposed on DDT in the early 1970s helped bring about the revival of the eagle and many other birds. America does not face the threat of silent springs.

Malaria has made a successful comeback around the world. Greatly reduced in the 1960s and 1970s in many places where it had long been a scourge, the disease has come back with a vengeance, now sickening more than 300 million people and killing 1 million a year, mostly children (Attaran et al. 2000). The major reason cited for the return of malaria, and other diseases, is the ban on DDT. Villages again face silence from the death and illness of children.

It is not acceptable to most people to trade children for birds. Should we return to the practices of decades past when mosquito and other pest eradication by DDT helped stop various plagues, but harmed wildlife? We will address the particulars of pest eradication, but the question just posed need not be relevant. It reflects the all-or-nothing approach that is so common to the command-and-control approach of government planning of the environment. Markets, under the rule of law, rarely force people to make all-or-nothing choices. We can have more birds and less malaria by allowing DDT use. To get this result we need strong enforcement of property rights.

To see why private decision makers, controlling their property, will allow for sensible and humane resolution of the complex issues involved in pesticides, human health, and environmental protection, we begin by reviewing the saga of DDT. The lesson learned from it is not specific to that pesticide, but DDT is one of the most studied pesticides and so illustrates the issue. We then turn to an analysis of the political forces at work that have caused terrible environmental damage and human misery—and show no sign of abating.

BETTER LIVING THROUGH CHEMISTRY

Traditionally, pests, not pesticides, were seen as a serious threat to human health and well-being. Indeed the first laws governing pesticide use were state laws, such as one enacted by Washington State to address a perceived problem in the apple industry: Not enough pesticides were being used (Whorton 1974, 72). Some farmers were seen as free-riding on the efforts of their neighbors to control pests by not applying the then-dominant insecticide, arsenic, to their apple trees. The second major problem with pre-DDT pesticides was consumer fraud; many simply did not work as advertised. Early federal and state regulatory efforts, such as the federal Insecticide Act of 1910, were aimed at removing ineffective products from the market. However, early pesticides that did work could pose acute health hazards. As a result, early regulatory efforts were largely aimed at avoiding acute poisoning and ineffective products (Morriss 1997, 137–38).

No wonder DDT was hailed as a modern miracle. Its first use was late in World War II when, sprayed on soldiers and civilians, it killed body lice, thereby stopping a typhus epidemic in Italy (Dunlap 1981, 61–63). Spraying DDT from the air on islands in the Pacific relieved the troops of the many miseries, especially malaria, caused by the mosquitoes that were eliminated or reduced. DDT was not only more effective against pests but also much safer than the inorganic pesticides, such as arsenic, that it replaced. Recognized as generally benign to humans, DDT's release to civilian use after the war was hailed as a boon and production rose rapidly. DDT was so popular it was even thrown instead of rice at some weddings (Whorton 1974, 248). Its inventor, Paul Müller, was awarded the Nobel Prize in medicine. Cheap and effective on a wide range of pests that inflict misery on humans, and safer than the alternatives, the new chemicals such as DDT became popular and their use spread rapidly. For example, pesticide use increased fivefold between 1950 and 1970 (Rogers 1994, 399).

For many years the U.S. Department of Agriculture promoted widespread spraying of DDT, and many other pesticides, as a public service to farmers and consumers. Under the leadership of Jamie Whitten (D-Miss.), long the power in the agriculture committee in the House of Representatives, pesticide operations under USDA control expanded in the 1950s. Support for pest control was bipartisan. As a Republican member of Whitten's committee said, "We expect the Department of Agriculture, in cooperation with the land grant colleges and experiment stations and . . . with insecticide producers and the chemical industry, to develop pesticides that will control what is left of the immune insects that attack what we produce and present to the American consumer" (quoted in Bosso 1987, 69). Enthusiasm was similar in the Senate, where in 1953 Sen. Allen Ellender said that pesticide use would help agriculture, thereby helping national security and defeat communism (Bosso 1987, 67–71).

Pesticide regulation had moved to the federal level after World War II in response to the concerns of pesticide manufacturers over increasing state regulation. Faced with potentially expensive and inconsistent labeling and other state requirements, the industry lobbied successfully for the 1947 Federal Insecticide, Fungicide, and Rodenticide Act (FIFRA). FIFRA was built around the same efficacy and acute health concerns as the earlier state and federal regulation. It did not, however, give the USDA any significant regulatory powers. For example, although the statute gave the USDA weak powers to require proof of efficacy and required manufacturers to register their products with the agency, it denied the agency the ability to refuse to register a product (Morriss 1997, 139). Manufacturers thus had the best of all possible worlds—no significant limitation on their ability to manufacture and sell effective pesticides, limits on competitors' ability to sell ineffective products, preemption of state regulatory ability in many areas, and federal regulatory authority located in a sympathetic agency whose mission was to assist farmers rather than consider third-party effects of chemical use.

Although this may not have been the military-industrial complex that President Eisenhower warned of, it was a set of interests that help form an enduring iron triangle in Washington. Members of Congress, overseeing diligent employees at the USDA, were happy to expend public money to help subsidize agricultural production, all the while encouraged by the makers of the assorted chemicals. Powerful political forces were at play. While we can look back skeptically upon their behavior now, no doubt the sense of mission was true and bolstered the special interests at work. DDT and other new pesticides were seen as cheap solutions not only for public health pest control problems but also for control of the boll weevil and other scourges that blighted agriculture.

The Need to Spray

From the vantage point of the 1950s, promotion of the use of DDT and other modern pesticides was no different economically than most government programs. An important role for government, economists taught, was the subsidization of "public goods," or those goods that no one person could capture all the economic benefits of providing. That is, if Farmer Jones sprayed his fields for a pest, he would save Farmer Smith next door some money, since fewer hungry critters would survive to migrate from Jones's farm to Smith's in search of food. Since Smith wouldn't be likely to pay Jones for the reduction in pests, he would be unfairly exploiting Jones. Furthermore, because Smith did not spray, thus allowing more pests to survive than if he did spray, there would be too many pests and too little pesticide use compared with the efficient optimum. Therefore, Smith should be required to spray (the approach taken by Washington State with apple growers in the early 1900s) or Jones should be subsidized. Because subsidies were (and are) a politically attractive option in agriculture, pesticide use was subsidized. Given that they were aids to farmers, it is not surprising that the pesticide programs were assigned to the USDA, an agency created to promote agriculture.

USDA pesticide spray programs expanded significantly in the 1950s (Bosso 1987, 81–106 is the basis of the discussion that follows). Millions of acres of trees in the Northeast were sprayed with DDT to kill gypsy moths. In 1957 Congress approved the Fire Ant Eradication Act. The USDA proposed to treat 20 million acres, with federal taxpayers bearing half the cost. To rationalize the program, as Rachel Carson (1962) noted in *Silent Spring*, the USDA asserted that fire ants were a major threat to agricultural production, animals, and even human life.

By the end of the 1950s, these expanding programs began to provoke some public opposition. The USDA knew little about the effects of widespread dispersion of many of the chemicals it promoted or used itself. The agency's ignorance stemmed from the political allocation of research dollars. Congress, for obvious political reasons, directed funds to providing services such as product promotion and spraying, not to background research needed to understand the environmental impacts of the programs. Although decision makers in Washington may have been ignorant of the effects of the spraying, the people who were sprayed weren't. Farmers began to balk at paying for even a share to spray chemicals that sometimes had unfortunate side effects. After a veterinarian in Georgia reported that more than 100 cattle died after one USDA aerial bombardment of dieldrin, farmers across the South increasingly refused to pay for spraying.

The USDA's solution in some cases was to offer certain chemicals for free to those who would take them. Even in Alabama, where fire ants had first appeared via the port of Mobile and where people were familiar with the problems the ants posed, the legislature withdrew funding for spraying in 1959 after state game officials estimated that up to 75 percent of the state's wildlife could be eliminated by the spraying program. The USDA continued to spray without state or farmer input, but opposition took its toll and the program gradually wound down.

By the end of the 1950s, the consequences of public subsidies for pesticide use so many could benefit from their use was joined by a second economic problem: that of externalities. New post–World War II pesticides such as dieldrin and DDT worked as advertised on pests, but they also "worked" on nontarget species. When pesticide spraying harmed valuable wildlife and domestic animals, the USDA generally did not have to compensate anyone and so failed to consider the full costs of the spraying. In part this problem arose because the USDA subsidies made pesticide spraying too cheap. Because the chemicals were inexpensive (or even free, as in the case of the fire ant program), pesticide users had little reason to economize on their use. Overapplication was common.

The public choice explanation for the USDA's activities is straightforward. Politicians in Congress and the bureaucrats at the agency had an incentive to maximize the net political benefits of spraying. The first spray programs were conducted when the marginal political benefits of spraying were largest, such as when controlling malaria. As the program expanded, spraying was done in areas in which the marginal benefits were smaller (gypsy moth control). Similarly, the spraying programs were first done where the marginal political costs of spraying were lowest (over swamps) and expanded into areas in which the marginal political costs increased (inhabited areas of Long Island). Because of the free-rider problem in organizing to influence the USDA and Congress, however, the dispersed political costs were less than the full costs incurred by individuals. Because Congress could mandate the use of tax dollars to pay, spraying programs were much bigger than they would have been if left to private decision makers. When the cost of organizing against spraying was reduced by the increase in public concern caused by the publication of *Silent Spring,* the USDA and Congress were suddenly faced with a sharp increase in the political costs of the program.

Public Fears of Spray Contamination

Growers have long been concerned about public reaction to negative publicity, true or not, about all food contaminants. Because many early pesticides were extremely acutely toxic (like arsenic), residues on foods had long been a public concern. In 1891 a scare about a fungicide used on grapes caused lurid headlines in the *New York Times* and other papers. Public health authorities destroyed grapes and consumption dropped as consumers avoided them, even though analysis by the USDA showed that "an adult would have to eat 300 pounds of grapes a day, including heavily coated stems, to get a harmful dose." The scare went away, but growers remembered the price they paid. When a similar situation arose in England in 1925, with respect to imported fruit from the United States, American growers hired independent chemists to inspect their products and assure the public that the fruit was safe. Testing was costly, however, and some producers sought to shift those costs to others. Beech-Nut, a baby-food manufacturer, had complained in the early 1950s about the cost of testing for insecticide residues and lobbied for increased regulation of pesticides (Dunlap 1981, 41, 68).

A major public scare about residues and improper use of chemicals came with the cranberry scare of 1959. In early November 1959, the secretary of Health, Education, and Welfare (HEW) announced that cranberries were contaminated with aminotriazole, a USDA-registered herbicide, which the FDA said caused cancer in lab rats (Bosso 1987, 98). Cranberry sales dropped just before Thanksgiving, the critical market period, and sales were halted in some states. The Department of Agriculture sputtered that there was no real threat; presidential candidates Richard Nixon and John F. Kennedy ate cranberries to demonstrate that they were safe, but sales still collapsed to one-third their normal level. The damage to cranberry sales eventually passed, but the scare left heightened public awareness that agricultural sprays might not be as beneficial as had been touted. Rachel Carson and other writers were inspired to dig into such matters.

DDT: FROM HERO TO SCAPEGOAT

Whereas DDT was every bit as effective at eliminating pests that carry diseases as had been learned in the war, its widespread effectiveness was also the key to its demise. DDT was a broad-spectrum pesticide—one that affected a wide range of species. From the start, some scientists warned that at a minimum more studies should be done regarding the effects of DDT before it was widely used. Cheap and effective, it was produced in large amounts.

Concern about widespread DDT application was growing. There was evidence that although DDT appeared harmless to people who even ingested large quantities, it affected things we do not generally consider to be pests. When the USDA began gypsy moth eradication in the mid-1950s, eastern New York, including Long Island, was subject to extensive aerial spraying. The rationale for the program was that the moth was destroying forests and no other effective control chemical had been discovered despite years of trying. The USDA solved this problem by mixing DDT with oil, so it would stick to the trees, and blanketed the area (Dunlap 1981, 87–91 is the basis for this discussion).

Residents complained about the scum that coated cars, swimming pools, and houses. Of greater concern were reports of large fish kills and charges that DDT, consumed by cows, would contaminate milk. Organic farmers were angry because they no longer had organic crops. In 1957, Robert Cushman Murphy, an authority on birds and curator-emeritus of the American Museum of Natural History in New York City, led some other Long Island residents in filing suit against the USDA to enjoin the spraying program. Dr.

Murphy and other plaintiffs charged that the spraying program deprived them "of property and possibly lives without due process of law and [took] their private property for public use without just compensation" and was a "trespass upon the persons and property of the plaintiffs" (*Murphy v. Benson* 1957, 789).

Murphy argued that DDT is a poison that can damage humans, animals, birds, and insects and that it made the food from gardens unsafe to eat. By definition, it made land unsuitable for organic cultivation. He argued that there was no public emergency that could justify the spraying program, especially since no trees on Long Island were infected with the gypsy moth and, even if they were, it would be best to let nature take its course.

The judge reviewed the program, noting that the spray consisted of one pound of DDT per one gallon of light oil sprayed by aircraft and that there was no doubt the spray irritated some people and damaged some wildlife. But science was on the side of the USDA. In 1955 the National Plant Board, representing all forty-eight states, passed a resolution urging the USDA to eradicate the gypsy moth. "Such a formulation of informed opinion could not be ignored . . . and the research conducted by the trained staffs of both Federal and New York State departments was directed to an intelligent program designed to deal with the realities of a perplexing situation" (*Murphy v. Benson* 1957, 792). Furthermore, USDA experts testified that there was no evidence of illness caused by DDT. Because the public benefit was great and plaintiffs failed to show that there was a threat of irreparable damage to them in excess of what the community would suffer from the gypsy moth, the program was not enjoined.

Murphy was back in federal district court again the next year with another try at enjoining the spray program. This time, he came armed with more evidence of dangers from DDT exposure. Dropping the claim of a violation of the Constitution for an uncompensated taking, the plaintiffs' claim was trespass by the aircraft and the spray it deposited. Again plaintiffs argued that they had the right to not have their property sprayed because the spray destroyed their ability to farm organically and it harmed wildlife. The court rejected these arguments because there was testimony that injured populations of insects were soon replenished and that crops sprayed with DDT were not unfit to eat, despite the preference of some people not to eat such crops. The court dismissed the plaintiffs' claims, holding that they really only complained of "annoyance" rather than damage. That bother was offset by a valid exercise of the government's police power. "The rights of individuals are not limitless. Individuals must yield to the requirements of the public as a whole" (*Murphy v. Benson* 1958, 128).

Murphy appealed, but the Second Circuit Court of Appeals made short shrift of his argument. The spraying program was over, so the case was moot. Besides, the court noted, Murphy failed to prove damages (*Murphy v. Benson*

1959). Murphy appealed to the U.S. Supreme Court, but it refused to review the lower court's decision. Justice Douglas dissented from the refusal, arguing the issue was not moot because spraying could resume and because the damage from DDT was not well understood enough for the courts to dismiss the possibility of danger (*Murphy v. Butler* 1960).[1]

Why did the legal system fail to control the externalities caused by DDT spraying? Two reasons stand out. First, the scientific evidence of significant harm did not support the plaintiffs' claims. Reasonable scientists might differ on the long-term impact of DDT, but the plaintiffs were unable to prove that the harms they faced were more serious. Second, the plaintiffs sought to restrain the government, not other individuals. There is no question that the plaintiffs could have won injunctive relief against a private entity that chartered a plane and sprayed even a harmless substance on the plaintiffs' land. But compared to the public interest, as articulated by the federal government, the plaintiffs could not hope to prevail without more dramatic and well-documented harm.

The Court of Public Opinion

Rachel Carson, a popular writer on nature subjects, made DDT the great Satan of the chemical world. *Silent Spring*, which was serialized in part in the *New Yorker* in 1962 before its publication as a book later that year, was well written, seemed to be based on scientific research, and painted a horrifying picture of the world that was coming if DDT usage was not restricted. Carson told her readers of a silent spring, when no birds sang because they were all dead from DDT exposure. And, although greatly exaggerating what little evidence existed, there was something to the story she told.

In the 1950s there was evidence that DDT, when sprayed over large areas, could cause fish kills and bird kills, as well as the intended insect kills. In particular, by the 1960s, scientists who studied birds were becoming increasingly convinced that DDT was decimating populations where it was sprayed widely. Studies of peregrine falcons and other raptors found evidence of a thinning of eggshells caused by DDT. Although not conclusive, qualified scientists produced credible studies that pointed to significant wildlife problems stemming from extensive use of DDT. The Environmental Defense Fund, at that time a small environmental pressure group, went on the offensive with high-profile lawsuits and scare-tactic campaigns that brought in a gush of revenues. General sensitivity to the presence of chemicals in food and the environment was increasing. The U.S. Food and Drug Administration, for example, banned the sweetener cyclamate on thin evidence and during this time was considering, with congressional support, banning assorted other substances (Dunlap 1981, 137, 197–200, 202–3).

Trying to stem uninformed public concerns about health hazards and increasing political support for banning DDT, the secretary of HEW established a commission to produce a report from the National Cancer Institute about DDT. Its report in 1969 was careful science. It noted suspicions about DDT, but found there was no firm evidence that it was carcinogenic to humans. More testing was recommended.

Environmentalists attacked the report (Dunlap 1981, 203–11 is the basis of this discussion). A wide range of groups pressed to have DDT banned as carcinogenic. Smelling victory, the Environmental Defense Fund (EDF) sued the USDA and was granted standing to challenge the propriety of USDA registration of DDT. The federal appeals court took the opportunity to excoriate USDA (*EDF v. Hardin* 1970). Moving quickly by Washington standards, federal agencies backpedaled and announced that DDT use would be phased out. The FDA asserted jurisdiction should DDT appear in any food product. The secretary of interior banned DDT from use on federal lands, a remarkable change given that earlier the federal government had been spraying private lands over the owners' objections. Perhaps most important, in 1970 Congress shifted responsibility for pesticide regulation from the USDA to the newly created Environmental Protection Agency (EPA).

One problem for a ban was that the alternatives to DDT were noticeably inferior in several respects—they cost more and did not work as well. DDT was recognized as harmful to some wildlife under certain conditions, but there was no good evidence of danger to humans. If banned, would cotton crops be wiped out by insects? And more generally, if banned, would not the alternative pesticides be more toxic and more costly? With the focus on the horrors of DDT use, however, those issues got little public attention and DDT was banned in June of 1972 by the first EPA administrator, William Ruckelshaus. That decision was not enough for the EDF; it then sued to have all production prohibited so the product could not be used for export or even in cases of domestic public health emergency, such as an outbreak of malaria (Dunlap 1981, 129, 214–22, 234). Environmental organizations have continued to press for bans on DDT in the intervening years and they have been imposed in many nations. The transformation of DDT from a public good to a public bad was complete.

The controversy over DDT also led to a major revision of FIFRA, the basic federal statute governing pesticides. Pesticides were now subject to an assessment of environmental harm as well as efficacy testing. The EPA, not the USDA, would take the primary role in regulation. Existing pesticides would be reexamined to ensure that they met the new environmental standards, a project that soon overwhelmed the EPA (Morriss 1997, 144–45).

One way to read the DDT story is as a triumph of political action and regulation over the tedious business of common law litigation. New Yorkers had tried the common law and failed; the federal government, responding to concerned citizens, put the interests of all in saving birds ahead of the profit-driven actions of a few, stepped in, and resolved the problem. This view is shortsighted, however. DDT was a problem, after all, because the federal government subsidized and promoted its use even to the extent of forcibly spraying private property. The common law actions to stop specific spraying programs failed, in part, because the federal government invoked the "public interest" against them.

Moreover, the DDT story suggests something important about the differences between common law and regulation. The plaintiffs in the early New York lawsuits sought to protect their property, not to ban DDT. The regulators of the 1970s, however, made all-or-nothing decisions for the entire country, raising the stakes and provoking everyone involved to invest considerable resources in influencing the political outcome.

Rolling Back Malaria

Banning DDT may have played a significant role in helping the bald eagle and other birds make a comeback in the past three decades, but it has also allowed malaria to make a comeback. The worry of scientists that there was no good, less toxic, cost-effective substitute for DDT to control mosquitoes is as true today as it was three decades ago. A disease that was on the way to being vanquished has returned with a vengeance.

In poor nations 1 million people, mostly children, die every year from malaria (World Health Organization [WHO] 1999b). As many as one-half billion people suffer from the disease (Stolberg 1999). Besides killing a child every thirty seconds, children who survive "suffer an average of six bouts each year," making it the most common reason to miss school; adult sufferers miss an average of ten working days a year (United Nations International Children's Emergency Fund [UNICEF] 1999, 4). Malaria, transmitted by parasites through the bites of mosquitoes, was estimated to infect 350 million people in 1952 before DDT spraying began. The infection collapsed in many countries, including Swaziland and Madagascar, that adopted effective spray programs (Roberts, Manguin, and Mouchet 2000, 331). But "DDT was widely discredited in the 1960s because of its harmful effects on the environment," so the disease is nearly back to where it was fifty years ago (UNICEF 1999, 6).

The tragedy is not being ignored, however. UNICEF, WHO, and the World Bank launched a new program, Roll Back Malaria (RBM), in October 1998, to "prevent and control this centuries-old scourge" (UNICEF 1999, 1). Even though DDT is available, politically it is unacceptable in most places, so RBM must rely on other measures: "insecticide-treated mosquito nets, mosquito coils, repellants and other materials; early detection, containment and prevention of malaria epidemics; and strengthening of local capacity to monitor malaria in affected regions" (UNICEF 1999, 8). If that list gives the impression that the results may not be as effective as DDT, the evidence is consistent with that. A UNICEF showcase effort in Laos, instituted in 1994, for example, reduced malaria by 25 percent over three years. The goal of RBM is to reduce infant mortality from the disease (not the incidence) by 50 percent by 2010 (UNICEF 1999, 3, 14), a far cry from the 97 percent reduction achieved decades ago with DDT.

Money is being pieced together from multiple sources for this project that has a hoped-for budget of $1 billion per year. By 2000, $27 million had been collected from or pledged by various countries and international agencies (WHO 1999a). Although that sum is trivial for the task at hand, the World Bank has promised to fund up to half the budget *(Lancet* 2000b). Funds are solicited from governments, agencies, nongovernmental organizations (NGOs), and the private sector, including pharmaceutical companies that can provide drugs to relieve symptoms as well as perhaps invent a cure. The World Bank is spearheading this private-public partnership, called "New Medicines for Malaria Venture," which is hoped to provide new medicines at prices affordable for impoverished people (World Bank 1999).

The focus of RBM in malaria prevention is on the use mosquito nets and a hope that more treatment for sufferers can be developed. People in the tropical regions of the world are all to sleep under such nets. At a price of $5 to $10 each, the nets are expensive for people in countries where per capita personal income is measured in the hundreds of dollars per year. Moreover, the nets require continual retreatment—soaking the nets in insecticide (UNICEF 1999, 3). Treating the nets exposes people to insecticide directly through unprotected skin contact during retreatment and through exposure to air filtered through the insecticide-impregnated nets. Substituting pesticide-impregnated mosquito nets for DDT has thus reduced exposure to DDT but increased exposure for many people to malaria and to the insecticides now being used. Given the terrible cost of the disease, most people probably willingly accept the minor risks of using the new limited prevention measures. They are denied, however, the choice between those risks and those of a DDT-spraying program. The ban on DDT thus substitutes RBM, a more expensive and less effective program with a different (and not necessarily smaller) set of risks, for the cost-effective program of DDT spraying.

As might be expected, in regions where malaria is a scourge, people question the viability and morality of RBM when a proven cost-effective malaria-control product, DDT, already exists. Delegates to the WHO Regional Consultation to Prepare African Countries Towards Reduction on Reliance on DDT for Malaria Control in Harare, Zimbabwe, in 2000, issued a statement expressing the "deep concerns of the participating member states on the possible economic and health implications of any restriction made on DDT use for malaria control" (WHO 2000). In sum, the delegates noted that no cost-effective or proven alternatives, that are less toxic, exist to replace the job DDT does.

Birds versus Children?

Because of DDT abuse in the United States before it was banned decades ago, must other nations face a tradeoff between a widespread deadly disease and a healthy ecosystem? Greenpeace still considers DDT an active environmental issue. According to its Website, it sponsors protests at factories in various nations where DDT is produced. The World Wildlife Federation is also pushing to eliminate all DDT use (Tren and Bate 2001, 23). None of the organizations have anything to say in their public literature about DDT and malaria control; it is simply an evil that governments must prohibit.

But perhaps the groups that have championed the banning of DDT are chagrined to have the issue publicly discussed. Trading lives and unmeasurable human misery, on the basis of limited evidence in the 1960s that extensive DDT application may have caused eggshell thinning on some bird species may strike many people as harsh. Should people be sacrificed in poor nations because wealthy residents of Western nations are worried about bird populations? If the risk of DDT is such that it could lead to silent springs, then billions should be spent on alternative malaria eradication, prevention, and treatment techniques. But as the RBM program indicates, present technology indicates only modest improvements are likely. Who must bear the burden while these alternatives are developed: birds or children?

In the decades that have passed since the banning of DDT in the United States, research on it has continued. Although we are not qualified to review the details of scientific studies about chemicals, we will try to give the gist of the state of knowledge reported in reputable journals. Because some nations still spray DDT to control mosquitoes, because some quit and then resumed spraying, and because others quit at a certain time, data have been collected from studies around the world. A review article covering numerous studies in the respected British medical journal the *Lancet* provides the basis for this discussion (Roberts, Manguin, and Mouchet 2000). An overview of much of the literature is to be found at www.fightingmalaria.org.

When DDT spraying is ended, malaria's incidence rises markedly (Tren and Bate 2001, 15–18). In the high and moderate risk regions of Colombia and Peru, for example, the risk of malaria doubled when spraying ceased in the 1990s. The disease has returned to areas in which it had been eradicated: urban areas of the Amazon Basin, Korea, Armenia, Azerbaijan, and Tajikistan. In Sri Lanka malaria fell from 2,800,000 cases and 7,300 deaths per year before DDT spraying, to 17 cases and no deaths. When the spraying stopped in 1961, malaria jumped back to 500,000 cases by 1969 (Attaran et al. 2000, 729). Ending DDT use thus led to an increase in human suffering from malaria. The spread of the disease elsewhere has led to its reappearance in the United States and Europe. And evidence indicates that DDT works as well today as it did decades ago in the United States.

Of course, that DDT works has never been the main issue.[2] The key questions concern toxicity and environmental damage. As of now, the best evidence is that "toxicity of DDT in human beings and effects on the environment are questionable and require further investigation" and that "claims of risks of DDT to human health and the environment have not been confirmed by replicated scientific inquiry" (Roberts, Manguin, and Mouchet 2000, 330). More than fifty years of use fails to indicate that, properly applied, DDT is harmful to humans or the environment in general (Tren and Bate 2001, 28ff.).

The reason DDT appeared to be so harmful in the 1950s and 1960s was due to its widespread use in heavy doses. In massive doses, birds can suffer acute effects. "The fault for this lies in the massive agricultural use of DDT. Dusting a single 100-hectare cotton field, for example, can require more than 1,200 kg of DDT over four weeks" (Attaran et al. 2000, 729). Even if sprayed from the air for mosquitoes, the volume and frequency are far less than common agricultural practices in earlier years. However, aerial spraying for mosquitoes, although it works very well, is not needed for DDT to provide significant protection to people against mosquitoes:

> The current practice is to spray the interior surfaces only of houses at risk, leaving a residue of DDT at a concentration of 2 g/m^2 on the walls, ceiling and eaves, once or twice a year. Half a kilogram can treat a large house and protect all its inhabitants. Doubtless some fraction of this escapes to the outdoors, but even assuming it all did, the environmental effect is just 0.04% of the effect of spraying a cotton field. Guyana's entire high-risk population for malaria can be protected with the DDT that might otherwise be sprayed on 0.4 km^2 of cotton in a season. (Attaran et al. 2000, 729)

Indeed, developing application methods that minimize input costs and maximize effective delivery against target pests is just what disease control agencies in resource-starved developing nations and nonprofits naturally do—and just what rich-country agencies such as the USDA do not.

Years of evidence indicate that DDT can be applied in manners much more cautious than was the case decades ago, saving lives at a low cost and with minimal environmental damage. Even if one subscribes to the highly restrictive "precautionary principle," one would have to justify the use of DDT for mosquito control (Goklany 2000). Since we now know this, why does the old policy persist? Why are we engaged in programs such as RBM that promise, at very high cost, to only dent malaria, not come close to eradicating it as can happen with DDT use? Hundreds of independent scientists, including three Nobel laureates in medicine, signed a public letter in 2000 advocating the use of DDT for house spraying (*Lancet* 2000a).

Good science rarely forms the basis of public policy. Most policy, especially in the details, is based on special interests that have little interest having their well-feathered nests blow away, as happens when an issue disappears. Science may indicate that careful use of DDT will be greatly beneficial and poses trivial environmental threats, but "environmentalists are still seeking a global ban, arguing that if DDT is produced for use in improving public health, it will also be used for agriculture and lead to global pollution of the environment" (Roberts, Manguin, and Mouchet 2000, 331).

Special Interest Politics Wins Again

The sufferers of malaria and the families that lose infants to malaria (the equivalent of "filling seven Boeing 747s with children, and then crashing them, every day") are denied an effective solution (Attaran et al. 2000, 729). The number of countries using DDT has been whittled down to twenty-three. It is produced in only three countries and is becoming difficult to obtain. The United Nations Environment Program has put it on the hit list for extinction. The U.N. seeks a global ban by treaty. What explains the march against DDT in the face of increasing scientific evidence that the ban is not justified?

Recall that back in the 1950s, special interests for agriculture pressed for public money to be used to spray DDT over massive areas to attack gypsy moths and other pests. The USDA benefited as an agency from this expansion into active pest management, which traditionally had been left to individual farmers or to states. Members of Congress who sat on the agriculture committees could report to their constituents that they were generating benefits for them—the government would spray for pests and, at most, they would only have to pay a fraction of the bill. And chemical companies that made DDT and other sprays no doubt lobbied for expanded spray programs, since it meant more sales of their products.

The world of politics is no different today, except that it is bigger and more complex, especially at the international level. The special interests today that want DDT banned are clear because they are self-identified. The World Bank, UNICEF, WHO, U.S. Agency for International Development (USAID), and other international government agencies are simply not needed in the area of malaria control without a DDT ban. DDT is cheap and simple; decades ago some countries and local folks were handling the situation. Without DDT, malaria is a tragedy that easily justifies an annual $1 billion budget for RBM, a program whose ineffectiveness makes it likely to become a permanent endeavor. The plague will never go away; it may be made smaller and less tragic, but a permanent program is growing to mitigate a persistent problem that was well under way to control three decades ago. Offices in Geneva, New York, and Washington must be staffed and billions of dollars must be raised and dispensed.

The World Bank benefits from its participation in RBM because, as Matthew Brown (2002) notes in chapter 8, it is routinely blasted (with good reason) by environmentalists for supporting programs that are environmentally (and economically) destructive. RBM gives the bank a public health role that is hard to criticize, one with a plausible impact on economic development (sick people cannot work as well as healthy people). So the World Bank finds a way to make peace with its environmental critics, yet justify its continued existence for years to come. The World Bank is not alone among agencies that have changed their agenda. As Terry Anderson and Henry Miller (2000) have documented in *The Greening of U.S. Foreign Policy*, a host of federal agencies have, with the waning of the cold war in particular, turned into agencies with environmental agendas or, at least, agendas that will not offend the politically potent environmental organizations. To survive without old enemies to fight, they need new friends.

RBM will have only limited success, even if it meets its goals. Its political virtue is not its efficiency, however, but that it does not irritate environmental organizations, who applaud the use of mosquito nets rather than DDT to deal with mosquitoes. Knowing that nets will not prevent many people from getting malaria, the major focus must be on developing a vaccine. Even though there is nothing on the horizon, drug companies and other researchers are willing to accept funds from government agencies to work on the project. Whereas DDT is banned in most nations due to outside pressure, and some countries that use it have been told they could lose foreign aid (Attaran et al. 2000, 730), alternative sprays will be allowed under RBM.

Other sprays present two problems: They cost much more and they have toxicity problems. Malathion, considered the next cheapest alternative, costs three times as much to apply (Attaran et al. 2000, 730). Similarly, pyrethroids also cost about three times more than DDT does to treat a house for mosquitoes. That high cost, an entomologist at the EPA asserts, is likely to lead many countries to abandon house spraying altogether (Stolberg 1999).

The alternatives also do not appear to work as well as DDT. According to an entomologist in South Africa, certain malaria-carrying species of mosquitoes "are completely resistant to the new, softer pyrethroid insecticides that were introduced by the National Department of Health" (Villet 2000). Whereas these newer, more costly, and less effective insecticides may help, and are believed to be less toxic to birds than DDT, they have not been subject to as much study as DDT, and so they may pose other environmental problems yet unknown (Tren and Bate 2001, 28–32).

In any event, chemical companies are no doubt pleased to supply more costly and less effective chemicals in lieu of cheap, generic DDT. The "insistence of environmental advocacy seems to have won approval of powerful pesticide companies because it allows them to sell their more expensive insecticides. The replacement of DDT by organophosphate, carbamate, or pyrethroid insecticides is commonly proposed even though price, efficacy, duration or effectiveness, and side effects (e.g., unpleasant smell) are major barriers to use in poor countries" (Roberts, Manguin, and Mouchet 2000, 331). Those cost barriers will disappear if sufficient money is poured in by the World Bank, UNICEF, WHO, and other government agencies—perhaps much like the USDA expanded the use of DDT in the United States in the 1950s.

The major environmental groups will not back down on the DDT issue and admit that the result of its ban is a loss of human life, primarily among the world's poorest nations, on a scale of the worst natural or man-made disasters. Although we hear much in the media about AIDS in Africa, almost nothing is said about the malaria epidemic. Media shyness aside, the wealthy nations' current policies on DDT led some public health experts to assert that the insistence of "rich countries" that poor countries "do without DDT is 'eco-colonialism' that can impoverish no less than the imperial colonialism of the past did" (Attaran et al. 2000, 730).

Why would major environmental organizations, such as the EDF and WWF, refuse to admit that DDT can play an effective role with far less damage to the environment than comes from many other sources today? They are well informed about this matter and have staff members who can read scientific journals. It is possible that they have such a strong preference for *any* trivial amount of environmental protection that they are willing to sacrifice lives. But that is unlikely to be the case. We suggest that it has more to do with the issue of liability and its relationship to revenues.

Environmental organizations are nonprofit institutions that raise money from donors who wish to support their activities. Most of the organizations that are household names today were minor or nonexistent entities before the modern environmental era of federal command-and-control regulations. The EDF was created in the late 1960s in response to the DDT fight on Long Island. Latching on to an issue that grabbed national attention, it was soon attracting foundation grants and more in support from other donors (Bosso 1987, 135–48), successfully attacking DDT. It reported some real evidence about DDT, but also blew things out of proportion, strongly implying, as did Rachel Carson, that DDT caused cancer. It advertised that babies were poisoned by DDT through their mothers' milk.

Today the children poisoned by malaria, who may have been saved by DDT, appear to be of little concern to environmental organizations. These interest groups continue their assault on the product. To do otherwise would lead to a loss of credibility. Because there is a lot of competition for donor dollars in the environmental fund-raising movement, no doubt the groups have learned what works. That is not unlike other actors in the nonprofit, competitive world—politicians. It is rare they simply admit they lied or were wrong; better to deny, to attack the other side, or stonewall.

That is significantly different than organizations that operate in the for-profit sector. If they are caught in a lie or a mistake, they are likely to be punished by the consumer and therefore lose profits. Even more, if they engage in a practice that results in injury to others, they face legal liability. Firestone made a mistake in tire production; it is punished by the market as consumers go elsewhere for tires and its stock price suffers. Also, Firestone faces legal liability for its mistake because people were injured and killed due to (apparently) sloppy production practices. The impression that the company covered up its problem or lied about it simply compounds the costs of its error. If a jury believes that the company knew of the problem and hid it, the company could be subject to punitive damages on top of compensatory damages.

Environmental groups and, more important, government policy makers who decided that DDT should not be allowed in anyone's hands, face no liability for the consequence of babies dying and many more suffering from the devastating impact of malaria. There are no legal forces or market forces to help generate a correction except for the hope that serious scientific evidence will be considered by policy makers, who still risk the wrath of environmental groups, and therefore voter wrath, if they discuss allowing DDT for mosquito control. Because policy makers need not make decisions based on sound science, there is no reason to expect a change in policy.

WHY ALL THIS HAPPENED

The saga of DDT, now a half-century long, is the result of moving decision making from the private sector to government. It was public decision makers, spending other people's money and responding to special interest pressures, that sprayed DDT and other chemicals over huge areas, all in the name of the public good, exercising the legitimate "police power" as the courts that reviewed the spray policy said. Today it is public decision makers, spending other people's money, deciding that DDT may not be used and that other, less effective and more costly, measures will be taken instead. All legitimate police powers.

It was generally accepted in the 1950s that DDT should be sprayed to kill gypsy moths, let alone mosquitoes, but today such practices are held in great suspicion. When New York City sprayed for mosquitoes (not with DDT) because of the West Nile virus in the summers of 1999 and 2000, there were reports of hysterical people calling assorted public offices and environmental groups asking if the spray would kill or harm them. But a lawsuit to stop that spraying was no more effectual than the ones filed in the late 1950s (*No Spray Coalition, Inc. v. City of New York* 2000).

We posit that, except for the spraying of soldiers in World War II, the government had little justification for spraying DDT (and other pesticides). To spray was a violation of property rights. We agree with Dr. Murphy and the original plaintiffs who sued the USDA in 1957, contending that the spray program was a trespass on their property and deprived them of the full value of their property without compensation. Those who preferred to have pesticide-free crops may have been "irrational" in their preferences, in that there was no scientific basis for them, but there was no reason they should not have been able to enjoy such a preference on their own property. They asked for no forced subsidy from taxpayers; they merely asked to be left alone on their property and for their preferences to be respected.

Public decision makers have little reason to respect such preferences because it weakens the latitude of the legislature and the agencies that execute their wishes. As an assistant secretary of agriculture told Congress, with respect to the fire ant spray program, "All infestations must be treated without regard to location, land use, or ownership" (Bosso 1987, 87). Private property rights are no more than an inconvenience to public decision makers. As one critic noted about the spray program, it is "a monument to the power which key congressmen on strategic committees can exercise over environmental policy" (Bosso 1987, 86, citing Wellford 1972, 291). The fire ant spray program drew the same kind of reaction among some farmers in the South that the DDT spray program drew in New York. As the USDA began to back down it admitted that "areas have been aerially treated contrary to the wishes of property owners" (Bosso 1987, 102). Not everyone agrees with "public health" measures or even programs specifically designed to help a specific interest group, such as farmers whose land contains fire ants. Those who did not like the programs, not having legal protection, had to turn to political action to get their way. Had the courts held, in the early challenges to the DDT spraying, that it was a trespass or a taking without compensation, the bald eagle and other species may have not suffered such large population drops that they needed the protection of the Endangered Species Act.

Political action, not markets and the rule of law, dictate one-size-fits-all solutions. If you are on the winning side, you get to have your preferences forced on others and make them help pay for what you want. If you are on the losing side, you may not exercise your preferences and you are forced to pay for what the winning coalition wants.

Since the early 1970s the winning coalition is the opposite of what it was in the previous two decades. Opponents of DDT have the upper hand politically, and, rather than force people to have their property sprayed with DDT as happened before, they have gotten the same political actors and government agencies to act on behalf of their preferences by prohibiting anyone from using DDT on their own property, even in their own house, to protect themselves from mosquitoes and the deadly diseases they carry. To lessen the risk of birds suffering and dying, many humans now suffer and die; the cause is the same—public decision makers running roughshod over the rights of citizens to protect themselves and their property in the way they most see fit. Worse, they have used their political power to attack the ability of people in other countries to make their own choices.

The standard answer of those who favor the DDT ban will be, of course, that DDT harms the environment. Ignoring the scientific evidence that spraying one's own house with DDT will have no measurable impact on any environment except the mosquitoes, let us consider this valid concern. Again, we posit that there is no need for legislative or agency action. Private parties, looking out for their own interests, will use spray in a manner they believe to be economically beneficial, given that they are paying for it, and will be subject to liability for damage done to their neighbors if they trespass on their property with the spray and cause damage.

COMMON LAW ENVIRONMENTALISM

The strongest protection for the environment comes from common law property rights enforced by the courts. As Dr. Murphy and other plaintiffs argued to the federal courts in 1957 and 1958, spraying was trespass. It wasn't even a close case under common law—intentionally physically invading another's property was clearly contrary to traditional rules of law. Dr. Murphy and his co-plaintiffs had a common law right not to have their property invaded by a substance they believed to be damaging to the vegetation and wildlife on their property and possibly to themselves. The court rejected their claim in part because there was no clear evidence of significant damage (and in those days, organic farming was probably a very foreign notion) and in large part because, even if there was some damage, the greater good, as defined by the legislature, required that the plaintiffs submit to collective action.

The debate about DDT became political, a debate about all-or-nothing solutions. Either we all get sprayed or no one gets sprayed. That tends to be the nature of political decisions—winners get more than what they are willing to pay for personally; losers are denied what they prefer and must contribute to the other side. Markets and the common law generally make decisions at the margin: Is it worth buying some spray, and, if so, how much will work for me? If I spray, some molecules of spray will drift on to my neighbor's property; if I spray too much, it will rise to the level of actionable damage and I will pay for violating my obligation to protect my neighbor from my actions.

The fact that one is responsible for spraying pesticides carelessly and inflicting injury on the property of another has long been the rule of law: "Common law tort theories imposing liability for crop, livestock and personal damages on those responsible for creating the pesticide drift should be understood as social efforts to internalize those external costs by making the polluter pay" (Blomquist 1995, 397). Cases from the 1950s concerning agricultural spraying of pesticides show that the general rule was that a farmer and the sprayer he hired could be held liable for spray that was accidentally dumped on a neighbor's property or drifted onto a neighbor's property and did measurable damage to crops, livestock, or persons (e.g., *Crouse v. Wilbur-Ellis Co.* 1954). No bad intention was needed, and usually did not exist because neither the farmer nor the spray pilot had reason to waste money by dumping spray on the property of another or spraying when it was windy (e.g., *Faire v. Burke* 1952). Quite a number of cases concern spraying that drifted and killed bees; liability was imposed (e.g., *Lundberg v. Bolon* 1948). Other cases concerned spray that caused dairy milk to be infected with unacceptable levels of pesticide (e.g., *Smith v. Okerson* 1950). If one was careless and sprayed too much because directions from the manufacturer were not followed, the action rose to the level of negligence per se (e.g., *Bennett v. Larsen* 1984). By the 1970s, when organic crops had come into vogue, farmers won cases for having their crops damaged by pesticide sprays that made them ineligible for organic certification, even though the level of pesticides on the crops was within federal standards for human consumption (e.g., *Langan v. Valicopters, Inc.* 1977).

Clearly, under the common law, we would be free to spray the inside of our houses to reduce the risk of mosquito bite, and such spraying would almost never inflict injury on a neighbor's property. Yet that level of personal protection is now prohibited because of command-and-control rules that dictate minuscule details of management of others' property even in other nations.

Common law protections against careless neighbors aside, what about careless governments? There is no doubt that under the Constitution, governments can condemn property for public purpose, which would include spraying property with DDT or bulldozing the property for a public school. The difference is that as the Supreme Court usually reads the Constitution, if the government wishes to bulldoze property, it pays the fair market value of the property; if it sprays property, tough luck. The Court need not take such an all-or-nothing approach. In some cases it did not. For example, in *U.S. v. Causby* (1946) the government was sued for killing chickens. During World War II, the military used an airfield in North Carolina. Aircraft flew over a chicken coop owned by the Causbys. Some chickens killed themselves in hysteria due to the low-flying planes. The government fought, all the way to the Supreme Court, arguing that since it did not destroy all value of the property by flying low over it, it did not have to compensate the owners for their inability to raise chickens. The Court, in a split decision, held for the property owners. It held that the government had the power to install an airfield wherever it wished, but when the effect of that was to deprive a property owner of the use and enjoyment of the land for the purpose of raising chickens, there was a taking that was entitled to just compensation. If only the bald eagles had been so lucky. Had the Court stuck with this view of the Fifth Amendment, much less DDT and other pesticides would have been sprayed because the price paid by Congress and its agencies would have been much higher. Because there is competition for budget dollars, more careful consideration would have been given to the costs and benefits of pesticide spray programs.

CONCLUSION

Political actors have no interest to see such decisions leave politics. Politicians are managers of crises and control agencies and their budgets. They have little interest in letting ordinary people control and protect the uses of their property that the owners think best. Crises are political opportunities regardless of the outcome of the situation—DDT for everyone or DDT for no one. The fact that such issues rise to the level of political action mean that politicians cannot lose—they respond to one set of special interests or another on one side of the issue or the other (McChesney 1997). Campaign support flows on both sides. Spray or no spray, dead birds or dead babies, the livelihood of politicians has been improved while we are all the poorer.

NOTES

1. The same issue arose again in 1967 in New York state court. This time, the newly formed Environmental Defense Fund, which was formed that year largely due to the DDT issue, was behind a suit to try to enjoin government spraying of DDT to control mosquitoes on Long Island (Dunlap 1981, 142–45). Perhaps being more savvy politically, the plaintiff did not argue on the basis of trespass or takings, but proposed a theory that they had the right to enjoin actions that adversely affects natural resources (*Yannacone v. Dennison,* 1967). That novel argument had no basis in common law or statutory law, so no injunction was issued, but plaintiffs were well aware that the issue was moving to the political level, so impact on the media may have the most real purpose of this and similar suits brought by the new organization (Dunlap 1981, 142–62). Coverage of such litigation added to the drumbeat against DDT that was very public after publication of *Silent Spring* in 1962. The product was not long for the market.

2. Some opponents argue that overuse of particular pesticides like DDT led to resistant strains of insects. Intensive use of DDT in agriculture in its early years of use caused resistance to it to arise slowly, but there is only limited resistance to DDT by mosquitoes in particular areas.

REFERENCES

Anderson, Terry L., and Henry I. Miller, eds. 2000. *The Greening of U.S. Foreign Policy*. Stanford, CA: Hoover Institution Press.

Attaran, Amir, Donald R. Roberts, Chris F. Curtis, and Wenceslaus L. Kilama. 2000. Balancing Risks on the Backs of the Poor. *Nature Medicine* 6(7): 729–31.

Blomquist, Robert F. 1995. Applying Pesticides: Toward Reconceptualizing Liability to Neighbors for Crop, Livestock, and Personal Damages from Agricultural Chemical Drift. *Oklahoma Law Review* 48 (Summer): 393–416.

Bosso, Christopher J. 1987. *Pesticides and Politics: The Life Cycle of a Public Issue*. Pittsburgh, PA: University of Pittsburgh Press.

Brown, Matthew. 2002. Banking on Disaster: The World Bank and Environmental Destruction. This volume.

Carlton, Jim. 1999. Clinton Administration Plans to Remove Bald Eagles from "Endangered" List. *Wall Street Journal*, July 6.

Carson, Rachel. 1962. *Silent Spring*. Boston: Houghton Mifflin Co.

Dunlap, Thomas R. 1981. *DDT: Scientists, Citizens, and Public Policy*. Princeton, NJ: Princeton University Press.

Goklany, Indur M. 2000. Applying the Precautionary Principle to DDT. December 2. Online: www.fightingmalaria.org (cited: March 6, 2001).

Lancet. 2000a. Commentary: Caution Required with the Precautionary Principle, 356: 265.

Lancet. 2000b. Commentary: Donor Responsibilities in Rolling Back Malaria, 356: 521.

McChesney, Fred S. 1997. *Money for Nothing: Politicians, Rent Extraction, and Political Extortion*. Cambridge, MA: Harvard University Press.

Morriss, Andrew P. 1997. Pesticides and Environmental Federalism: An Empirical and Qualitative Analysis of § 24(c) Registrations. In *Environmental Federalism*, ed. Terry L. Anderson and Peter J. Hill. Lanham, MD: Rowman & Littlefield, 133–74.

Roberts, D. R., S. Manguin, and J. Mouchet. 2000. DDT House Spraying and Reemerging Malaria. *Lancet* 356: 330–32.

Rogers, William. 1994. *Environmental Law*, 2nd ed. St. Paul, MN: West.

Stolberg, Sheryl Gay. 1999. DDT, Target of Global Ban, Finds Defenders in Experts on Malaria. *New York Times*, August 29.

Tren, Richard, and Roger Bate. 2001. When Politics Kills: Malaria and the DDT Story. Online: www.fightingmalaria.org (cited: March 5, 2001).

UNICEF. 1999. *Rolling Back Malaria*. New York.

Villet, Martin. 2000. Malaria Epidemic in KwaZulu-Natal and DDT—The Facts. Online: www.malaria.org/news227.html (cited: April 3, 2001).

Wellford, Harrison. 1972. *Sowing the Wind*. New York: Grossman.

Whorton, James. 1974. *Before Silent Spring: Pesticides and Public Health in Pre-DDT America*. Princeton, NJ: Princeton University Press.

World Bank. 1999. *Roll Back Malaria Partnership: Defining the Role of the World Bank*. Africa Region Findings No. 144. Washington, DC, October.

World Health Organization. 1999a. Cabinet Project: Roll Back Malaria Financial Situation. December 1. Online: mosquito.who.int/docs/3gpm_financial.htm (cited: March 5, 2001).

———. 1999b. *The World Health Report 1999*. Geneva, Switzerland.

———. 2000. Delegates' Report. Report of the Regional Consultation to Prepare African Countries towards Reduction of Reliance on DDT for Malaria Control, Harare, Zimbabwe, February 8–10. Online: www.who.int/rbm/DDT/ddt_Zimbabwe.htm (cited: March 5, 2001).

CASES CITED

Bennett v. Larsen, 118 Wis.2d 681, 348 N.W.2d 540 (1984).

Crouse v. Wilbur-Ellis Co., 77 Ariz. 359, 272 P.2d 352 (1954).

Environmental Defense Fund, Inc. v. Hardin, 428 F.2d 1093 (D.C. Cir., 1970).

Faire v. Burke, 363 Mo. 562, 252 S.W.2d 289 (1952).

Langan v. Valicopters, Inc., 88 Wash.2d 855, 567 P.2d 218 (1977).

Lundberg v. Bolon, 67 Ariz. 259, 194 P.2d 454 (1948).

Murphy v. Benson, 151 F. Supp. 786 (1957).

Murphy v. Benson, 164 F. Supp. 120 (1958).

Murphy v. Benson, 270 F.2d 419 (2nd Cir., 1959).

Murphy v. Butler, 362 U.S. 929, 80 S.Ct. 750 (1960).

No Spray Coalition, Inc. v. City of New York, 2000 WL 1401458 (S.D.N.Y., 2000).

Smith v. Okerson, 8 N.J. Super. 560, 73 A.2d 857 (1950).

United States v. Causby, 328 U.S. 256, 66 S.Ct. 1062 (1946).

Yannacone v. Dennison, 55 Misc.2d 468, 285 N.Y.S. 2d 476 (1967).

3

Fueling the Race to the Fish

Donald R. Leal

Mainstream environmentalism promotes government ownership of resources as the preferred approach for conservation. There are basically two related arguments behind this promotion. The first is greed, i.e., the pursuit of profits in the private sector forces individuals to disregard all else, including the long-term health of a resource. The corollary to this argument is the removal of greed, i.e., acting without motivation for profits, government decision makers are free to practice good stewardship. Indeed these were among the prevailing arguments early conservationists used to justify government ownership of resources in the United States (Anderson and Leal 1991, 38; 1997, 65–67).

These two arguments fail to recognize the importance of private property rights and the incentives decision makers face in the public sector. Property rights that are exclusively held by one owner (or group of owners) and transferable to others ensure that there is a strong incentive to protect the resource against harm or neglect because being careless would reduce the value of the resource both to the owner and to any future owner. In other words, private property rights give the owner a strong incentive for good stewardship. A host of historical and contemporary cases clearly illustrate the use of private property rights in promoting good stewardship (Anderson and Leal 1997). But problems of overexploitation often arise when resources are not owned by anyone. The near extermination of bison on the American frontier provides a classic example. In the public sector the wealth of government decision makers is not tied to the condition of the resource per se, but in the ability to cater to constituencies who use a resource but do not actually own it. Government-managed fisheries provide one of the classic cases in which the incentive to cater to constituencies in the public sector runs counter to good resource stewardship.

This chapter presents two poignant examples of government mismanagement of ocean fisheries and the logic behind them. This is followed by an examination of two prevailing failures in government fishery management: regulation and subsidies.

CANADA'S GREAT COD COLLAPSE

Consider the case of Atlantic Canada's cod fishery. The fishery was once reputed to have one of the world's largest stocks of cod. Indeed, the resource seemed almost limitless. Cod had been fished for nearly five centuries without interruption. Then thanks to the presence of large high-powered factory trawlers, the view that the resource was boundless changed. Cod landings rose dramatically between 1960 and 1975 as fishers caught as many cod as they had in the 250 years following John Cabot's arrival in Newfoundland (Harris 1998, 63–64). The high harvest rate proved to be unsustainable. Once thought to be limitless, cod abundance declined by more than 80 percent over the period (Hutchings and Myers 1995, 59).

In 1977 the fishery received a much needed respite. Canada extended its jurisdiction to 200 miles from shore and removed the foreign trawlers from its newly claimed waters. Over the next five years fishing pressure in the Grand Banks fishery was cut almost in half. Cod abundance nearly doubled in five years, but remained far below historical highs (Hutchings and Myers 1995, 78).

Unfortunately cod never had a chance to recover fully. In the late 1970s, the Canadian federal government increased its involvement in the management of the Grand Banks fishery to promote what it called an "expansionist development philosophy" centered on creating jobs in fishing communities (Brubaker 1998, 10). In quest of short-term political payoffs, government officials set annual catch limits above what could be sustained over the long term. They supported fishers, boat owners, and processors with construction and insurance subsidies, tax breaks, and loan guarantees. They maintained a labor force well in excess of what could be sustained in the long run by the resource by providing overly generous unemployment benefits relative to fisher incomes (Grafton 1996, 145).

Scientists predicted dire consequences for the Grand Banks fishery if such policies continued, but government officials had other priorities. A 1982 government task force "suggested that the economic viability of the industry, maximization of employment subject to income constraint, and Canadian harvesting and processing should be priorities" (Canada, Task Force on Atlantic Fisheries 1982, 60). According to an internal government document, scientific advice was "gruesomely mangled and corrupted to meet political ends" (Canada, Department of Fisheries and Oceans 1993). The document went on to accuse fishery managers of "scientific deception, misinformation, and obfuscation."

By 1992 the scientists' predictions had come true. The cod stock had collapsed to a level never seen before. As an illustration, the estimated spawner biomass (fish age seven years and older) had gone from a high of 1.6 million tons in 1962 to just 22,000 tons in 1992 (Bishop et al. 1993). The story was repeated on a lesser scale for hake, halibut, redfish, haddock, plaice, and flounder. That year the Canadian government was forced to close the Grand Banks cod fishery; as a result, about 40,000 Canadian fishers and processors lost their jobs (Brubaker 1998, 2). A government task force was set up to investigate the crisis and more than $2 billion worth of taxpayer money was allocated to reduce the size of the fishing sector of Atlantic Canada through license buyouts for inshore and nearshore fishers, government-subsidized early retirement for older processing workers, and special retraining and capacity reduction programs (Grafton 1996, 146).

MIMICKING CANADA'S FAILURE

Down the coast, New England's Georges Bank mixed groundfish fishery suffered a similar fate. Like the Grand Banks fishery, the Georges Bank had been one of the most productive demersal fisheries in the world, but it too had been severely overfished during the 1960s and early 1970s. By the mid-1970s, overfishing had resulted in a 70 percent decline in annual landings. Government officials had a chance to sustain a long-term recovery in the fishery when in 1976 the United States extended its claim to ocean resources from 12 to 200 nautical miles from shore. Foreign fishing fleets were banished and groundfish stocks began to recover. Unfortunately this recovery was also short-lived. Along with the elimination of foreign fishers came a concerted effort to expand and modernize the American fishing fleet.

Assisting in the expansion were federal subsidies and a fishery policy that allowed American fishers unlimited access to the Georges Bank fishery. For example, the Fishing Vessel Construction Fund program allowed fishing vessel owners to defer federal income taxes on fishing vessel income if that income was set aside for future vessel construction, reconstruction, and acquisition costs. The program's tax benefits led to the development of newer, larger, better-equipped, and harder-fishing boats, the so-called highliners, in the fishery (Gautman and Kitts 1996, 2, 5). In addition, the Fishing Fleet Vessel Obligation Guarantee program provided a federal guarantee for private loan long-term debt that finances or refinances the costs of fishing vessels and shore-side facilities (National Marine Fisheries Service [NMFS] 1996, 17).

On the management side, the federal government refused to limit the number of fishers despite warnings from government scientists that excessive fishing pressure was again depleting groundfish stocks. Instead federal managers tried various indirect approaches, such as promoting harvest of less popular fish species and limiting the amount of fish that could be caught on a single trip. Not surprisingly such approaches failed to stem fishing pressure, and fish stocks declined further. By 1994 the index of groundfish abundance in Georges Bank off New England had reached a thirty-two-year low.

In the face of continued depletion, the Conservation Law Foundation (CLF) and the Massachusetts Audubon Society filed a lawsuit to force the federal government to protect the fishery. In 1993 a consent decree was entered into between the government and CLF stipulating that measures be developed that would eliminate the overfished condition of cod in five years and haddock in ten years. Subsequently, Amendment 5 to the New England Multispecies Fishery Management Plan (FMP) specified these measures in terms of a moratorium on new vessel entrants, a schedule of reduction in days at sea for trawl and gill net vessels, increases in net mesh size, and expanded areas of closed fishing to protect haddock. Based on a later assessment that stocks of haddock and yellowtail flounder had collapsed and that cod was in immediate danger of the same fate, the federal government issued Amendment 7 to accelerate the existing days at sea reduction schedule established in Amendment 5 as well as carry out other restrictions of fishing (NMFS 1999, 5).

Substantial reductions in fishing effort have taken place in the New England fishery in the past few years. Like the Canadian situation, the domestic fishing industry has paid a heavy price for the government's mismanagement of the fishery, which subsidized a boom and then the inevitable bust. Amendment 5 resulted in a five-year, 50 percent reduction in days at sea, which forced hardships on many fishers who needed the income from higher catches to pay for their earlier fishing investments. A vessel buyout program was initiated in 1995 by the secretary of commerce. The program, which was concluded in 1998, removed seventy-nine fishing vessels at a cost of $25 million and resulted in an approximate 20 percent reduction in fishing effort in the Northeast groundfish fishery (NMFS 1999, 8).

As a result of these measures, there have been modest improvements in the numbers of cod and haddock in recent years. In addition, yellowtail flounder has rebounded to levels not seen since the early 1970s. Meanwhile, fishers displaced from forced reductions on Georges Bank have turned their attention to inshore areas in the Gulf of Maine. Spawning stocks of cod, American plaice, and white hake have declined to record lows in these areas (NMFS 1999, 9).

THE PERVERSITY OF POLITICAL CONTROL

There is a logic behind these two tragedies that explains why they are not flukes. In the public sector, politicians gain favor by doling out goodies to special interests, be they fishers or defense contractors. The benefits are concentrated, and the recipients demonstrate their gratitude by providing a dedicated base of voters for reelection. Bureaucrats, be they generals or fishery managers, are also part of this governmental gravy train. Knowing full well that agency budgets can more easily expand when the constituency it serves is growing, it is easier to go along with programs that promote gifts to the constituency. The costs, however, are diffused among the hundreds of millions of taxpayers, most of whom are unaware that such programs exist. In any event, the cost to any one taxpayer is too small for the taxpayer to devote resources to fight such waste. Just as they do not actively oppose government programs that raise sugar prices, taxpayers do not actively oppose programs that lead to scarcer fish and higher fish prices.

When the outcome is an environmental tragedy, such as the collapse of a fishery, the same politicians who helped expedite the collapse with government handouts can now come to the rescue—spending more taxpayer dollars in temporary relief measures, such as dictating how to fish and providing bailouts to fishers The recipients are "trapped" in an industry that should never have developed so large. They must continue to rely on government prescriptions or face bankruptcy. Politicians, who bear none of the financial costs of their decisions, can tell worried environmentalists that help is along the way vis-à-vis more restrictions on how to fish. Breaking this vicious cycle by establishing exclusive property rights in the fishery is difficult because politicians have little interest in enacting policies that reduce the scope of their power, preferring instead to let nature take its course (Leal 2000).

Specifically, the collapse of Atlantic Canada cod and New England groundfish stocks serves to illustrate three problems of politically controlled resources.

1. Politicians tend to choose actions with short-run political payoffs. In these cases, expanding employment in the fishery served to garner votes for the next election, even though such actions proved to be ecologically, economically, and socially disastrous in the long run.
2. Politics can and does override sound science. Scientific advice that fish stocks were declining rapidly was ignored for the sake of expanding the fishing sector.
3. Politicians and bureaucrats are not held personally accountable for their decisions. Since the moratorium on fishing in the Grand Banks was imposed in 1992, 40,000 fishers and processors in Atlantic Canada have been thrown out of work, but no one in government has been fired, demoted, or even reprimanded (Brubaker 1998, 10).

Although most of the world's fisheries are not in a state of collapse, many are in danger of becoming casualties. The Food and Agriculture Organization

(FAO) of the United Nations reports that at the beginning of the 1990s, about 69 percent of the world's commercial species were fully fished or overfished: 44 percent were fully exploited,[1] 16 percent were overexploited, 6 percent were depleted, and 3 percent were very slowly recovering from overfishing (FAO 1998, 6).

In the United States, the National Marine Fisheries Service reported to Congress in its annual *Status of Fisheries of the United States* that 90 species are overfished and another 10 species are approaching an overfished condition—one-third of the 300 species whose status is known. As usual, Congress finds little motivation to invest in research that would make clear the extent of the problem its deeds have wrought. Unknown is the status of 544 species that are being commercially fished (NMFS 1998, 1).

In addition, there is concern that as conventional high-value species decline, fishers focus their efforts on catching species lower on the food chain and lower in value. This strategy, some argue, not only hurts fisher income but could also jeopardize the chances of recovery for earlier targeted species (McGinn 1998; Pauley et al. 1998).

The rest of this chapter examines the problem of the ocean commons and the two types of government failure plaguing ocean fisheries today. The first is the failure of government regulation to halt overexploitation, as well as its tendency to generate additional wastes in the fishery. The second, which has adversely affected other natural resources (Anderson and Leal 1991, 51–59), is the use of government subsidies and government tax incentives to expand the size of the fishery in spite of clear signs of overcapacity. This type of government failure only serves to create and entrench special interests against meaningful change from the status quo.

THE OCEAN COMMONS

The fundamental reason for depleted fisheries has been known for decades (Clark 1981; Gordon 1954). Ocean fisheries provide the classic case of the tragedy of the commons, in which lack of ownership of jointly exploited fish stocks often leads to depletion of the stocks (Hardin 1968).[2] There are two reasons for this outcome.

- Fishers cannot save fish for the future; if they restrain their harvest to leave enough to reproduce for the following season, the fish may be taken by someone else. Without ownership, any fish left remain available for harvest by any other fisher. The rule of capture prevails.
- Each fisher can capture all the benefits of catching more fish while facing only a fraction of the costs—the harm caused by overfishing—because the cost of stock depletion is split among all fishers. As a result of

this disparity between full benefits received and fractional costs paid, there will be too many fishers in the fishery and too many fish taken. This is the tragedy that no one wants but that commons tend to dictate.

In a commons situation, entering the fishing grounds first and capturing the fish fastest is a compelling strategy. That is when search and capture costs are the lowest. Thus each fisher is motivated to invest in equipment (e.g., faster boats and better detection devices) that improve the chances of winning the race for the fish—equipment that would not be necessary if the fishery were not under the strain of such competition. Not only do the stocks decline, but fishing becomes wastefully expensive as too many fishers invest in too much capital to catch too few fish.

Because costs tend to rise rapidly as fish become scarcer, fisheries have historically reached commercial extinction before they are totally depleted. The additional costs of capturing the few fish exceed the returns, so that it becomes unprofitable to continue (Keen 1988, 32). Thus while extinction may be avoided, the fishery frequently results in a lower than optimal (and perhaps severely depleted) fish population and an overinvestment in fishing capacity. According to recent studies, the world's fishing fleet suffers from overcapacity, with estimates ranging from 30 percent to as high as 50 percent or more (Garcia and Newton 1997, 16–19; Porter 1998, 12).

Economist Frederick Bell provided one of the first empirical verifications of the overexploitation of a commons fishery. Studying New England's northen lobster fishery in 1966, he estimated that an efficient output of lobster would have occurred at 17.2 million pounds. To attain this output, the efficient number of lobster traps would have been 433,000 traps. However, Bell (1972, 156) found that in 1966 fishers employed too much capital (891,000 traps) to harvest too many lobsters (25 million pounds).

In more recent cases, capacity excesses and lost benefits have been assessed for a number of U.S. fisheries suffering from the commons problem. For example:

- It was estimated that 1989 profits in New England's groundfish otter trawl fishery, which at the time comprised 1,100 vessels and 5,300 fishers, could be increased by $150 million annually (90 percent in resource rents and the remainder in consumer surplus). To realize these returns, however, the fishing effort would need to be reduced by 70 percent, and the stock size of groundfish would have to return to a historic level seven times larger than reported in 1989 (Edwards and Murawski 1993). Only a complete collapse of fish stocks and subsequent lawsuit prompted government overseers to begin to reduce the size of the fishery in the late 1990s.
- The number of full-time vessels in the Gulf of Mexico shrimp fishery more than doubled between 1966 and 1991, but annual net revenues

per vessel decreased about 75 percent to approximately $25,000 (in 1990 dollars). Total landings by full-time vessels were virtually unchanged over the period. With a fleet of more than 16,000 vessels and boats operating in 1988, it was estimated that one-third of the fleet could harvest the same amount of shrimp; that is, two-thirds of the fleet could be retired, with the excess capital shifted to other sectors of the economy (Ward and Sutinen 1994).

- A study of the Bering Sea pollock fishery off Alaska estimates that the "catching capacity of vessels . . . appears to be double or more the annual quota" and observes that given the current market conditions "considerable downsizing would be needed to restore profitability" (Miller, Lipton, and Hooker 1994, 37).

- In the Atlantic surf clam fishery, which implemented a quasi-property rights system of individual tradable quotas (ITQs) in 1990, the fleet was reduced by 54 percent within two years; landings per vessel increased while total landings increased slightly. The value of the surf clam resource was estimated to be $57 million in 1992, with a resource rent of more than $11 million accruing to the surf clam industry. Resource rent that was being dissipated before the assignment of ITQs was now being captured by ITQ holders (NMFS 1996).

These examples illustrate the excesses created by the economic waste and subsequent environmental damage created by the commons problem and the benefits that can be achieved by solving it.

REGULATORY FAILURE

Unfortunately today's tragedy is that government regulation has not been able to halt overexploitation in fisheries but has greatly increased costs. For decades government fishery managers have attempted to overcome the commons problem by applying regulations on the harvest (total allowable catch), on fishing effort (e.g., boat size limits, seasonal closures, trip limits), and on vessel entry (limited vessel licensing). Unfortunately all these regulatory approaches have proven to be ineffective as well as wasteful. The reason: Fishers simply increase their reliance on inputs not under regulatory control to maximize their catch. For example, restrictions on the number of fishing days have typically resulted in a surge of investment in larger and faster boats. Restrictions on boat-holding capacity have typically brought more boats into the fishery. Restrictions on fishing areas have led to overfishing in areas that remain open to fishing. Restrictions on one type of gear have led to a surge in the use of another type of gear (Anthony 1990; Kingston 1988). And restrictions on the number of boats through limited

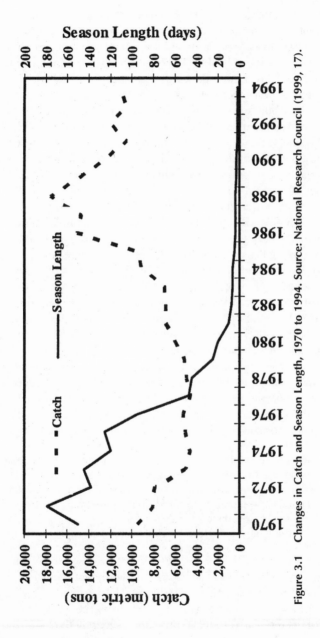

Figure 3.1   Changes in Catch and Season Length, 1970 to 1994. Source: National Research Council (1999, 17).

licensing have resulted in the replacement of existing vessels with more capital-intensive vessels.[3]

An extreme example of regulatory failure is Alaska's halibut fishery, which had no limits on entry from 1970 to 1994. As more fishers entered the fishery, government managers shortened the fishing season in an effort to satisfy the overall catch limit of halibut. Fishers responded by finding ways to catch halibut more quickly, before the total catch limit was reached. Many invested in bigger and more powerful boats, exacerbating the problem of overcapacity created by open access. Before long, a season that used to take several months now was compressed into just two or three days (fig. 3.1). The fishery had become a dangerous derby, held often in bad weather with frequent loss of life. In addition, the price for halibut was believed to be below what it could have been if product deliveries were more evenly distributed throughout the year (Parfit 1995, 30–34).

In addition to overcapitalization, the regulatory process has spurred sometimes absurd regulations on fishing methods. For example, Maryland oystermen at one time could use dredges but had to tow them behind sailboats on all but two days of the week, when motorized boats were allowed (Christy and Scott 1965, 15–16). And in some Alaskan fisheries, fishing boats were required to be no more than fifty feet long (Crutchfield and Pontecorvo 1969, 46).

Such restrictions often favored one user group over another. After examining a host of regulatory data during the 1960s and 1970s, economist James Crutchfield (1973, 115) observed the regulatory process has "generated an ever-increasing mass of restrictive legislation, most of it clothed in the rhetoric of conservation, but bearing the clear marks of pressure politics." The overwhelming majority of these restrictions, Crutchfield decided, reflect "power plays by one ethnic group of fishermen against another, by owners of one gear against another, or by fishermen of one state against another." The combined costs of regulations led Robert Higgs (1982, 82) to conclude:

> The social resource waste has therefore grown steadily larger over time. Today, from a comprehensive point of view, the Washington salmon fishery almost certainly makes a negative contribution to net national product. The opportunity costs of the socially unnecessary resources employed there, plus the socially unnecessary costs of governmental research, management, and regulation, are greater than the total value added by all the labor and capital employed in the fishery.

Without property rights, fishers in a government-regulated fishery still have an incentive to maximize individual catches, instead of the value of the resource. In addition, such a fishery suffers from the additional wastes created by fishers motivated to make investments merely to circumvent the regulations imposed on them. Government regulation is one of the two types of government failure plaguing ocean fisheries today.

SUBSIDIZED FISHING

Subsidized fishing is the other. These subsidies exacerbate the commons problem in three ways. First, by artificially lowering costs and inflating estimates of profits, government subsidies attract more entrants in a fishery. Second, by hiding the true cost of capital, these subsidies spur overinvestments in boats, nets, and other equipment in a fishery. Third, by propping up incomes the subsidies encourage less-efficient fishers to remain in a fishery that is incapable of supporting them based on harvests alone. In short, subsidies to the fishing sector prevent market signals from encouraging members of the industry to stop investing time, labor, and capital in already overfished, overcapitalized fisheries.

Five types of subsidies encourage fishing excesses around the globe. They are income support, capital cost, operating cost, foreign access, resource management, and indirect or cross-sectoral subsidies.

Income Support Subsidies

Income support subsidies discourage exits from fishing, and thus sustain a state of overcapacity in a fishery even in the face of declining harvests due to stock depletion. For example, Norway, Sweden, France, and Finland provide fish price supports as a social welfare scheme for producers. The European Union (EU) through its Common Fisheries Policy implements a number of measures to support domestic fishery prices, including a minimum import price program and programs to remove excess supplies from the market. During the 1980s these programs were funded at about $25 million annually. The EU also co-funds a program to promote the sale of fish at about $50 million per year (Milazzo 1999, 22). Japan, Norway, and France provide compensation when necessary to provide a guaranteed wage specifically for fishers. As noted previously, Canada has a generous unemployment insurance program for fishers that essentially doubles the net earnings of the average fisher and serves as a strong incentive to remain in the industry. Another type of income support subsidy, frequently used in European fisheries, is the "laying-up" grant to fishing vessel owners to remove vessels temporarily from active fishing (Porter 1998, 14–15). The subsidy is usually allocated in the aftermath of moratoria on fishing for depleted species. It allows financially hard-pressed fishers to wait for fish stocks to rebound before resuming fishing.

The United States supplies a limited amount of income support to fishers through the Department of Agriculture's Surplus Commodity Program. In 1998 the department allocated $14.4 million under this program for fisheries products, all of which was designated for Pacific salmon products. Also carried out is an export promotion program that includes fishery products.

About $7 million in government funds is used to promote the exportation of fish from U.S. fisheries (Milazzo 1999, 25).

Capital Cost Subsidies

Huge investments in vessel construction led to a doubling of the world's commercial fishing fleet from 1970 to 1989, when new tonnage was added at an annual average rate of 4.6 percent. Over the same period, total marine landings increased from 60 million to more than 86 million metric tons in the peak year of 1989. This translates to an average annual increase of 2.4 percent (FAO 1992). Thus new fishing capacity was being added at nearly twice the rate of increase in marine catches.

Government subsidies were behind the inordinate increase in the world's fishing fleet, relative to the world catch trend. For example, the European Union increased spending on its commercial fleets from $80 million in 1983 to more than $500 million a year in 1990, of which one-fifth went to boat building or upgrading. By the early 1990s Japan's national government had extended an estimated $19 billion worth of credit to its commercial fishing fleet (*Economist* 1994, 13, 21). And in the United States, $1.6 billion of government and private investment was used to build up the domestic factory trawler fleet in Alaskan waters (Stump and Batker 1996, 3).

Government grants, low-interest loans, loan guarantees, and income tax preferences are the main contributors to sizable leaps in fishing capacity. In some cases they have also paved the way for fishery collapses. For example, the Canadian government's construction and modernization program in the 1950s and 1960s led to a major buildup in the northwestern Atlantic fleet that was at least twice the size needed to catch the maximum sustainable yield of fish each year (Porter 1998, 15). In the early 1980s the government bankrolled a struggling fishing industry suffering from depleted fish stocks with income support subsidies. It then subsidized another buildup of the domestic fleet following the removal of foreign fishing, which led to the disastrous decline in Atlantic cod in the early 1990s. Similarly, the EU financed a major fleet buildup and modernization for its member countries during the 1970s and 1980s. As harvests remained the same and then plummeted in the 1980s, it became obvious that the EU's funding resulted in fishing far in excess of what could be sustained by the resource. Current funding by the EU indicates an inability to learn from its previous mistakes. From 1994 to 1999 the EU budgeted $747.7 million in "fleet renewal and modernization" (Porter 1998, 22).

In the United States a number of federal programs encouraged the development of the domestic fishing fleet from the 1960s through the 1980s. The 1964 Amendment to the Fishing Fleet Improvement Act financed up to 50 percent of vessel construction costs. The 1969 Fishermen's Protection Act defrayed the costs of foreign seizure of U.S. vessels. The 1970 Fishing Vessel Construction Fund program (later known as the Capital Construction Fund [CCF]) deferred payment of federal income taxes provided the money was used to construct or reconstruct a vessel. The 1973 Fishing Fleet Vessel Obligation Guarantee program (FOG) financed up to 87.5 percent of the cost of construction, reconstruction, or reconditioning of fishing vessels and shoreside facilities.[4] New guarantees in 1995 totaled $25 million, and the outstanding loan portfolio reached $200 million (Milazzo 1999, 45). Notably, both CCF and FOG contributed to the rapid buildup of the domestic fleet in the Georges Bank fishery after the removal of foreign fishing in the late 1970s. In addition, the federal government funds much scientific, gear, and marketing research, supported by taxes from the Dingell-Johnson Act of 1950 and Wallop-Breaux Amendments, the Saltonstall-Kennedy Act of 1954, and the Commercial Fisheries Research and Development Act of 1964. Research conducted with these funds has primarily been aimed at promoting development of the fishing industry.

The huge buildup of the world's fishing fleet can be linked to state-owned or state-run fishing enterprises as well. For decades the Soviet government made huge capital investments in expanding and modernizing its distant-water fishing fleet. By the mid-1970s annual capital investments in the fleet averaged more than $1 billion. At the time, the Soviet fleet of larger vessels accounted for an incredible 50 percent of the total world high-seas and distant-water fishing vessel tonnage, but accounted for only 15 percent of total world landings (Milazzo 1999, 26–27). The Soviet fleet was grossly overcapitalized and required massive state support to keep operating. A U.S. government assessment from the mid-1970s determined that the average Soviet catch per tonnage in the high-seas fleet was less than one-third the world average. Following the collapse of the Soviet Union, the fishing industry experienced a precipitous drop in government financial support, and the industry contracted dramatically in the 1990s.

China is poised to take up the slack. In a 1995 government publication on its long-term fishery development policy, one of its stated goals is to significantly expand distant-water fishing through government investments. Its distant-water fleet is dominated by a few state-run enterprises that operate mainly in the Pacific and Indian Oceans and off western Africa. From 1986 to 1991 the fleet grew from practically nothing to 275 vessels, and the distant-water catch jumped from 0.02 to 0.323 million metric tons (Milazzo 1999, 39).

Operating Cost Subsidies

Government-funded insurance and compensation programs for vessels and equipment are among the most important in this category. These programs are designed to help defray the industry's cost of marine insurance and damage to and loss of their boats, gear, and other equipment, and as such, they encourage greater investments in capital than would be the case if fishers faced the true costs of insurance and equipment losses. A revealing example comes again from Japan. The Fisheries Agency of Japan has a special account in the amount of $500 million that funds vessel and other equipment insurance and losses for the fishing industry (Milazzo 1999, 19).

Foreign Access Subsidies

Another type of subsidy is the financial assistance that governments provide their fishing fleets to obtain access to foreign waters. A World Bank study estimates that between $.5 and $1 billion is spent annually by countries on foreign access subsidies (Milazzo 1999, 42). This type of subsidy is especially troubling because it effectively transfers excess fishing capacity from northern to southern hemispheres and probably tends to undermine the economic and perhaps even the conservation interests of coastal developing nations. Such a subsidy can assume many forms, but the most important type is government-to-government payment for foreign fishing access.

A good example of how these subsidies work is the access arrangement the EU, a major player in subsidized foreign access, has with the West African nation of Mauritania (Milazzo 1999, 36–37). In June 1996, the EU signed a five-year access for trade agreement with the government of Mauritania that lifted an EU embargo on fishery imports from that nation in return for EU payments of $70 million per year. The agreement also permits an increase in EU fishing access to Mauritanian waters, authorizes higher EU total harvests, and, for the first time, specifically allows EU-directed fisheries for high-valued squid and octopus. The Mauritanian fishing industry expressed alarm over the agreement because it sanctions increased fishing in already fully and overharvested fisheries. The EU subsidizes similar access arrangements with other West African countries, including Cape Verde, Gambia, Morocco, and Sierra Leone. The governments are unstable and corrupt, so the subsidies can be expected only to line the pockets of government officials, not help impoverished citizens.

Another major player in this area is Japan. It spends almost $100 million on distant-water access arrangements, mainly for the benefit of vessels operating in waters of developing countries in the western Pacific and elsewhere. In addition, another $100 million is spent on foreign fisheries assistance, an objective of which is to secure continued access for its own fleet in waters of the recipient developing nations (Milazzo 1999, 39).

American involvement in foreign fishing subsidies is limited to the tuna purse seine fleet's operations in the southwest Pacific. Under the terms of a 1987 agreement with a number of Pacific island states, the United States gained access for up to fifty-five U.S.-flag purse seiners for five years in exchange for fees paid by industry and $10 million in annual economic development assistance provided by the government. The agreement was extended in 1991, with the government increasing its annual payment to $14 million (Milazzo 1999, 41).

Resource Management Subsidies

Most countries allow their fishers practically free access to their fisheries. If fishers do not pay user fees sufficient to cover the full costs of managing the resource, fishers do not internalize those social costs but instead pass them along to the population at large. The result is a misallocation of the resource and another incentive for overfishing.

A look at the United States provides some insight into the extent of the subsidy. The latest amendments to the Magnuson-Stevens Fishery Conservation and Management Act[5] appropriate the following sums to carry out management of federal fisheries: $147 million in 1996, $151 million in 1997, $155 million in 1998, and $159 million in 1999. In addition, the U.S. Coast Guard allocated $353 million for fisheries law enforcement in 1997. Therefore, the federal government spends about $500 million annually on management and enforcement of federally managed fisheries. In fiscal year 1993, the secretary of commerce collected less than $900,000 from commercial fishers for various fishing permits, or nearly 0.2 percent of the cost of management and enforcement (Gorte 1995, 10–11). Thus the federal government has a long way to go in recovering the federal taxpayers' considerable investment in marine fishery management.

Indirect or Cross-Sectoral Subsidies

Indirect or cross-sectoral subsidies are not supplied directly to fishers, but indirectly benefit them and tend to stimulate additional fishing effort and capacity in ocean fisheries. Standing out in this category are subsidies supplied directly to shipyards. According to a recent World Bank study, subsidies to the global shipbuilding sector that are passed along to the fishing industry total $1 billion annually (Milazzo 1999, 52). As an example, Norway provided generous subsidies in the 1980s to its shipbuilders to refurbish vessels for use as factory trawlers in Alaskan waters. Recently the owners of two of these factory trawlers had to pay a considerably higher tax bill when the IRS ruled that the subsidies—in this case $1.75 million—constituted taxable income (*World Fishing* 1996, 4). Shipbuilding subsidies take on a variety of forms. In Japan they include vessel export credits, vessel export credit insurance, and government funds for vessel research and development; in Spain they are tax exemptions for exported vessels and government loans with below-market interest rates to shipyards; and in Norway government guarantees of loans to shipyards and government funds for vessel research and development. Not surprisingly, nations that provide generous subsidies to their shipbuilders are also major fishing nations.

Because many subsidy programs are either not budgeted (e.g., subsidized lending) or provided by government agencies not directly involved in the commercial fishing industry (public infrastructure programs), estimating the total amount of worldwide fishing subsidies is difficult. In 1992 the FAO estimated that most of the global fishing industry's annual deficit of $54 billion in the late 1980s was covered by government subsidies (FAO 1993, 32). It was hardly an exact number, but it did give some idea of their potential magnitude. A more recent estimate comes from a 1998 World Bank study, which reports that annual global fishing subsidies range from $15 to $21 billion, or about 20 and 25 percent of annual revenues from global ex-vessel fish sales (Milazzo 1999, 74). Not included in these estimates are subsidies provided by subnational governments, such as the U.S. states, the Chinese provinces, and the Japanese prefectures.

CONCLUSION

In the political setting, government decision makers have incentives to provide constituents with products and services they want at little or no cost to them. Political entrepreneurs in this arena are rewarded with more votes, more authority, and more control over taxpayer dollars, but they do not face the reality check of profitability that entrepreneurs in the private sector face. Moreover, in the case of commercial fisheries the long-term health of the resource is being sacrificed for short-term political goals.

Government regulation fails to curtail the incentive that fishers face to overfish in a commons, which generates wastes. An effective cure to overfishing must be organized around well-defined property rights to either the resource or shares of the catch. A step in this direction is the application of individual, transferable quotas (ITQs) in ocean fisheries. ITQs have already registered major successes in curtailing overcapacity and in helping rebuild fish stocks in ocean fisheries in New Zealand and Iceland (Leal 2000, 8–10).

Government subsidies exacerbate the commons and regulatory problems plaguing ocean fisheries. They also create vested interests in the status quo of overcapitalized fisheries. They may be politically expedient in the short term, but they inevitably harm the resource and the economy down the road. Canadian citizens found this out when the federal government doled out tax breaks, loan guarantees, and lavish unemployment benefits to boost employment in Atlantic Canada's fishing industry, all of which contributed to the creation and perpetuation of fishing excesses and subsequent collapse of the northern cod fishery.

Given the pervasiveness of ineffective regulation and subsidies, effective policy reform in ocean fisheries must not only include the establishment of property rights but also the elimination of harmful effort-enhancing government subsidies to the fishing industry.

NOTES

1. Fully exploited stocks are those producing catches that are close to their maximum sustainable yield. This implies that there is no room for expanding fishing without a stock being overfished. Given that few countries have established effective incentives for aligning fishing capacity—vessels, gear, and technology associated with fishing power—with sustainable harvests, these stocks bear carefully monitoring.

2. Community-run, coastal fisheries are an exception. See Leal (1996).

3. For example, despite limited entry in the Scotia-Fundy fishery off Atlantic Canada, the gross registered tonnage of registered inshore vessels increased by 35 percent from 1978 to 1981. See Halliday, Peacock, and Burke (1992).

4. This act was intended to make U.S.-built vessels as affordable as foreign-built vessels.

5. 16 U.S.C. 1801.

REFERENCES

Anderson, Terry L., and Donald R. Leal. 1991. *Free Market Environmentalism*. San Francisco: Pacific Research Institute for Public Policy.

Anderson, Terry L., and Donald R. Leal. 1997. *Enviro-Capitalists: Doing Good While Doing Well*. Lanham, MD: Rowman & Littlefield.

Anthony, V. C. 1990. The New England Groundfish Fishery after Ten Years under the Magnuson Fishery Conservation and Management Act. *North American Journal of Fisheries Management* 10: 175–84.

Bishop, C. A., E. F. Murphy, M. B. Davis, J. W. Baird, and G. A. Rose. 1993. *An Assessment of the Cod Stock in NAFO Divisions 2j+3k*. NAFO Scientific Council Research Document 93/86, serial number N2771, Dartmouth, NS, Canada.

Bell, Frederick W. 1972. Technological Externalities and Common-Property Resources: An Empirical Study of the U.S. Northern Lobster Fishery. *Journal of Political Economy* 80 (January/February): 148–58.

Brubaker, Elizabeth. 1998. Property Rights: Creating Incentives and Tools for Sustainable Fisheries Management. *Fraser Forum*. Vancouver, BC: Fraser Institute, April.

Canada, Department of Fisheries and Oceans. 1993. *Science Branch Council Final Report*. Ottawa, ON.

Canada, Task Force on Atlantic Fisheries. 1982. *Navigating Troubled Waters for the Atlantic Fisheries*. Report prepared by the Task Force on Atlantic Fisheries. Ottawa, ON: Ministry of Supply and Services.

Christy, Francis T., Jr., and Anthony Scott. 1965. *The Common Wealth in Ocean Fisheries*. Baltimore: Johns Hopkins University Press.

Clark, Colin W. 1981. Profit Maximization and the Extinction of Animal Species. *Journal of Political Economy* 81 (August): 950–60.

Crutchfield, James A. 1973. Resources from the Sea. In *Ocean Resources and Public Policy*, ed. T. Saunders English. Seattle: University of Washington Press, 105–33.

Crutchfield, J. A., and G. Pontecorvo. 1969. *The Pacific Salmon Fisheries: A Study of Irrational Conservation*. Baltimore: Johns Hopkins University Press.

Economist. 1994. The Catch about Fish. March 19.

Edwards, Steven F., and Steven A. Murawski. 1993. Potential Economic Benefits from Efficient Harvest of New England Groundfish. *North American Journal of Fisheries Management* 13 (Summer): 437–49.

Food and Agriculture Organization. 1992. *World Fisheries Situation*. Prepared for the International Conference on Responsible Fishing in Cancun, Mexico, May 6–8.

———. 1993. *Marine Fisheries and the Law of the Sea: A Decade of Change*. Rome, Italy.

———. 1998. *The State of World Fisheries and Aquaculture*. Online: www.fao.org/docrep/w9900e/w9900e00.htm.

Garcia, S. M., and C. Newton. 1997. Current Situation, Trends, and Prospects in World Capture Fisheries. In *Global Trends: Fisheries Management*, ed. Ellen K. Pikitch, Daniel D. Huppert, and Michael P. Sissenwine. Bethesda, MD: American Fisheries Society.

Gautman, Amy B., and Andrew W. Kitts. 1996. *Data Description and Statistical Summary of the 1983–92 Cost-Earnings Data Base for Northeast U.S. Commercial Fishing Vessels*. NOAA Technical Memorandum NMFS-NE-112. Silver Spring, MD, December.

Gordon, H. Scott. 1954. The Economic Theory of a Common Property Resource: The Fishery. *Journal of Political Economy* 62 (April): 124–42.

Gorte, Ross W. 1995. *Natural Resource "Subsidy" Issues*. Washington, DC: Congressional Research Service.

Grafton, R. Quentin. 1996. Rights-Based Fisheries Management. In *Taking Ownership: Property Rights and Fishery Management on the Atlantic Coast*, ed. Brian Lee Crowley. Halifax, Nova Scotia: Atlantic Institute for Market Studies, 148–81.

Halliday, R. G., F. G. Peacock, and D. L. Burke. 1992. Development of Management Measures for the Groundfish Fishery in Atlantic Canada. *Marine Policy* 16: 411–26.

Hardin, Garrett. 1968. The Tragedy of the Commons. *Science* 162: 1243–48.

Harris, Michael. 1998. *Lament for an Ocean: The Collapse of the Atlantic Cod Fishery: A True Story*. Toronto, ON: McCelland & Stewart.

Higgs, Robert. 1982. Legally Induced Technical Regress in the Washington Salmon Fishery. *Research in Economic History* 7: 82–95.

Hutchings, J. A., and R. A. Myers. 1995. The Biological Collapse of Atlantic Cod off Newfoundland and Labrador: An Exploration of Historical Changes in Exploitation, Harvesting Technology, and Management. In *The North Atlantic Fishery: Strengths, Weaknesses, and Challenges*, ed. R. Arnason and L. F. Felt. Charlottetown, PEI: Institute of Island Studies, University of Prince Edward Island, 37–93.

Keen, Elmer A. 1988. *Ownership and Productivity of Marine Fishery Resources*. Blacksburg, VA: McDonald and Woodward Publishing.

Kingston, Jennifer A. 1988. Northeast Fishermen Catch Everything, and That's a Problem. *New York Times*, November 13.

Leal, Donald R. 1996. Community-Run Fisheries: Preventing the Tragedy of the Commons. In *Taking Ownership: Property Rights and Fishery Management on the Atlantic Coast*, ed. Brian Lee Crowley. Halifax, NS: Atlantic Institute for Market Studies, 183–220.

———. 2000. Homesteading the Oceans: The Case for Property Rights in U.S. Fisheries. *PERC Policy Series*, PS-19. Bozeman, MT: PERC, August.

McGinn, Anne Platt. 1998. The Worldwatch Report: Free Fall in Global Fish Stocks. *Environmental News Network*, May 7. Online: www.enn.com/enn-features-archive/1998/05/050798/0507fea-21854.asp.

Milazzo, Matteo. 1999. *Subsidies in World Fisheries: A Reexamination*. World Bank Technical Paper No. 406 (Fisheries Series). Washington, DC: National Academy Press.

Miller, M., D. Lipton, and P. Hooker. 1994. *Profile of Change: A Review of Offshore Factory Trawler Operations in the Bering Sea/Aleutian Islands Pollock Fishery*. Report to the National Marine Fisheries Service, Silver Spring, MD.

National Marine Fisheries Service. 1996. Our Living Oceans: The Economic Status of U.S. Fisheries, 1996. December. Online: www.st.nmfs.gov/econ/oleo/oleo.html (cited: August 12, 1999).

———. 1998. Report to Congress: Status of Fisheries of the United States. September. Online: www.nmfs.noaa.gov/sfa/98stat.pdf (cited: July 10, 2000).

———. 1999. Our Living Oceans: Report on the Status of U.S. Living Marine Resources. 1999. U.S. Department of Commerce, NOAA Technical Memorandum NMFS-F/SPO-41. Online: spo.nwr.noaa.gov/olo99.htm (cited: July 10, 2000).

National Research Council. 1999. *Sharing the Fish: Toward a National Policy in Individual Fishing Quotas*. Washington, DC: National Academy Press.

Parfit, Michael. 1995. Diminishing Returns: Exploiting the Ocean's Bounty. *National Geographic*, November.

Pauley, Daniel, Villy Christensen, Johanne Dalsgaard, Rainer Froese, and Francisco Torres Jr. 1998. Fishing Down the Marine Food Webs. *Science* 279: 860–63.

Porter, Gareth. 1998. Too Much Fishing Fleet, Too Few Fish: A Proposal for Eliminating Global Fishing Overcapacity. Draft. World Wildlife Fund, Washington, DC, August.

Stump, Ken, and Dave Batker. 1996. Sinking Fast—How Factory Trawlers Are Destroying U.S. Fisheries. Online: www.greenpeace.org/~oceans/ (cited: May 15, 2001).

Ward, J., and J. G. Sutinen. 1994. Vessel Entry-Exit Behavior in the Gulf of Mexico Shrimp Fishery. *American Journal Agricultural Economics* 76(4): 916–23.

World Fishing. 1996. Factory Trawlers Face Tax Demand. April.

4

Federal Flood Policies: 150 Years of Environmental Mischief

David E. Gerard

Extensive media coverage of the 1993 floods in the Midwest vividly exposed the fallibility of flood control measures. The public looked on as communities prepared for the flood waters, fled for higher ground, and picked up the pieces when the waters receded. The flooding damaged 100,000 homes, inundated thousands of acres of cropland, and left entire communities submerged. The 1993 floods caused $12 to $16 billion in property damage, and the federal government doled out more than $4 billion in various forms of disaster aid.

Although the personal tragedies of the flood were well documented, what the television cameras failed to capture is how federal flood policies have subverted market processes, resulting in overinvestment of public and private resources into the floodplain, transfers of billions of dollars of wealth, and "continental-scale ecological damage" (Weiner 1996, 322). As is the case with most riverine flooding, the midwestern flooding was a disaster waiting to happen. It is impossible to predict with any certainty *when* major flooding will occur, but there are few questions concerning *where* it will occur (National Science Foundation 1980, 14–15).

The buildup of capital and infrastructure and the conversion of floodplain wetlands into cropland ensured that when the flood waters came the damage would be momentous. The federal government has spent upward of $100 billion on flood control measures, yet if anything, flood damages continue to rise. And flood damages will continue to escalate, not because there is more flooding but because there is more stuff in the way to be damaged.

Federal flood control policies can be traced back to the mid-nineteenth century when land policy promoted the conversion of wetlands (then known as swamp or overflow lands) to what were considered more productive uses. The federal government granted lands to the states with the

understanding that the states sell these lands and use the proceeds to finance construction of structural flood control measures, such as levees,
dams, flood walls, high-flow diversions, and storage reservoirs.

Otherwise there was limited direct federal involvement until the political climate of the New Deal led to the nationalization of flood control. Following the
Flood Control Act in 1936, flood control quickly became a multibillion-dollar
federal program. The U.S. Army Corps of Engineers, the chief architect of federal flood control, offers a textbook example of government versus the environment. As mandated by congressional appropriations, the agency promotes,
builds, and maintains billions of dollars' worth of fiscally questionable and environmentally disruptive projects along thousands of miles of waterways.

In addition to these structural measures, the federal government also runs the
National Flood Insurance Program (NFIP). For a variety of reasons, private insurers do not consider flood damages to be insurable risks. In response Congress introduced subsidized flood insurance through the NFIP as a means to alleviate the pressure of mounting disaster relief payments. Although it is
tempting to argue that subsidized insurance encourages extensive floodplain
development, this is a difficult case to make empirically. Only 20 to 30 percent
of those eligible to purchase federal flood insurance do so, and many of these
policies are issued to extremely high-risk properties. Predictably the NFIP is
plagued by the same problems that frustrate the emergence of private flood insurance markets, and consequently the program is awash in red ink.

Generous disaster relief may well be the Achilles' heel for the NFIP. Expanded since the New Deal, federal disaster relief now creates significant expectations for taxpayer-provided resources, and disaster assistance is viewed
by many as an entitlement. Generous relief programs also reduce the expected
costs of locating in harm's way, and therefore these programs encourage
floodplain development. People see little reason to purchase even subsidized
insurance if there is an expectation that disaster relief will be forthcoming.

Finally, approximately 70 percent of the floodplains affected by the 1993
midwestern flood were in agricultural use, so agricultural policies have significant implications on floodplain development decisions. These policies include price and income support programs, export policies, crop insurance,
and myriad tax code provisions that influence cropping and tilling decisions.
Although these programs are all important, this paper will focus on federal
flood control policies.

BACKGROUND: FLOODS, FLOODPLAIN INVESTMENT, AND ENVIRONMENTAL DAMAGES

A riverine flood is a temporary inundation of lands adjacent to a waterway,
and such flooding occurs periodically as the result of the breakup of ice

jams, natural or man-made dams, or simply a lot of rain. The area that gets inundated is the floodplain. In general, an area is classified as a floodplain when the chance of flooding is 1 percent or greater in any year. If the probability of a flood is estimated to be 1 percent, the area is called a 100-year floodplain. Likewise, a 50-year floodplain is an area with a one in fifty (2 percent) chance of flooding in any given year.

The widespread flooding in 1993 resulted from a combination of unusual, but not unique, factors—the persistence of rainfall on already saturated soil, coupled with the confluence of heavy flows from the upper Mississippi and lower Missouri River basins. Although President Clinton called the flooding a 500-year event (i.e., a 0.2 percent chance of occurring in any given year), and indeed water flows were at 500-year levels at some gauging stations, water flows were below the 100-year level at many stations. Moreover, flood waters were less than 50-year flood heights at four of the six Mississippi River stations (Philippi 1995, 72). Many of the farms and communities affected by the midwestern flooding were located in five- or twenty-year floodplains, so it should not have come as a shock when the flood waters rolled in.

Not all floodplain development is undesirable or inefficient. Individuals will plant or build in a floodplain if the expected benefits exceed the expected costs. Such a decision is generally considered to be socially efficient if individuals bear all the costs and reap all the benefits of development. In some cases the benefits of floodplain development will outweigh the costs. The floodplain can indeed be a tempting place to locate, given the scenic and aesthetic values, access to water, and transportation benefits. With respect to agricultural potential, the flat topography and rich soil of the floodplain bottomlands have tremendous appeal. Corn yields in Missouri floodplains, for instance, average 15 percent higher than those across the rest of the state (Galloway Report 1994, 38).[1] Floodplains, of course, are often adjacent to navigable waters that facilitate transportation of agricultural commodities. Given the expansiveness of floodplains in the United States—almost 7 percent of the lower forty-eight states is part of a 100-year floodplain (National Science Foundation 1980, 30)—we would expect to see some degree of floodplain development even without the helping hand of government.

Still one cannot ignore the fact that the federal government spends billions of dollars on capital and infrastructure to prevent or reduce flood damages, offers subsidized flood insurance, and provides generous disaster relief to flood victims. These policies alter the individual decision calculus by reducing the individual costs of floodplain development. Consequently, the policies induce further investment, whether in the form of residential construction, community development, or farming. There is no reason to believe that people are making irrational decisions because the costs of structural flood control measures and disaster relief have been incurred by the government. We would, however, expect many people currently located in the floodplain to seek higher ground if they had to bear all these costs.

Environmental Impacts of Flood Control

Alterations of streams and rivers to facilitate navigation, irrigation, and flood control constitute some of the greatest engineering feats of the twentieth century. These hydrological modifications, as they are known, include measures to regularize or modify stream flow, channelization, dredging, and dam and levee construction. There are a number of incredible examples of the impacts of such alterations. For example, to facilitate navigation on the Missouri River the Army Corps of Engineers narrowed the average width of the river from 2,363 to 789 feet. Narrowing the channel allowed farmers to plant crops on 180,000 acres of what was largely open water (Faber 1996, 4). The corps has also gone to incredible lengths to prevent the Atchafalaya River from capturing the flow and essentially changing the course of the Mississippi River (McPhee 1989). At the same time, much of Louisiana would be submerged without structural control measures, but it seems that these measures are causing large sections of the state to sink into the sea. The ecological impacts of these projects are certainly fantastic, though the exact nature of the impacts is unknown and probably unknowable.

Hydrological modifications carried out by the corps are also a significant source of water quality degradation. A recent survey of states and tribal governments shows that the alteration of free-flowing rivers is a major source of water-quality impairment to U.S. rivers and streams (Environmental Protection Agency [EPA] 2000). The EPA surveyed 840,402 miles of rivers and streams, and found that 57,763 miles (about 7 percent) were impaired by hydrological modifications. After agricultural runoff, the next leading source of water-quality impairment in the United States is the modification of rivers and streams. And, of course, a major rationale for modifying streams and rivers is flood control.

Federal flood control policies and floodplain development have also directly encouraged the conversion of wetlands to alternative uses. Although vaguely defined, a wetlands encompasses coastal and inland areas, and includes such diverse ecosystems as forested wetlands, bogs, marshes, and swamps. The salient characteristic of a wetland is that the soil was formed by water, and the plants in the system have adapted to water. For these lands the water table is generally at or close to the surface, or else the land is entirely submerged. Lands adjacent to rivers and streams are often wetlands (wetlands are also found in field potholes and around standing bodies of water) and provide a variety of functions, including flood conveyance, flood

storage, storm buffers, habitat for fish, waterfowl and other wildlife, water fil-
tration, sediment control, groundwater recharge, and timber production (National Research Council [NRC], 1992, 265).

There has been extensive wetland loss in the United States. Dahl (1990)
found that more than half of the wetlands that existed in the 1780s have
been depleted, and in the upper Midwest these figures approach 90 percent. Wetland depletion on this scale almost certainly has substantial impacts on their ecological functions, most visibly on water quality and on fish
and wildlife habitat. Many rivers receive effluent discharges and runoff, including agricultural chemicals and industrial and municipal wastewater. To
the extent that flood control encourages wetland conversion, federal policies can have substantial impacts. For example, Stavins and Jaffe (1990) find
that forested wetlands have been particularly hard hit by federal flood control projects that have promoted conversion of forested wetlands to cropland by making agricultural use feasible. They estimate that federal flood
control policies were responsible for 30 percent of wetland deforestation in
Arkansas, Louisiana, and Mississippi between 1935 and 1984. This figure
likely understates the total impact of federal policies—the federal government began encouraging the depletion and deforestation of wetlands as far
back as 1850.

Together hydrological modifications and land conversion have substantial
implications for the water quality and fish and wildlife habitat. According to
the EPA (2000, 75): "[s]eparating the river channel from the floodplain
through flood control and land use conversion measures has reduced the
ability of the [Mississippi] river to cleanse itself of nutrients and has starved
the marshes of Louisiana of sediment needed to offset subsidence of sea-
level rise." The impacts on habitat have also been pronounced. For instance,
commercial fishing harvests on the Missouri River have declined by more
than 80 percent, and forty-six species along the Mississippi River are listed as
rare, threatened, endangered, or of special concern (Galloway Report 1994,
53–55).

FEDERAL LAND POLICIES AND WETLAND CONVERSION

Federal involvement in floodplain management and flood control predates
what is considered the era of big government that accelerated during the
New Deal. In fact early federal policies that emerged in response to riverine
flooding in the lower Mississippi basin explicitly targeted the conversion of
wetlands.

Through the swampland acts of 1849, 1850, and 1860 the federal government granted millions of acres of lands to the states with the understanding that the states would sell the land to finance development of

levees and other internal improvements. The constituency was initially confined to Louisiana, Mississippi, and Arkansas, but soon grew to include Alabama, California, Florida, Indiana, Iowa, Michigan, Minnesota, Missouri, Ohio, Oregon, and Wisconsin. Overall, the swampland acts led to privatization of nearly 65 million acres. Notably, substantial portions of land transferred did not even remotely meet the criteria of "swampland" (Gates 1968, 321–30).

Table 4.1 compares total wetland loss and total lands transferred under the swampland acts. Obviously there is not a one-to-one correspondence between what passed as a swamp and what Dahl (1990) considers a wetland. That coupled with widespread corruption associated with the swampland acts (Gates 1968, 321–30) certainly dampens any strong inferences about the precise magnitude of the effects of the federal policies. Nevertheless, it is clear that a high percentage of wetlands was destroyed. Federal policy encouraged this devastation and continued to encourage wetland conversion into the 1970s (NRC 1992, 264–65). The underlying influence was flood control.

The transfer, drainage, and conversion of the so-called swamplands to alternate uses bolstered demand for new and better structural flood control measures. These demands were not immediately accommodated, but the next century would see the physical transformation of virtually every significant inland waterway in the United States for irrigation, navigation, and flood control, and the federal government led the way.

Table 4.1 Wetland Depletion and Land Transfers under the Swampland Acts (Million Acres)

State	Total Acres	Wetlands 1780s	Wetlands 1980s	Depletion (%)	Depletion	Land Transfers
Alabama	33.03	7.57	3.78	50	3.79	0.44
Arkansas	33.99	9.85	2.76	72	7.09	7.69
California	101.56	5.00	0.45	91	4.55	2.19
Florida	37.48	20.33	11.04	46	9.29	20.33
Illinois	36.10	8.21	1.25	85	6.96	1.46
Indiana	23.23	5.60	0.75	87	4.85	1.26
Iowa	36.03	4.00	0.42	89	3.58	1.20
Louisiana	52.65	16.19	8.78	46	7.41	9.58
Michigan	37.26	11.20	5.58	50	5.62	5.68
Minnesota	53.80	15.07	8.70	42	6.37	4.71
Mississippi	30.54	9.87	4.07	59	5.80	3.35
Missouri	44.60	4.84	0.64	87	4.20	3.43
Ohio	26.38	5.00	0.48	90	4.52	0.03
Oregon	62.07	2.26	1.39	38	0.87	0.29
Wisconsin	35.94	9.80	5.33	46	4.47	3.36

Sources: Dahl and Johnson (1991) and Gates (1968).

BUREAUCRACY VERSUS THE ENVIRONMENT:
THE U.S. ARMY CORPS OF ENGINEERS

The economic theory of bureaucracy begins with the assumption that government officials, like everyone else, act in their self-interest. Specifically they seek to maximize their budgets, expand the scope of their power, secure perks, or pursue other objectives that may not square with the public interest.[2] Government agencies pursue such objectives because congressional oversight is generally handled by legislators with the highest demand for the agency's output. That is, members of Congress who want flood control subsidies for their states are likely to dominate oversight committees. In some instances congressional review may be limited because information is generally provided and controlled by the agencies. Agencies become their own vested special interests, producing too much output at too high a cost.

In terms of expansion of its budget and its responsibilities, the U.S. Army Corps of Engineers has been one of the most successful agencies ever. Its primary responsibilities are navigation and flood control, but its projects are expansive: The corps "dams rivers, deepens rivers, straightens rivers, ripraps rivers, builds bridges across rivers, builds huge navigation locks and dams, builds groins on rivers and beaches, builds hatcheries, builds breakwaters, builds piers, and repairs beach erosion." The prolific output, the dubious fiscal soundness of the projects, and the selective crafting of information enshrine the corps as an exemplary case study in the economics of bureaucracy. Unfortunately the environmental consequences of the agency's projects have been substantial. In the process of its myriad activities, it has "ruined more wetlands than anyone in history, except perhaps its counterpart in the Soviet Union" (Reisner 1986, 179–80).

The corps had modest beginnings. In response to a series of Mississippi floods during and following the Civil War, Congress established the Mississippi River Commission in 1879. The commission, with corps involvement, surveyed the basin and determined that a system of levees was the best course of action. Congress and the states provided funding for projects (Moore and Moore 1989, 2). At the time, however, Congress showed little interest in building and maintaining a nationwide system of levees and dams, and total federal outlays were limited. Between 1882 and 1916 federal and local governments spent $120 million on flood control.

The congressional restraint was at least in part due to the questionable federal authority to oversee flood control projects. The concept of limiting congressional powers to those enumerated in the Constitution was taken seriously a century ago when the federal government was considerably smaller. Aside from the Mississippi, the only other rivers with corps involvement were in California, where debris from hydraulic mining operations had dreadful downstream impacts. In 1893 Congress set up the California Debris Commission to address these matters. Otherwise, federal involvement remained confined to flood control projects along the Mississippi River. These projects were often clothed as navigation projects, which did not involve the same thorny constitutional issues as flood control.

A series of federal laws, which typically were enacted in response to severe flooding episodes, slowly ratcheted up federal involvement. The Flood Control Act of 1917 took an important step by being the first to authorize direct funding for federal flood control. Following disastrous flooding in 1927, Congress exercised its newfound authority with the authorization of an unprecedented amount of flood control expenditures—$325 million (Philippi 1994).

The political and judicial environments of the New Deal set the stage for massive federal involvement in flood control projects, and severe flooding across the United States in 1935 provided the impetus for the transition. The Flood Control Act of 1936 confirmed that nationalization was complete, stating that "flood control is the proper activity of the federal government." Congress wasted little time exercising its new authority, bankrolling $11.1 billion in flood control projects over the next fifteen years. The corps was the primary beneficiary, and the agency put several hundred projects into motion. By 1960 the agency was working on or had completed 219 reservoirs, 9,000 miles of levees and flood walls, and 7,400 miles of channel improvements. Of the $6.2 billion spent on these projects, more than 90 percent came from the federal coffers (Moore and Moore 1989, 17).

The Importance of Information: Data Control

The 1936 legislation contained a supposed safeguard against profligate federal spending. Specifically the legislation required a formal analysis to demonstrate that the benefits of public works projects exceed the costs of the projects. There was just one problem. The corps was responsible for generating and providing this information.

The control of information is integral to successful agency expansion, and allowing the corps to conduct its own cost-benefit analysis greatly biased federal funding decisions. For instance, the agency routinely used unreasonably low discount rates to mask extensive front-loading of project costs. A more fundamental methodological flaw concerned the calculation of flood control benefits. Consider the case in which a farmer has a choice of planting one additional acre either inside or outside the floodplain, and further assume that the acre within the floodplain has a 10 percent higher yield than an acre outside the floodplain. In this case the benefit of providing flood control is the value of the increased yield. The costs include the monetary expenditure of constricting and maintaining the flood control structures, as well as the value of environmental amenities (e.g., recreation, wetland functions, etc.). The corps certainly did not include environmental amenities on the cost side of its ledger. It did, however, include the total value of the floodplain development on the benefit side, apparently assuming that people who build or plant in the floodplain have no viable alternatives for their capital. This generates a tremendous bias toward a pro-development decision.

Along with its dubious accounting methods, the viability of many corps projects also relied on inducing further floodplain development. As discussed, even without government intervention it is reasonable to expect some degree of floodplain development. The agency, in fact, assumed that its projects would induce further development; the inflated benefit projections allowed it to justify projects on a cost-benefit basis (Congress allocated $38 billion to spend on flood control projects from 1960 to 1985).

It is unfair to say that all the flood control projects were inefficient, but there is plenty of research showing how sensitive the agency's cost-benefit analyses were to the choice of a discount rate; how benefits were routinely mischaracterized; and how it relied on induced development to justify its projects. Weiner (1996, 324–29) summarizes the major concerns of cost-benefit analysis, as well as evaluations of the corps's own project analysis:

> In the important sample examined by Krutilla, use of deliberately low rates during the period 1952–1964 overstated benefits from many projects. Claimed [benefit-cost analysis] ratios of up to 1.2 (20 percent positive return) may actually have been less than 1 (Krutilla 1966b). Analyzing 1962 authorizations, Fox and Herfindahl (1964) found that use of rates of 4, 6, and 8 percent (instead of the federal policy rate of 2⅝ percent) would have produced failure to break even in 9, 64, and 80 percent of the projects respectively! In 1965 more than half of authorized projects would have failed with defensible rates (Krutilla 1966a; Freeman 1993).

Presumably, if environmental values had been recognized at the time—even if these values were confined only to recreation benefits—still more projects would have failed the cost-benefit test. Thus, corps projects led to major wealth transfers from general taxpayers to floodplain communities as well as major allocative inefficiencies. Resources were diverted to unjustified projects, and the resulting floods destroyed capital and created disruptions, compounding the wastefulness.

Even with the prodigious expenditures, the overall effectiveness of flood control measures at abating property damages is unclear. It is true that structural measures reduce some property damages, but it is also true that they encourage more development. Even if we assume corps projects were justified on the basis of questionable cost-benefit tests, the more problematic aspects of flood control concern the subsidization of these projects by the many to benefit the few, and the attendant ecological consequences. The agency also continues to be called to task for its appetite for construction. Recently it delayed plans to implement major construction projects along the Mississippi River "after an independent review concluded the study's forecasts were riddled with serious flaws and unrealistic assumptions" (Grunwald 2000b, A33).

In addition to the dubious fiscal soundness of corps activities, the real and potential ecological consequences are a continuing source of consternation for environmental groups. Stein et al. (2000) begin a recent report with the assertion: "No other federal agency has had—and continues to have—such a profound impact on the nation's environmentally sensitive floodplains, waterways, and coastal areas as the U.S. Army Corps of Engineers." The report then proceeds to detail environmental and fiscal problems of twenty-five of its projects, including a number of proposed flood control projects across the nation. These include the Auburn Dam project in Sacramento, California; the St. John's Bayou project in East Prairie, Missouri; the Devils Lake Emergency Outlet in Devils Lake, North Dakota; the Clear Creek Flood Control project near Houston; and the Dallas Floodway Extension. These are likely to attract further development in the floodplain, and lead to the degradation of water quality and elimination of fish and wildlife habitat.

The most notorious projects discussed are the Big Sunflower Dredging and Yazoo Backwater Pumping Station in western Mississippi. The dredging and pumping activities from these sites would do demonstrable harm to the environment:

> Productive wetlands would be drained, destroying bottomland hardwood forests that are home to waterfowl, eagles, deer, bear, fish, and alligators. The river itself houses a thousand-year old colony of mussels, thought to be the densest mass of life in the world. Water quality would deteriorate through shoreline erosion. . . . (Stein et al. 2000, 20)

These projects are entirely federally funded, making them classic cases in which potential monetary benefits are concentrated and costs are diffuse.

Michael Grunwald published a series of five articles exploring the Army Corps of Engineers. The summary of his findings is consistent with our understanding of government versus the environment:

> A *Washington Post* review of Corps activities across the nation, supported by thousands of interviews and tens of thousands of pages of documents, found that the agency is converting its strong congressional relationships into billions of dollars' worth of taxpayer-funded water construction projects, many with significant environmental costs and minimal economic benefits. (Grunwald 2000a, A01)

THE NATIONAL FLOOD INSURANCE PROGRAM:
INSURING OR ENSURING DISASTER?

Despite billions of dollars in capital investments, structural flood control measures do not eliminate damages to crops and other property located in floodplains. Insurance is a way for individuals and communities to hedge against these risks. For a risk to be insurable, the provider must be able to identify the risk and set a premium. An individual pays a fixed premium in exchange for compensation in the case of damage from some unforeseen event (e.g., a flood). In a competitive market the expected value of payments to any individual should equal the premium. Insurance spreads risks across individuals and reduces overall risk by offering lower premiums and/or deductibles to those who take steps to mitigate the probability of being harmed.

Yet private insurance providers do not consider all risks to be insurable. The emergence and continued availability of insurance against certain hazards is confounded by factors such as:

- adverse selection and moral hazard
- uncertainty
- correlated risk

Adverse selection is when the insured knows about the risks of an activity and the insurer knows very little. In such cases, insurers cannot distinguish between low- and high-risk individuals, and thus must treat all customers as if they were high risk—that is, only the high-risk premium will be charged. If insurance is available at all, only high-risk individuals will be willing to purchase coverage because those at low risk know that the expected benefits of insurance are far below the expected costs.

To illustrate, consider the case in which there are two groups of 100 people each. The high-risk group has a 5 percent chance of suffering a $1,000 loss, whereas the low-risk group has a 1 percent chance of suffering the same loss. The expected losses are $50 and $10, respectively. Thus, if the insurance company could sort out the individuals, it would charge premiums equal to the expected losses plus some administrative charges. But if the insurance company cannot distinguish between the groups, it will not split the difference and charge a $30 premium. Why? Because if the premium is $30, all the high-risk and none of the low-risk individuals will demand insurance, making this a losing proposition for the insurance provider. Therefore, the insurer has to treat everyone the same and charge a high-risk premium to avoid certain losses. In such cases, regulators could make insurance coverage mandatory, allowing the provider to set an actuarially sound $30 premium. Such regulation would result in a wealth transfer from low- to high-risk individuals.

The problem of moral hazard arises when the insured party begins to behave more recklessly after purchasing a policy. Private insurers address this problem in a number of ways: by raising the amount of the deductible the insured person is required to pay; by making the insured pay for a percentage of the total loss; by capping total coverage of the loss; or by refusing to provide insurance, as in the case of repeat offenders of drunk driving.

A major problem for private insurance providers is uncertainty over the probability and extent of potential damages. There is a difference between risk and uncertainty. Risk assumes the probability distribution of outcomes is fairly well understood. For instance, insurance companies have a very good idea of the likelihood that a twenty-five-year-old single male will have an auto accident, as well as the expected damages. In contrast, if there is true uncertainty, the probability distribution over expected damages is not well understood. To hedge against this uncertainty, insurance providers must charge substantially higher premiums (Kunreuther 1998, 34), in which case there may or may not be a market for such insurance based on the willingness of people to pay.

Another problem stifling the emergence of private insurance is correlated risk. For many types of hazards people either suffer no damage or they face some catastrophic event. In these cases, the possible damage for anyone is either zero or very high. For instance, a person might have no damage with a probability of 0.99 and $1 million in damage with a probability of 0.01. The expected damage and actuarially fair premium for a single policy is $10,000, and the variance of damages is $9,900. Private insurance providers are able to respond in these cases because of the law of large numbers—the variance of outcomes decreases as the number of outcomes increases. If 100 identical individuals purchase coverage, the expected loss for each person remains $10,000, but the group variance decreases to $99. For the law of large numbers to apply, however, potential outcomes must be independent of one another. On one hand, if my neighbor smashes his car into a tree, there is no reason to believe that thousands of other drivers smashed their cars into trees at the same time. The probabilities of these events occurring are independent of one another. On the other hand, if my neighbor's house is inundated by high waters, in all likelihood my house will also be similarly affected. That is, the risks of flood damages are correlated. Unless these risks can be effectively spread, correlated risks can devastate insurance providers.

In sum, adverse selection and moral hazard make it difficult for providers to set premiums, and uncertainty and correlated risks force insurance providers to charge premiums that may greatly exceed what people would reasonably be willing to pay. In these circumstances the quantity demanded of insurance is very low, and consequently providers fail to market a product either because there are not enough parties to spread the risk or the benefits do not warrant the costs of marketing the line of such policies.

THE NATIONAL FLOOD INSURANCE PROGRAM—
A BILLION DOLLARS IN LOSSES AND COUNTING

Given the pervasiveness of people living and farming in floodplains, especially after the development of federal flood control projects, it is hard to imagine that insurance companies (at least in an unregulated environment) would not offer some policies if a profit opportunity existed. There are, however, a number of confounding factors. Although areas that are likely to be flooded are easy to identify, the frequency and magnitude of floods are uncertain, and flood risks are correlated. These factors stymie the development of private insurance markets. Indeed, in the 1890s and the 1920s private flood insurance markets flourished, but catastrophic losses overwhelmed providers, and the private flood insurance market all but disappeared (Kunreuther, 1998, 40). In response, the federal government introduced the National Flood Insurance Program in 1968 (NFIP). The NFIP offers subsidized insurance to people already living in harm's way, provided that their community adopts regulations that meet certain federal minimum standards, such as the development of community flood maps and building codes that make properties less susceptible to flood damage. Once a community has complied with these regulations, individuals are eligible to purchase insurance through the NFIP. The NFIP helped to develop mapping programs, which provide information about flood risks that can be used to enforce zoning codes and set insurance premiums.

Response to the program has been less than expected for a variety of reasons. In its first year, four communities joined the program and a total of twenty policies were issued. A major impediment was the slow pace of the mapping program required for community eligibility. Congress amended the NFIP to relax the requirement, but only 3,000 communities out of 21,000 had enrolled by 1973, and only 275,000 policies had been issued.

It seems odd that the NFIP offered insurance at below actuarially fair rates, yet floodplain dwellers still refused to buy it. Undeterred by the disinterest, Congress made NFIP participation mandatory for eligibility for federal assistance in 1973, including any federally related mortgage on a property in flood hazard areas. Lenders, for their part, required insurance, but never bothered to make sure that the parties renewed the policies. As a result, many people allowed their flood insurance policies to lapse. Congress addressed this situation by mandating fines for lenders that failed to enforce the provision. As a result, the number of communities involved in the NFIP grew to more than 18,000, and the number of policies exceeds 4 million today. In the Midwest floods, roughly 20 to 30 percent of flood-prone structures were insured, mirroring the national participation rate.

Even so, the nature of the policy holders hardly conforms to a representative cross section of floodplain dwellers. The characteristics of those who buy insurance seem to fall into three major categories:

- where flood insurance is mandatory
- where properties are repeatedly damaged
- when flood damages are imminent

Not surprisingly, the NFIP loses a lot of money—nearly $1 billion between 1984 and 1997 (Platt 1999, 30).

Palm (1998, 56) argues that the central motivation for purchasing policies is that the government requires it: "Individuals purchase policies primarily to comply with regulations rather than because of perceived risk or a desire for the insurance per se." But this characterization is too narrow, as individuals who suffer damages or are aware of the danger have a sound understanding of their own risks. A significant amount of NFIP payments are from so-called repetitive loss properties—properties that have filed two or more damage claims since the inception of the program. Overall, repetitive loss properties account for 2 percent of total NFIP policies, but these properties have absorbed $2.58 billion—40 percent of total NFIP payments. Repetitive loss properties that have been hit three or more times account for 1 percent of all NFIP policies and 21.5 percent of total NFIP payments. Moreover, this amount understates the total amount from properties that have been repeatedly damaged by floods. Many people purchase insurance only after experiencing flood damages for the first time, and are subsequently flooded again. Notably, these people, if they located in the floodplain prior to the enactment of the NFIP, would not have to pay what the NFIP considers to be actuarially fair rates.

Environmental groups, including the National Wildlife Federation, American Rivers, and Friends of the Earth, view the voluntary government buyout program of repetitive loss properties as a viable alternative to costly and environmentally disruptive structural flood control measures (Conrad 1998). This buyout program was expanded as part of legislation following the 1993 floods, and in some cases entire communities have been relocated.

The final class of insurance purchasers includes those who are in immediate danger. The NFIP requires a five-day waiting period between the purchase of the policy and the coverage date. There were 13,310 claims filed following the 1993 floods, 4,588 of them (35 percent) purchased when flooding appeared imminent.

- 1,828 policies with disbursements of $45 million were purchased within fifteen days of the flooding event.
- 1,562 policies with disbursements of $37 million were purchased between sixteen and thirty days of flooding.

- 1,198 policies with disbursements of $60 million were purchased between thirty-one and sixty days.

More policies likely would have been purchased if people had known that they could get insurance coverage for something that was inevitable. After all, skydivers cannot buy life insurance after discovering that their parachutes are inoperable. Not so for the NFIP. At any rate, responses to the NFIP waiting period illustrate that incentives matter: "In at least one instance, a community undertook a gallant flood fight not in expectation of protecting a school but rather to keep it from flooding until the 5-day waiting period had expired" (Galloway Report 1994, 136).

Losses from insurance policies are not the only costs that taxpayers have incurred under the NFIP. A major factor confounding the emergence of private insurance markets is uncertainty, which is often costly to resolve. Ironically, concluding that there is a market failure requires that we assume that uncertainty is *not* costly to resolve. The NFIP set up the Community Rating System to map floodplain risks for communities that participate in the NFIP. Consistent with this assumption that information should be free, the NFIP has allocated more than a billion dollars to its community mapping program (Platt 1999, 28). It is not clear why it is a federal responsibility to assess risks for investments for communities located in floodplains, yet the Galloway Report (1994) concluded that the mapping program is underfunded.

The NFIP has had mixed results. On the one hand, the program sometimes discourages floodplain development, and many structures that are built in floodplains have better flood-proofing. On the other hand, the NFIP has cost taxpayers several billion dollars, representing major transfers of wealth from taxpayers to federal agencies and flood-prone communities.

DISASTER RELIEF—THE HEMORRHAGING CONTINUES

Insurance programs, public or private, are undermined if people do not bear the full costs of their actions—"A government that cannot say no to generous disaster assistance is unlikely to implement an insurance program with strong incentives for risk management" (Harrington 2000, 40). There are a number of reasons that property owners do not bear the full costs of their actions: Uninsured losses are tax deductible, owners can declare bankruptcy, and disaster assistance is available. Any one of these confounds development of private insurance markets as well as market penetration for federal insurance policies. High prices elicit low quantity demanded for disaster insurance. In addition, when the government externalizes the costs of floodplain development, the demand for insurance decreases.

Disaster relief, in particular, externalizes costs of floodplain development, and the federal government has been generous when it comes to issuing disaster relief. Following the midwestern flooding, a number of federal agencies doled out various forms of disaster relief, totaling more than $4 billion. The Department of Agriculture spent the most ($1.7 billion), followed by the Federal Emergency Management Agency ($1.1 billion), the Department of Housing and Urban Development ($500 million), the Army Corps of Engineers ($253.1 million), the Department of Commerce ($201.3 million), the Department of Transportation ($146.7 million), the Department of Education ($100 million), the Department of Labor ($64.6 million), the Department of the Interior ($41.2 million), and the Environmental Protection Agency ($34 million).

Given the number of agencies involved, it is clear that disaster relief has many faces. Many authors point to the fact that disaster relief is often contingent upon a presidential disaster declaration, and assistance is often less generous than the benefits of insurance coverage. No matter. These facts do not change the basic economics of the situation—that expectation of disaster relief payments lowers the expected cost of floodplain development.

WHAT POLICY SHIFT?

The introduction of the NFIP in 1968 is said to have marked a shift from structural to nonstructural approaches to flood control.

> The Flood Insurance Program signaled a shift from reducing the floods through structural controls to reducing the damages by limiting the development in flood prone areas. It did this with a carrot and a stick: The carrot was federally subsidized flood insurance available to property owners in flood-prone areas; the stick was making that insurance available to property owners only in those communities that adopted floodplain zoning. The federal government also offered to pay for the floodplain mapping upon which the zoning restrictions would be based. (Philippi 1994, n.p.)

In principle, the expected shift would alleviate some of the burden on taxpayers. In practice, however, there was no policy shift. Communities were slow to enroll in the federal program, and the insurance program was almost universally ignored.

In fact, economists recognized an entirely different type of shift occurring during the mid-1960s: "[John] Krutilla noted that by 1965 there had clearly been a shift in federal programs from protection of existing floodplain uses to supporting new invasion of the floodplains; in effect, use of public funds to transfer wealth from uphill landowners to floodplain owners, with some unknown but very much smaller element of true creation of new wealth" (Weiner 1996, 325). The voluntary buyout program, a program strongly endorsed by environmental groups, shows that federal policies have come full circle. Massive federal expenditures on structural flood control measures, among other policies, encouraged floodplain development. Now, environmental groups are touting voluntary buyouts to mitigate pressures on the floodplains. The government pays to get people into the floodplain; the government pays to get them out. Of course, if people believe that federal buyouts are becoming the norm, there will be a limited incentive to purchase flood insurance.

CONCLUSIONS

For the greater part of human history people had a healthy aversion to floods. Many religions and cultures make references to great floods, emphasizing that they are devastating and beyond human control. Noah's ark, a formative story of Judaism, Christianity, and Islam, is but one example in which an angry God, upset with human wickedness, inundates the earth with flood waters. In the *Ovid,* Jupiter, also displeased with human wickedness, teams up with Neptune to flood the earth. There are also similar stories from the Assyrians, the Babylonians, the Celtics, Australians, Pacific Islanders, Native Americans, Latin Americans, and just about every other ethnic and religious background (Dundes 1988). In these instances the best strategy was to avoid the floodplain altogether, but if people have to build there, for at least 2,000 years it has been recognized that rock, not sand, is the prudent place to lay the foundation. In fact, these points are among the few things that have been universally agreed upon across time, space, religious beliefs, and scientific observation.

What could have reversed several millennia of impeccable common sense, prompting businesses, communities, and farms to invest billions of dollars' worth of resources in floodplains? As we have seen in this chapter, a large part of the blame can be laid at the feet of the government. There is nothing more central to economic analysis than if you subsidize an activity, you get more of it. What we find in this chapter is a host of government programs that reduce the costs of placing capital in harm's way.

> During the past 50 years, Congress has created a legal edifice of byzantine complexity to cope with natural disasters consisting of laws, agencies, programs, policies, and strategies, many of them intended to operate in "partnership" with state and local governments. Federal assistance is provided to households, businesses, farms, states, municipalities, special districts, and nongovernmental organizations under approximately 50 different laws and executive orders. (Platt 1999, 277)

These programs distort the decision-making processes, either by inflating the benefits or deflating the costs of an activity. The result is a host of inane programs that are fiscally and environmentally irresponsible.

In contrast, markets left to their own devices, would produce more efficient, equitable, and environmentally friendly outcomes. Scott Harrington (2000, 46) frames the issues matter of factly: "Government intervention undercuts private markets and thus creates pressure for expansive government programs. The predictable result is less economic efficiency and more government spending." The New Deal is rarely called to task for sowing the seeds of widespread environmental malfeasance, yet it was the promiscuous judicial attitude toward federal authority that opened the door to the appetites of the legislative and executive branches to expand their authority. In the case of federal flood control policies, taxpayers and the environment continue to suffer the consequences of another sad chapter in the saga of the government versus the environment.

NOTES

1. Following the midwestern floods, the Interagency Floodplain Management Review Committee—a thirty-one-member taskforce headed by Gen. Gerald E. Galloway—issued *Sharing the Challenge: Floodplain Management into the 21st Century*. The report is known as the Galloway Report.

2. The literature on the economics of bureaucracy is vast. Johnson and Libecap (1994, ch. 7) provide a superior overview.

REFERENCES

Conrad, David. 1998. *Higher Ground*. Washington, DC: National Wildlife Federation.

Dahl, T. E. 1990. *Wetland Losses in the United States, 1780s to 1980s*. Washington, DC: U.S. Department of the Interior, Fish and Wildlife Service.

Dahl, T. E., and C. E. Johnson. 1991. *Status and Trends of Wetlands in the Conterminous United States, Mid-1970s to Mid-1980s*. Washington, DC: U.S. Department of the Interior, Fish and Wildlife Service.

Dundes, Alan, ed. 1988. *The Flood Myth*. Berkeley: University of California Press.

Environmental Protection Agency. 2000. National Water Quality Inventory: 1998 Report to Congress, 841-R-00-001. Online: www.epa.gov/305b/ (cited: May 15, 2001).

Faber, Scott. 1996. *On Borrowed Land: Public Policies for Floodplains*. Cambridge, MA: Lincoln Institute of Public Policy.

Fox, I. K., and Orris C. Herfindahl. 1964. Attainment of Efficiency in Satisfying Demands for Water Resources. *Papers and Proceedings of the American Economic Association* 54: 198–206.

Freeman, A. Myrick. 1993. *The Measurement of Environmental Resource Values: Theory and Methods*. Washington, DC: Resources for the Future.

Galloway Report (Interagency Floodplain Management Review Committee). 1994. *Sharing the Challenge: Floodplain Management into the 21st Century*. Washington, DC: Government Printing Office.

Gates, Paul W. 1968. *History of Public Land Law Development.* Washington, DC: Zenger.

Grunwald, Michael. 2000a. Engineers of Power: An Agency of Unchecked Clout. *Washington Post,* September 10.

———. 2000b. Army Corps Delays Studies over Flawed Forecasts. *Washington Post,* October 12.

Harrington, Scott E. 2000. Rethinking Disaster Policy. *Regulation* 23(1): 40–46.

Johnson, Ronald N., and Gary D. Libecap. 1994. *The Federal Civil Service System and the Problem of Bureaucracy: The Economics and Politics of Institutional Change.* Chicago: University of Chicago Press.

Krutilla, John V. 1966a. An Economic Approach to Coping with Flood Damage. *Water Resources Research* 2(2): 183–90.

———. 1966b. Is Public Intervention in Water Resource Development Conducive to Economic Efficiency? *Natural Resources Journal* 6(1): 60–75.

Kunreuther, Howard. 1998. Insurability Conditions and the Supply of Coverage. In *Paying the Price: The Status and Role of Insurance against Natural Disasters in the United States,* ed. Howard Kunreuther and Richard J. Roth. Washington, DC: Joseph Henry Press, 17–50.

McPhee, John. 1989. *The Control of Nature.* New York: Noonday Press.

Moore, Jamie W., and Dorothy P. Moore. 1989. *Army Corps of Engineers and the Evolution of Federal Flood Plain Management Policy.* Boulder: University of Colorado, Institute of Behavior Science.

National Research Council. 1992. *Restoration of Aquatic Ecosystems.* Washington, DC.

National Science Foundation. 1980. *Report on Flood Hazard Mitigation.* Washington, DC.

Palm, Risa. 1998. Demand for Disaster Insurance: Residential Coverage. In *Paying the Price: The Status and Role of Insurance against Natural Disasters in the United States,* ed. Howard Kunreuther and Richard J. Roth. Washington, DC: Joseph Henry Press, 51–66.

Philippi, Nancy S. 1994–1995. Plugging the Gaps in Flood-Control Policy. *Issues in Science and Technology* 11(2): 71–78.

———. 1994. *Revisiting Flood Control: An Examination of Federal Flood Control Policy in Light of the 1993 Flood Event on the Upper Mississippi River.* Chicago: Wetlands Initiative, Inc.

Platt, Rutherford H. 1999. *Disasters and Democracy: The Politics of Extreme Natural Events.* Washington, DC: Island Press.

Reisner, Marc. 1986. *Cadillac Desert: The American West and Its Disappearing Water.* New York: Penguin Books.

Stavins, Robert N., and Adam B. Jaffe. 1990. Unintended Impacts of Public Investments on Private Decisions: The Depletion of Forested Wetlands. *American Economic Review* 80(3): 337–52.

Stein, Jeff, Peter Moreno, David Conrad, and Steve Ellis. 2000. Troubled Waters: Congress, the Corps of Engineers, and Wasteful Water Projects. A Report by Taxpayers for Common Sense and the National Wildlife Federation. Online: www.taxpayer.net/corpswatch/troubledwaters/index.htm (cited: February 26, 2001).

Weiner, John D. 1996. Research Opportunities in Search of Federal Flood Policy. *Policy Sciences* 29: 321–44.

5

Unplugging the Everglades

Clay J. Landry

For more than 5,000 years, the Florida Everglades has supported extraordinarily diverse plant and animal life, thanks largely to its natural water flows. Government policy has taken less than a century to disrupt and pollute the Everglades's water system. Indeed this is a poignant case of how federal and state governments externalized the costs and inflated the benefits for select groups at the expense of taxpayers and the environment. Early settlers to Florida thought that draining the 'Glades would be as simple as pulling the plug in a bathtub (Blake 1980, 4). At the turn of the twentieth century, numerous private efforts to drain large areas of the swamp failed because the undertaking proved too costly and too enormous a task. As was the case for so many water projects implemented in the first half of the century, "success" required federal involvement. With enough time and taxpayer money, the federal government succeeded in reducing the Everglades to half its historic size.

Federally funded projects lowered the water levels, exposing rich fertile soils. Farming flourished, but farmers soon discovered that the prized soils were highly combustible. Ground fires raged through the newly drained lands. In addition, the land itself began to disappear. As fields were drained, the top layer of soil started decomposing through oxidation. Soil subsidence data showed that the rich soil that was attractive to many farmers would soon be gone in many agricultural areas. These and other nutrient problems prompted another round of public funding—this time for research on soil depletion and fertility.

Federal protectionist policies for domestic sugar growers have further exacerbated environmental problems in the Everglades. Tariffs on imported sugar and federal price supports for domestic sugar encouraged expansion of sugarcane production in the region. The federal government diverted water and drained more lands to make room for more sugarcane. As a result, the Everglades now receives less than one-third of its historic water flow. Water that is received is contaminated by fertilizer and other nutrient-laden runoff from the cane fields. Removing the federal government's "helping hand" in the region would not only save consumers and taxpayers money but also reverse the trend of shrinking habitat for numerous endangered species as well as protect coastal coral reefs (Organization for Economic Co-operation and Development 1996, 64).

This chapter chronicles federal and state involvement in the demise of the Everglades. It looks at the history of early drainage efforts and the public policies that encouraged private investment in the grandiose scheme. The impact of federal reclamation policies is discussed, followed by a review of U.S. sugar policies that prompted further drainage for sugarcane production. Finally, the current federal Everglades restoration proposal is reviewed.

THE EARLY DAYS: FAILED PRIVATE VENTURES

At statehood, the federal government owned more than three-quarters of Florida. The Swamp and Overflowed Lands Act of 1850 had enormous consequences for the subsequent change of ownership and development of the state and gave it title to all "swamped and submerged land" that it could drain, providing Florida with an opportunity to expand its size, economic opportunities, and population (Carter 1974, 58, 60). Under the act, the federal government eventually gave Florida title to more than 20 million of its 35 million acres (Snell and Boggess 1994, 7).

The Florida legislature used the swampland act to encourage settlement of an area near Lake Okeechobee, most of which was part of the Everglades. The first attempts to drain this unique natural area began in 1855 with the formation of the Internal Improvement Fund (IIF), a state agency that administered the swamplands act by enticing private developers with public money for draining projects. The money was raised through the sale of swampland, taxes on settlers of drained lands, and the sale of state-backed bonds. The IIF also raised money for dredging and draining operations through drainage taxes on land developers and installments on their land purchases. The developers in turn collected payments from people who purchased undrained swampland with the hope of someday building successful farms (Blake 1980, 113, 143). The entire scheme hinged on the efforts of the IIF.

Accusations of corruption and underhanded dealings lingered throughout the IIF's existence. Lucrative construction contracts were routinely granted to dredging companies with close ties to the IIF's board, which included the governor and several elected cabinet officers of the state. Excessive construction costs and poor investments left the IIF's finances depleted. By the end of the Civil War, holding largely worthless assets, including railroad stocks and Confederate bonds, the IIF was essentially bankrupt. Under court order to settle its debts, the IIF desperately needed an investor who could pay cash in exchange for lands yet to be drained (Carter 1974, 84). It soon found such a person—Hamilton Disston, a wealthy industrialist from Philadelphia.

HAMILTON DISSTON: FINANCIALLY SWAMPED IN THE EVERGLADES

Stories of failed commercial drainage operations in the Everglades are nearly as numerous as its alligators. Perhaps the most tragic tale is that of Hamilton Disston. From his first visit to the area on a fishing trip, Disston dreamed of the economic potential beneath the swamp waters. He envisioned expanding his empire by draining the Everglades. With ample financial resources, he was the first person to carry out extensive drainage. The millionaire purchased 4 million acres of land around Lake Okeechobee and the Kissimmee River for twenty-five cents an acre (Hanna and Hanna 1948, 380). The sale price was just enough to pay off the IIF's creditors, thus alleviating the board of financial liability (McCally 1999, 89).

But Disston needed to drain the land he purchased to obtain clear title; then he could sell the land to people who dreamed of farming in the Florida sun and realize a return on his investment. To do this he established land sales offices around the country to attract potential customers and the capital to begin draining projects. He leveraged his position by selling land before it was drained. Disston initiated his grand plan by attempting to drain land around Lake Okeechobee. Channels were dug so that water was diverted into the lake and then routed to the Gulf of Mexico and the Atlantic Ocean. Soon he claimed to have drained more than 2 million acres, although by most accounts, only a fraction of that was actually drained. Eager to see Disston succeed, the IIF readily supported his claim and hastily granted ownership to nearly all the 2 million acres (McCally 1999, 89)—land that was already claimed by farmers and ranchers under the Armed Settlement Act of the Seminole War and other federal laws (Blake 1980, 80). The settlers argued that much of the land Disston claimed was not swampland to begin with and should never have been passed to him. The state intervened, offering to sell disputed lands to the settlers for one dollar an acre and then crediting the sales to the millionaire's account.

The land dispute brought Disston's drainage projects under more scrutiny. Critics asserted that he had not drained 2 million acres, but rather was claiming land that dried up naturally from several years of abnormally low rainfall. Responding to these accusations, the legislature ordered a special investigation. After two years it determined that Disston had drained only 50,000 acres (Blake 1980, 81). Eager to realize Everglades farming and development, the state struck another compromise with the developer. He was allowed to retain ownership if he invested an additional $125,000 to adequately drain the land. Disston accepted the terms, though the lands were never completely drained.

Disston continued to make heavy investments in the south Florida region. In addition to his drainage projects, the entrepreneur became the first person to experiment with sugarcane on a commercial scale. He established more than 1,000 acres of sugarcane and built a large mill for processing.

These projects, along with the draining endeavors, were financed primarily through land sales to individuals. Additional cash was raised by selling half of his original 4-million-acre purchase to a prominent British investor and Everglades developer. The cash from the land sale was not enough, however, to cover costs on Disston's other investments. During the depression of the 1890s, the Philadelphia millionaire fell on hard times. Unable to pay his workers, he suspended dredging operations. Banks called his loans due, forcing him to default on bonds issued to underwrite various enterprises. In financial and emotional despair, Disston returned home from a Philadelphia theater one spring evening in 1896 and took his life. His family, who all along had opposed the Florida development project, let the state recover some of the lands for taxes and eventually sold the remaining estate for $70,000, a fraction of his original investment (Harner 1973, 17).

Although the Disston operations dug less than eleven miles of canal, the idea stirred ambitions around the state. Draining the Everglades seemed more feasible than ever. However, it was not long before other commercial drainage and development operations experienced financial problems. As an economic enterprise, Everglades development struggled to sustain itself. Even with public assistance, draining and clearing proved much more difficult than envisioned, and by 1912 commercial drainage efforts had all but stopped (McCally 1999, 89, 100).

INVESTIGATING THE INTERNAL IMPROVEMENT FUND

Most Everglades land was sold to people in northern states who dreamed of warm winters and farming year-round. But when drainage efforts stopped, the majority of land purchased was still under water. Disillusioned buyers stopped payments. Lacking a flow of cash, developers were unable to continue to make needed payments to the IIF to ensure that dredging operations continued. With drainage stopped and dreams unrealized, public sentiment grew to have developers sent to prison.

Newspapers picked up the story, reporting on the "Florida Scandal." Dismayed by the attacks, state officials passed resolutions deploring newspaper reports as "derogatory to the practicality of the plans which are being followed for the drainage and reclamation of the Everglades and derogatory to the value and utility of the Everglades land for agricultural and horticultural purpose." To counter the attacks, the IIF's board invited reporters from around the country on an all-expenses-paid junket (McCally 1999, 107). The tour was planned for April, at the end of the dry season when the region's water was at its lowest. The tactic seemed to work. Impressed by what they saw, the reporters sent enthusiastic stories to their papers. One impressed reporter wrote, "In the Everglades you simply tickle the soil and the bounteous crops respond to feed hungry humanity" (quoted in Blake 1980, 118). But favorable reports did not last long.

Many small land development companies went bankrupt when they were unable to collect payments from disgruntled would-be farmers. The trend worried larger developers. If reclamation was not resumed, Everglades land would never sell. One of the largest development companies, Everglades Land Sales Company, commissioned a study during the summer of 1912 to review the IIF's drainage program. Its findings were disturbing. The report found the state's overall approach was ill-conceived because it was too expensive and too difficult to drain the entire region. It recommended that smaller projects in which private developers would build their own levees and ditches was a more economically sound strategy. The study suggested that without public financing, Everglades development and drainage would have been far less extensive. Finally, the report called on the state legislature to pass a "sound drainage act" that would minimize government involvement in private drainage operations (McCally 1999, 109, 110).

On release of this critical report, many of the large land development companies refused to make further drainage tax payments until the state revised its drainage strategy. Construction stopped. By the end of 1912, canals all across Florida stood partially completed. The state legislature needed to act fast to solve the crisis of confidence that threatened to halt Everglades development. The legislature responded with a drainage act that concentrated on so-called financial reforms. The act attempted to reassure investors and ensure their continued support for reclamation.

The new drainage law established a tax system that was based on a sliding scale so that each acre of land would bear its part of the expense according to the benefit received (Blake 1980, 123). In addition, the law allowed the state to borrow money for up to one year as well as sell bonds. The new law also allowed for the creation of drainage districts with taxing and borrowing powers of their own (McCally 1999, 111).

The IIF resumed development projects by exercising its newly created powers to borrow money and issue public bonds. However, the law did not

solve the crisis entirely. The tangled finances of reclamation projects still relied on taxes, which in turn relied on the state's ability to drain lands and collect taxes from landowners. The law also created other financial problems.
With newly gained taxing and borrowing powers, drainage districts quickly
overextended themselves.

The Everglades Drainage District, the oldest and largest drainage district,
sold more than $10 million in bonds to pay for drainage projects (Blake 1980,
137). The bonds were drawn into question when drainage progress slowed.
In order to continue construction, the IIF scraped together money wherever
it could. Most of it was raised through sleight-of-hand accounting by borrowing money from other state agencies; however, the IIF had no intentions
of repaying the money. State-backed loans were also issued to pay contractors so that drainage projects continued. With its finances in a perilous condition, state officials turned to the federal government to bail Florida out of
its drainage woes.

In sum, despite the efforts of the IIF, early drainage projects in the Everglades experienced limited success. By 1920 fewer than 900,000 acres had
been successfully drained, but this situation changed dramatically with fed-

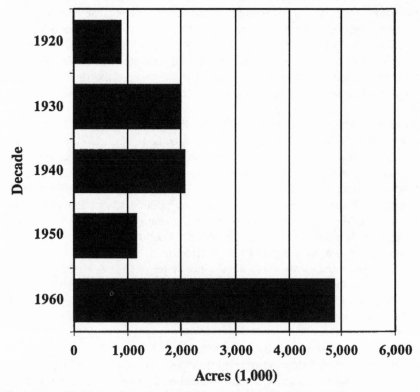

Figure 5.1   Florida Lands Drained, 1920 to 1960. Source: USDA (1978).

eral involvement. Figure 5.1 shows the amount of Florida land drained by decade. Federal reclamation projects in central and south Florida vastly expanded the amount of land drained in the Everglades. Notably, the amount of land drained jumped dramatically between 1950 and 1960, when several federal flood control projects were initiated. The largest was the Central and South Florida Flood Control District, which began in 1949 and replaced the Everglades Drainage District (McCally 1999, 153).

THE RECLAMATION ERA, 1930–70: THE FLOW OF FEDERAL FUNDS

Reclamation of the Everglades has developed into a national as well as a state problem with the federal government giving promise of co-operation that will insure the completion of this project in a proper way.

—Doyle E. Carlton, governor of Florida, 1929

Florida's reclamation efforts were paralyzed by financial failure. In practice, drainage efforts from 1910 to 1930 represented little more than an uncoordinated effort to develop the Everglades. Unable to collect drainage taxes, borrow more money, or meet bond payments, the state was in search of new funds, and federal aid was the most obvious source. Federal reclamation funds began trickling into the Everglades in the 1930s, and by 1950, a federal assault on the Everglades led by the U.S. Army Corps of Engineers reached full operation.

One of the first projects undertaken by the corps was a flood control project on Lake Okeechobee. The project was largely in response to the flooding and tragic deaths that occurred during the 1926 and 1928 hurricanes. Many people blamed the catastrophic flooding on poorly designed and unfinished drainage projects left by early developers. To alleviate future flooding problems, the corps constructed the Herbert Hoover Dike, which was eighty-five miles long and at least three times the size of the old state-built mud levee. In total, the project cost just over $19 million, about twice the original estimate. Florida was initially required to kick in $2 million for the flood control project, but Congress reduced the state's obligation to $500,000 when it was unable to raise the money (McCally 1999, 140).

The National Industrial Recovery Act of 1933 gave Pres. Franklin Roosevelt the authority to spend an unprecedented $3.3 billion on construction projects (Blake 1980, 147). The Florida delegation quickly eyed the money as a way to revive old reclamation projects and launched a campaign to fund the Cross-Florida Canal project. For more than 100 years the canal had been a pork barrel project of Florida politics. Congress first allotted money in 1826 to conduct an initial evaluation; the project continued to receive other small appropriations until the 1930s. Early reports by the U.S. Army Corps of Engineers (USACE) that emphasized the difficulties and questionable benefits of the project repeatedly chilled enthusiasm for the idea until New Deal public works projects revived support for the canal (Blake 1980, 151).

The corps began splitting its attention between draining the Everglades and dissecting the upper peninsula with the Cross-Florida Canal. In 1935 Franklin Roosevelt transferred $5 million to the agency to begin constructing the canal. This was only a token installment for a dubious project never to be completed. President Nixon finally killed the Cross-Florida Canal project in 1969, but not before it left a legacy of financial and environmental ruin still realized today.

Rodman Dam provides an apt illustration. In 1968 the corps dammed the Ocklawaha River while constructing the Cross-Florida Canal. The dam flooded sixteen miles of river, destroying 9,000 acres of the river and its floodplain forest. One year later the project was decommissioned, and Rodman never served its original purpose of moving barges across the state. It did, however, virtually eliminate species like striped bass, shad, mullet, and American eels from the river by blocking migratory paths. In addition, the dam requires maintenance at a cost to taxpayers of about $500,000 annually.

Federal funding grew in Florida as a result of one of the worst storms on record. In 1947 a severe tropical storm flooded nearly 2.5 million acres, leaving 90 percent of south Florida under water (General Accounting Office [GAO] 1999, 3). The corps estimated that the storm caused more than $59 million worth of damage (Johnson 1974, 135). To dramatize the severity of flooding to the nation, Florida published what became known as the "weeping cow" book (Light and Dineen 1994, 58). The cover of the book depicted a cow standing in belly-deep water that completely blanketed the landscape. Despite the book's depiction, much of the flooding occurred in the urbanized coastal regions. The affected cities blamed the flooding on inadequate and ailing drainage canals.

The weeping cow must have made quite an impression in Washington because federal funds for Florida flood control projects gushed for more than two decades. Figure 5.2 presents annual expenditures in 1998 dollars, by the U.S. Army Corps of Engineers on flood control projects in central and south Florida from 1947 to 1976. During that period, the state lost nearly 1.5 million acres of wetlands, almost entirely in the Everglades region (Kriz 1994, 590). Federal spending peaked in 1964 when nearly $100 million was spent to redirect Everglades water.

The first major federal appropriation of money for drainage projects was issued in the storm's wake. In 1948 Congress approved a bill for $208 million to provide flood control for 700,000 acres in the region later known as the Everglades Agricultural Area (Kriz 1994, 590). The money established the Central and South Florida Flood Control Project, an extensive system of more than 1,700 miles of canals and levees and sixteen major pumping stations (GAO 1999, 4). The project drains lands south of Lake Okeechobee in the Everglades Agricultural Area, which is now farmed primarily by sugar grow-

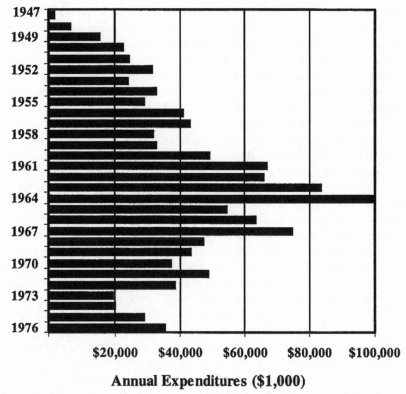

$20,000 $40,000 $60,000 $80,000 $100,000

Annual Expenditures ($1,000)

Figure 5.2   Central and South Florida Flood Control Project, 1947 to 1976. Source: USACE (1976).

ers. Completed in 1979, the Central and South Florida Flood Control Project arrived ten years past its deadline and nearly $100 million over budget (Snell and Boggess 1994, 21).

The Central and South Florida Flood Control Project severely disrupted the flow of water in the Everglades. Environmental problems were first noticed in the summer of 1966 when heavy rains caused extensive pumping of excess water from farmlands. The water was pumped onto land that was reserved for wildlife and home to much of south Florida's deer population. Hundreds of deer drowned and smaller animals like wild hogs and raccoons died because high water covered their food supply. The *New York Times* (1966, 8) reported the event as a "man-made flood" where "mindless technology is triumphing over life."

More deer problems came in 1968 and 1969, when large quantities of water were again pumped onto land managed for wildlife. Concerned about the deer population, sportsmen and conservationists attempted to rescue the deer by hazing them to higher ground. But the frightened animals merely exhausted themselves running away. Contending that kindness was killing more deer than high water, wildlife managers urged the Samaritans to leave the animals alone (Blake 1980, 187). To prevent future problems, the state established a deer sanctuary in the Big Cypress Swamp, but water problems persisted in the Everglades.

Water disruption is Everglades National Park's foremost problem. The construction of levees and drainage canals has blocked the flow of water to the Everglades. During years of adequate rainfall the park has enough water, but in dry years, water is held in drainage canals and diverted from the park. After a series of droughts in the late 1960s, Congress tried to fix the water problem by pouring more money into reclamation projects. The Army Corps of Engineers was brought in to dig additional ditches and rework existing canals so that more water would reach the Everglades. This solution bore a hefty price tag of $3 million and was only temporary.

Everglades protection gained national attention in 1970 when a former U.S. Fish and Wildlife Service biologist compared flood control projects in the Everglades to delicate heart surgery performed with a meat cleaver. The complex system of natural rivers and estuaries had been carved up by canals to control water flow. The park was last in line in the 250-mile system and thus at the mercy of other uses, from flood control for agricultural lands to municipal water demands. For years the park had little control over the timing and quantity of water it received (during normal water years, it received only about a third of the amount needed). In recent years, flows to the park have improved, but water problems still exist. A severe drought in 1989 left South Florida in short supply of water, with water restrictions imposed on Miami residents. Even with water rationing, the 'Glades was short on water (Duplaix 1990, 96, 104).

In other years too much water is a problem for the Everglades. After large rainstorms water control districts relieve flooded farmlands by releasing large volumes of fresh water in brackish estuaries adjacent to the park. The excess water wreaks havoc on estuary shrimp and fish, a valuable food source for many coastal birds because it disrupts the delicate mix of brackish water needed to produce shrimp and fish. When these aquatic creatures are not abundant, coastal birds will desert their nests and nestlings in search of new food supplies, further disrupting the ecological balance.

SWEETENING THE SWAMP: THE CUBAN EMBARGO AND FEDERAL SUGAR SUBSIDIES

Water drainage and control, paid for largely with federal funds, opened the door for commercial sugar production in the Everglades. Sugar was among the first cash crops considered suitable for the drained lands. In addition, the state and federal government pumped millions of dollars into scientific re-search on soil fertility and sugarcane harvest, but these publicly funded stim-ulants resulted in only modest levels of sugarcane production—federal sugar policies provided the real impetus.

Federal sugar policies have always played a prominent role in the devel-opment of the Everglades. In fact the revenue potential created by favorable federal sugar policies figured prominently into Hamilton Disston's decision to invest heavily in his development scheme. The Philadelphia millionaire saw an opportunity to take advantage of a policy that offered a two cents per pound bounty to domestic raw sugar producers. In addition, as early as 1789 the federal government implemented protectionist tariffs for the domestic sugar industry. The United States relaxed the protection policy from 1890 to 1894, but continued to offer a bounty to growers. Ever since then, sugar pro-duction changes in Florida have roughly followed changes in federal sugar policies.

No single policy affected the development of the Everglades more than the sugar embargo on Cuba. In 1960 fewer than 50,000 acres of sugarcane were planted in all of Florida; however, the post-Castro embargo on imports changed all that. Domestic sugarcane growth exploded from 1961 as Cuban sugar was entirely eliminated from the U.S. market. During the embargo Florida's sugar acreage production increased nearly fourfold, from 50,000 acres in 1959 to more than 200,000 acres five years later.

Federal price supports also ensured that more land would be drained and planted into sugarcane. Domestic sugar prices are supported by the federal government through a complex arrangement of loans and import restric-tions. The mainstay of sugar supports are through nonrecourse loans offered by the federally funded Commodity Credit Corporation (CCC). In addition to the loans, the U.S. Department of Agriculture (USDA) has established a tar-iff-based quota on imported sugar. Combined, these programs have effec-tively kept domestic prices well above the world price.

The CCC nonrecourse loans are an elaborate way for the government to guarantee a minimum price for sugar. Loans are made to the sugarcane processors who purchase the crop at a guaranteed price. The processors can store the final product for up to nine months, the time limit of the loan, to determine whether the domestic market price exceeds the USDA's estab-lished minimum price. If prices fail to meet the minimum rate, the processors can default on their loan and give their harvest to the USDA, which accepts it as payment-in-full (Tolman 1995, 6). In 1998 the domestic price was about 17.37 cents per pound, nearly twice the going rate in the world marketplace (Koo and Taylor 1999, 2).

To ensure that the loan system works and that processors do not default, the USDA imposes restrictions on imported sugar. In recent years the USDA has restricted imports to about 20 percent of total U.S. consumption (Koo and Taylor 1999, 2). Without import restrictions, domestic buyers would purchase sugar from the lower-priced world market. Left to the world market, domestic producers would default on CCC loans and take the guaranteed price of eighteen cents per pound, rather than selling their sugar at the lower world price. The import restrictions prevent the government from being left with millions of tons of overpriced sugar. Under the quota system, foreign countries pay a low-level tariff up until the point they reach the USDA quota (Tolman 1995, 6). Once the quota is reached, additional sugar exported to the United States is subject to a sixteen-cent-per-pound tariff. Each year the duty is evaluated and set by the USDA to control the amount of refined sugar coming into the country so that a high domestic price is maintained. A GAO (1993, 3) study estimates that overall, the sugar program costs American consumers $1.4 billion a year.

Much like the Cuban embargo, current U.S. sugar policy has artificially bolstered Florida sugarcane production. Sugar consumption in the United States has remained relatively constant over the past few years even though cane production in Florida and the United States, as a whole, has grown. This in turn has resulted in increases in acreage: From 1980 to 1994, acreage in the United States increased by approximately 25 percent, while acreage in Florida increased by 35 percent. The much higher increase in Florida is largely due to the sugar tariff barriers set up by Congress and embraced by the USDA in an effort to maintain the domestic price of sugar. Over a comparable period imports fell approximately 77 percent, from a high of 6.1 million tons in 1977 to a tariff quota of approximately 1.4 million tons in 1998.

Federal sugar policy is taking its toll on the Everglades, with price supports and import restrictions serving as major contributors. In addition, the mechanisms encourage extensive use of other inputs such as fertilizers and chemicals to bolster yields. The buildup of fertilizer concentrations, in particular, in the Everglades ecosystem is causing problems. A major component of fertilizer is phosphorus, a chemical not abundantly found in the region's natural water supply. Due to the extensive use of fertilizers in sugarcane agriculture, phosphorus leaches into groundwater supplies. The water is then pumped out to Everglades National Park and Loxahatchee Wildlife Refuge. Studies estimate that nearly 80 percent of phosphorus used in fertilizing crops is transferred with drainage water into the Everglades (Coale, Izuno, and Bottcher 1994). Phosphorus concentrations in agricultural runoff water are also increasing. A study by the South Florida Water Management District showed that concentrations increased from 0.095 to 0.314 milligrams per liter (mg/l) between 1973 and 1979 to a level of 0.188 to 0.573 mg/l from 1983 to 1985. The high phosphorus levels are contributing to ecological imbalances in the Everglades. Many nonnative plants that thrive on the phosphorus are crowding out naturally occurring species. For example, the once abundant native sawgrass is being choked out by nonnative cattails. Bird populations have also been reduced dramatically: avian numbers are only 10 percent of what they were at the turn of the century (Tolman 1995, 3, 6–7). Habitat loss to sugarcane production and reductions in food sources due to polluted runoff are the main culprits.

The financial and environmental costs that the sugar program has wrought have brought together an unlikely coalition of environmental and fiscally conservative taxpayer groups called the Green Scissors Coalition, which contends that eliminating federal entitlement makes far too much economic and environmental sense. It estimates that sugar farming has destroyed native wildlife habitat at a rate of three to five acres per day. Further, the activities of the sugar industry are directly responsible for an estimated $1.5 billion in Everglades restoration costs, which will mostly come from federal taxpayers' pockets. The Green Scissors Coalition contends that eliminating the federal sugar program would help restore the Everglades while saving taxpayers billions of dollars. Despite the coalition's efforts, Congress seems to have a sweet tooth for the sugar industry and refuses to ax the federal sugar program.

REPLUGGING THE EVERGLADES: A CHANCE AT REDEMPTION

Draining the Everglades proved to be more difficult than simply pulling the plug on a bathtub. The original vision of development was never achieved even after hundreds of millions of dollars and nearly a century of dredging and pumping. But these efforts have severely changed the region's character. The corps played a significant role by building a maze of canals, levees, and pumps to reroute billions of gallons of fresh water out of the sawgrass prairies and cypress swamps of the Everglades to the residents of south Florida. As a consequence, half of the original land has been swallowed up by development, and the remaining area is without enough clean water to support its flora and fauna.

To rectify years of federal abuse, in 1998 the corps unveiled an $8 billion, thirty-year plan—touted as the largest environmental restoration effort undertaken in the history of the United States—to restore water flow in the Everglades. The basic idea of the plan is to capture fresh water that has been flowing to the ocean, store it in new reservoirs, and then release some of it to mimic natural flows. The remaining water will be diverted to meet the needs of sugar plantations and thirsty cities throughout southern Florida. This portion of the plan, however, has raised the ire of some environmentalists and, at times, some National Park Service officials.

The main selling point to Congress is the restoration phase of the project, but critics such as Environmental Defense and the Natural Resources Defense Council charged that, like so many corps projects, the water supply features of the plan are given priority over restoration efforts. Their charges are not without merit. Many of the plan's water supply projects are funded up front, whereas full-scale restoration projects are scheduled two decades later. In fact according to a review by a University of Tennessee ecologist, the plan's first $4 billion worth of projects may result in almost no environmental benefits (Stevens 1999).

A more fundamental criticism of the corps plan is that it places a heavy emphasis on building elaborate structures to move water rather than eliminating old structures and letting nature take its course. Environmentalists have proposed several plans they contend would be more effective, faster, and far less expensive. But even these plans have their critics. Several of south Florida's water management districts who have a substantial stake in the outcome of the replumbing experiment say that the environmentalists' proposals oversimplify complex problems. The districts contend that such "let 'er rip," schemes by the environmentalists would worsen flooding problems for wildlife, as well as for the Miccosukee tribe north of the park.

Ironically, preliminary restoration efforts are already causing conflicts and problems for the tribe. The Cape Sable seaside sparrow, according to some biologists, is the Everglades version of the canary in the coal mine. Efforts to save the small olive-drab bird have created an enormous political game of tug-of-water between the tribe and the federal government. The sparrow's nesting cycle coincides with the region's dry season. As the land dries, the sparrows build nests just four inches above the ground. But the birds' nests have been submerged by water released by south Florida's massive flood control system. Scientists estimate that flooding has reduced sparrow populations as much as 90 percent in the past ten years.

Since 1996 environmental groups tried to protect the sparrow by threatening lawsuits under the Endangered Species Act. State water managers have responded by diverting excess water from the bird's breeding grounds and onto land owned by the Miccosukee Indian tribe. The U.S. Fish and Wildlife Service requires state water managers to ensure that the breeding grounds remain dry because the bird is in danger of extinction; however, the tribe claims that the government is killing wildlife on their lands to save the sparrow. It contends that three years of controlled flooding have drowned nearly 85 percent of the white-tailed deer on islands in the reservation. The Miccosukee accuse environmentalists and the Department of the Interior of using the sparrow's endangered status to gain legal leverage over water management on tribal lands (McKinley 1999). The Department of the Interior is in a politically vulnerable position. It must choose between saving an endangered bird or violating the tribe's sovereignty by continuing to flood their land. Regardless of the department's decision, one thing is certain: The agency will be flooded with lawsuits.

Besides a strong bias toward large construction projects, the corps will have to overcome other institutional challenges to successfully pull off the Everglades restoration project. According to a Department of Defense (2000, 7) investigation, schedule delays and budget overruns are a routine problem that plague nearly every major corps project. These problems are already occurring in preliminary restoration efforts. For example, modifications to the Everglades National Park–South Dade canals are more than two years behind schedule and $80 million over budget because federal and state agencies failed to agree on all the components of the project beforehand. Poor communication among all agencies involved is also causing more delays. The corps, for example, expedited the construction of a water pumping station to provide immediate environmental benefits to the national park. Pump construction was completed in December 1997, but it was not activated because sufficient funds to operate the station were never allocated (GAO 1999, 15–16).

PRIVATE EFFORTS TO PROTECT THE EVERGLADES

The protection of the Everglades is steeped in history. One of the earliest efforts to protect the region was a unique partnership between a local civic group and a large land development company. In 1910 the Florida Federation of Women's Clubs entered a partnership with the Model Land Company to set aside Paradise Key, a small hammock fifteen miles southwest of Homestead. The area was growing in popularity among tourists, birders, and adventure seekers. The head of the land company, an avid birder, agreed to donate the land to the federation. The Royal Palm State Park, as it was named, was dedicated November 22, 1916, and was privately run and self-supporting for more than thirteen years. The federation raised revenues by renting rooms in the park's lodge, collecting donations from visitors, and leasing land to local farmers. But the park was not immune from the devastating hurricanes of 1926 and 1928. Within a year of the last hurricane the federation donated their faltering project to the federal government. Although the hurricanes caused serious damage, they paled in comparison to the years of abuse that were to ensue from misguided federal policies.

Ironically the private sector is again offering to help protect and restore the Everglades. In 1999 Azurix Corporation, a subsidiary of Enron, tendered an offer to the state to cover some of the restoration costs. Azurix sees a way to help the Everglades while improving their bottom line—a share of the state's water, which it proposes to market to thirsty coastal residents. But to do this would require Florida to establish private tradable water rights. This is an alien concept in a state that prides itself on a twenty-year-old law that treats water as a free resource owned by the public.

Florida has embraced privatization in other areas such as schools, prisons, and healthcare. Yet the water privatization proposal is causing some Floridians to thumb their nose at the idea. David Guest, an expert on water law for the Earthjustice Legal Defense Fund in Tallahassee, is fascinated by it, but finds the offer "utterly frightening" (King 1999). He warns that Azurix would "control the most precious commodity in the state."

State officials, however, see a lot of potential for turning water management over to the private market. The state needs to come up with $4 billion over twenty years to finance Everglades restoration, and the more money the private sector offers for restoration, the less state officials must take from taxpayers. State officials are quick to point out that water markets encourage people to conserve water, thus providing additional protection for the Everglades. Once water rights are established, Azurix, along with anyone else, can buy and sell them for any purpose including restoring flows.

This is not the first time water privatization has been proposed in Florida. In the early 1990s, water managers near Tampa Bay tried to solve shortages by legalizing the private sale of permits. The proposal was rejected by a state hearings officer after being challenged by environmentalists, who contended that Florida's water is free and should remain that way.

CONCLUSION

The Everglades epitomizes government programs gone awry. Early federal policy through the Swamp and Overflowed Lands Act of 1850 gave Florida strong incentives to begin draining the Everglades. At that time, the vast wetlands were viewed merely as a swamp to be drained for more productive uses. Lacking the financial capital, the state encouraged private investors and entrepreneurs to take on draining projects by offering state-backed bonds and tax schemes. Needless to say, draining the south Florida swamp was a costly undertaking. Numerous investors failed in their effort, and by 1920 fewer than 1 million acres were drained to a level suitable for farming.

Significantly, the federal government, not private efforts, took an interest in draining the Everglades. Congress ordered the Army Corps of Engineers to dredge and gouge the swamp to carry water to the sea. The corps constructed an extensive network of canals, levees, and pumping stations to control the flow of water so that crops could be grown in the rich soils. Today the canals and levees carry water away from farmland, as well as provide drainage and supply water to cities on Florida's south coast. The water bypasses much of the former Everglades and has dramatically altered the timing, quantity, and quality of water delivered to the coastal estuaries. These engineered changes, coupled with extensive and heavily subsidized agricultural activities have reduced the Everglades to about half its original size. Without federal involvement, the region is unlikely to have been drained to the extent that it is today. Nor would there be consideration of a multibillion-dollar recovery plan that may amount to nothing more than stuffing money down a drain.

Ironically the same agency that drained the area, the Army Corps of Engineers, will be the lead federal agency responsible for replugging the region. The $8 billion restoration phase of the federal project will attempt to restore a natural hue of green. But with the corps in charge the Everglades may end up taking a military green hue.

REFERENCES

Blake, Nelson Manfred. 1980. *Land into Water—Water into Land: A History of Water Management in Florida*. Tallahassee: University Presses of Florida.

Carter, Luther J. 1974. *The Florida Experience: Land and Water Policy in a Growth State*. Baltimore: Johns Hopkins University Press.

Coale, F. J., F. T. Izuno, and A. B. Bottcher. 1994. Phosphorus in Drainage Water from Sugarcane in the Everglades Agricultural Area as Affected by Drainage Rate. *Journal of Environmental Quality* (January/February): 121–26.

Department of Defense. 2000. *U. S. Army Inspector General Agency Report of Investigation. Case 00-019*. Washington, DC: Office of the Inspector General, November.

Duplaix, Nicole. 1990. South Florida Water: Paying the Price. *National Geographic*, July.

General Accounting Office. 1993. *Sugar Program: Changing Domestic and International Conditions Require Program Changes*. GAO/RCED-93-84. Washington, DC, April.

———. 1999. *South Florida Ecosystem Restoration: An Overall Strategic Plan and a Decision Making Process Are Needed to Keep the Effort on Track*. GAO/RCED-99-121. Washington, DC, April.

Hanna, Alfred Jackson, and Kathryn Abbey Hanna. 1948. *Lake Okeechobee: Wellsprings of the Everglades*. Miami, FL: Bobs-Merrill Company.

Harner, Charles E. 1973. *Florida's Promoters: The Men Who Made It Big*. Tampa Bay, FL: Tampa Trend House.

Johnson, Lamar. 1974. *Beyond the Fourth Generation*. Gainesville: University Press of Florida.

King, Robert P. 1999. Firm May Ante Up to Restore Everglades. *Palm Beach Post*, November 12.

Koo, Won W., and Richard D. Taylor. 1999. 1999 Outlook of the U.S. and World Sugar Markets. *Agricultural Economics Report* No. 420. Fargo: North Dakota State University, Department of Agricultural Economics.

Kriz, M. 1994. Mending the Marsh. *National Journal*, March 12.

Light, Stephen S., and J. Walter Dineen. 1994. Water Control in the Everglades: A Historical Perspective. In *Everglades: The Ecosystem and Its Restoration*, ed. Steven Davis and John Ogden. Delray Beach, FL: St. Lucie Press, 47–84.

McCally, David. 1999. *The Everglades: An Environmental History*. Gainesville, FL: University Press of Florida.

McKinley, James C. 1999. A Tiny Sparrow Is Cast as a Test of Will to Restore the Everglades. *New York Times*, June 3.

New York Times. 1996. Flooding in Florida. August 7.

Organization for Economic Cooperation and Development. 1996. *Saving Biological Diversity: Economic Incentives*. Paris, France.

Snell, Rand, and Bill Boggess. 1994. Everglades Case Study: Water Agriculture, and Environmental Policy Issues. Background paper prepared for the Congressional Office of Technology Assessment. Oregon State University, Corvallis.

Stevens, William K. 1999. Some Scientists Attack Plan to Restore Everglades. *New York Times*, February 22.

Tolman, Jonathan. 1995. *Federal Agricultural Policy: A Harvest of Environmental Abuse*. Washington, DC: Competitive Enterprise Institute.

U.S. Army Corps of Engineers. 1976. *Annual Report of the Chief of Engineers on Civil Works*, vols. 1 and 2. Washington, DC: Department of Defense.

U.S. Department of Agriculture. 1978. *Census of Agriculture and Drainage*, vol. 5, *Special Reports: Drainage of Agricultural Lands*, part 5. Washington, DC.

6

War on Wildlife

J. Bishop Grewell

"I may be considered too optimistic, but I believe that in three years, if allowed to take our course under an intensive campaign, with the support of Congress, we shall have practically exterminated the big wolf from the Rocky Mountain region. . . ." (quoted in McIntyre 1995, 176)

—Dr. A. K. Fisher
United States Biological Survey, 1916

Wildlife often symbolizes the state of environmental quality. Pictures of oil-soaked birds and marine mammals following the Santa Barbara and Valdez oil spills helped galvanize the environmental movement in the 1960s and 1990s. Conservation efforts to protect the furry and the cuddly, the slithery and the slimy, both predator and prey, from extinction or other harms are the foundation for groups like the National Audubon Society, Isaac Walton League, World Wildlife Federation, and Trout Unlimited. These organizations regularly turn to government for protection of species, but the political arena has been a double-edged sword. On the one hand, governments at the federal and state levels in the United States are entrusted with the authority to protect species from unlawful takings and to provide habitat when possible. On the other hand, both levels of government have been guilty of efforts to eliminate certain species when special interests exert their influence over politicians and bureaucrats. Overt government efforts to eliminate a species have generally arisen out of protest to the damages that the species does to favored species or to an economic activity, such as agriculture. As early as 1630, laws to encourage the destruction of wolves were passed by the Massachusetts Bay Colony for the threat that wolves posed to livestock. This came only ten years after the colonists had landed in America. The history of government-aided wolf killing continued for the next three centuries. Even in government-run sanctuaries such as Yellowstone National Park, wolves were killed to procure more elk for sportsmen. Although government's assault on the wolf ended in the continental United States by midcentury, governmental assaults on other wild animals have continued. In some cases it has led to the irony of one government agency trying to eliminate a species while another tries to save it.

This chapter examines government's role in the destruction of wild animal species. It begins with a history of wolf destruction in the United States and a brief account of wolf destruction in other countries. This is followed by an account of early efforts to eliminate hawks in the United States and an examination of state and federal efforts to destroy the prairie dog in the West, a species considered for listing under the Endangered Species Act (ESA). Then the chapter examines the history of the U.S. Department of Agriculture's Wildlife Services program to destroy predators and pests. The chapter concludes with a discussion of unintended destruction of wildlife by public bodies ostensibly trying to save species. The cases of the international ivory ban under the Convention on International Trade in Endangered Species (CITES) and preemptive habitat destruction under the Endangered Species Act in the United States fall into this category.

LOS LOBOS—A RECORD OF DESTRUCTION

In the spring of 1995, the federal government reintroduced wolves into the Yellowstone region. This reintroduction is in stark contrast to wolf management throughout the history of the nation. Wolves were the number one enemy of shepherds in Europe for centuries until the animals were largely eradicated there. Colonists to the New World brought their prejudices against wolves over with them from Europe along with fables, such as "Little Red Riding Hood." The predator's bad reputation with Europeans, earned by their propensity to kill livestock, continued when the animals were discovered in America.

In his history of American efforts to exterminate the wolf, author Rick McIntyre looked into laws encouraging the destruction of wolves from colonization of the New World to the present. He found that only ten years after colonists landed in Massachusetts Bay in 1620, bounties were put in place to encourage the killing of wolves. Records from the Governor and Company of the Massachusetts Bay[1] set the bounty as follows:

November 9, 1630
    It is ordered that every English man that killeth a wolf in any part within the limits of this patent shall have allowed him 1d [one penny] for every beast &

horse, & ob. [? penny] for every weaned swine and goat in every plantation, to be levied by the constables of the said plantations. (quoted in McIntyre 1995, 30)

The bounty rose to ten shillings per wolf seven years later. Finally, by 1640 the law paid forty shillings to a man who killed a wolf with dogs and ten shillings to a man who killed a wolf using other means. McIntyre notes that a 1638 law fixed the minimum wage for laborers at eighteen cents per day and as one shilling equaled twelve cents, a killed wolf was equivalent to twenty-seven days' worth of labor. The incentive for hunting wolves was high.

The colony of Virginia opted for a different form of payment, doling out tobacco instead. In 1646 the colony offered 100 pounds of tobacco for the head of a wolf. By 1691 the payment for a destroyed wolf was 300 pounds, if killed by pit or trap, and 200 pounds, if killed otherwise. In Pennsylvania in 1705, killers of male wolves could earn ten shillings; she-wolves would bring fifteen. Those who were willing to go so far as to make wolf killing their official job for at least three days a week could earn twenty-five shillings for every animal killed.

State-backed bounties on wolves continued into the next century. A rather humorous amendment was offered by Jarius Neal, Iowa state senator, to a wolf bounty law in 1856.

That any wolf or other voracious beast which shall feloniously, maliciously and unlawfully, attack with intent to kill, or do great bodily injury to any sheep, ass, or other domestic animal shall on being duly convicted thereof, be declared an enemy to our Republican institutions, and an outlaw, and it shall be lawful for the person aggrieved by such an attack, to pursue and kill such beast wherever it shall be found, and if such beast unlawfully resist, the injured party may notify the Governor, who shall thereupon call out the militia of the State to resist said voracious beast, and if the militia of the State should be overcome in such battle, then the Governor is authorized to make a requisition upon the President of the United States, for troops. (quoted in McIntyre 1995, 50–51)

Neal's amendment was voted down. Two years later, however, a $3 bounty on wolves in Iowa passed.

As farming and ranching moved westward, so did the laws encouraging wolf destruction in the hope of preventing the predators from threatening agricultural livelihoods. Colorado was the first territory in the Rocky Mountain region to pass a wolf bounty law, having done so in 1869. Wyoming followed with a bounty of fifty cents per wolf in 1875, which steadily rose to $8 in 1893 before dropping down to $3 in 1896. From 1897 to 1907, Wyoming paid out more than $65,000 in bounties on wolves. In 1884 Montana Territory was offering bounties for wolves as well as other wild species. A wolf

scalp brought $1, a coyote skin $.50, and $8 was paid for the pelt of a moun-
tain lion or a bear. The scalp law cost the Montana territoral treasury
$12,740.50 that year (McIntyre 1995, 84). Most counties in the territory were
offering at least as much. Scalp bounties apparently did not go far enough in
later years—in 1905, the Montana legislature passed a law that enlisted the
state veterinarian's help in destroying wolves. The veterinarian was required
to capture wolves and coyotes, and their pups, and then infect them with
mange in the hope that they would carry it back to their packs and infect fellow pack members (McIntyre, 120). This disease caused by mites, leads animals to lose their fur, and subsequently can cause the animals to freeze to
death in winter.

Dunlap (1983) reports that the federal government did not take a direct
role in eliminating predators until 1905 when the USDA Forest Service began
hiring trappers to reduce predator populations on grazing lands. Chase
(1986) reports that in 1907, U.S. Biological Survey officers eliminated more
than 1,800 wolves and 23,000 coyotes in thirty-nine national forests. A 1908
document written by U.S. Biological Survey biologist Vernon Bailey gives a
more precise number of 1,723 wolves exterminated in these forests during
1907 (McIntyre 1995, 160). Earlier that year, a study published by the Biological Survey recommended an all-out campaign to destroy wolves by
"killing young in breeding dens" (quoted in Chase 1986, 120). In 1914 Congress charged the Biological Survey with the task of "destroying wolves,
prairie dogs, and other animals injurious to agriculture and animal husbandry" (quoted in Chase 1986, 122). The next year Congress devoted
$125,000, or 28 percent of the Biological Survey's entire budget specifically
to "be used on the national forests and the public domain in destroying
wolves, coyotes, and other animals injurious to agriculture and animal husbandry" (quoted in McIntyre 1995, 172). The reason for the congressional
appropriation, according to Dunlap was to appease the complaints of western stockgrowers, mainly sheepmen. In following years the Biological Survey would encourage stockmen to contribute additional funds that eventually led to the cooperative program in which, according to Wagner (1988,
197), "states provide part of the control costs with monies obtained from
'head taxes' on the woolgrowers' sheep." Dunlap (1983, 55) found this cooperative funding, combined with the influence of western congressmen sit-
ting on appropriations committees and acting loyal to their agricultural constituents, made the Biological Survey more responsive to stockmen.

In a report from 1928, the supervisor of the Biological Survey's predator
control program lauds the success of the survey's work:

> In the year 1896, the State paid bounties of $3 each on 3,458 wolves. From 1895
> to 1927, 36,161 wolves have been taken in Wyoming by regular Federal, State,
> and bounty hunters. In the early stages of wolf control, bounties reduced them

greatly, but it was left to the expert State and Federal Government hunters to thin the ranks of the last few, and if possible exterminate them entirely. (quoted in McIntyre 1995, 96)

The supervisor went on to note that no more than five wolves remained in Wyoming. Federal, state, and county taxpayers doled out $338,013 on predator control in Wyoming from 1921 to 1928. In 1924 at a meeting of the American Society of Mammalogists, a senior biologist of the Biological Survey said, "Large predatory animals, destructive to livestock and game, no longer have a place in our advancing civilization" (quoted in Dunlap 1983, 57).

A final tally of 69,786 wolves killed between 1915 and 1970 is offered up by McIntyre (1995, 199) for the U.S. Biological Survey's twentieth-century wolfkill (including the later years when it was killing wolves as the U.S. Fish and Wildlife Service). Of those, 48,276 were killed between 1940 and 1970 and nearly 15,000 were killed between 1960 and 1970 (Cain et al. 1972, 22). These later wolfkill efforts were primarily from Biological Survey programs to exterminate the southern red wolf in the Southeast and Mexican wolves in New Mexico and Arizona.

Two states in the Great Lakes region also had long-running wolf control programs. In Minnesota a state bounty on wolves continued until 1965, after which the state Department of Natural Resources continued to kill the animals under a predator control program until 1974. About 250 wolves were destroyed each year (Wooley 2000, 48). The state of Michigan paid out $11,375 in wolf bounties between 1935 and 1959, though this pales in comparison with the $1.2 million in bounties it paid out to destroy coyotes over the same period (Cain et al. 1972, 75).

If there is anywhere wolves might be protected from government extermination, Yellowstone Park would seem to fill the bill. Yet even in Yellowstone wolves were under attack by Uncle Sam. The goal of killing wolves in the park, however, was not related so much to agriculture as to fostering big game populations. In February 1918, Stephen Mather the director of the National Park Service (NPS), ordered Chester Lindsley, Yellowstone's acting superintendent, to aid the U.S. Biological Survey in their program of "extermination of mountain lions and other predatory animals" (quoted in Chase 1986, 21). This extermination plan included wolves. The reason for the program was that park service officials blamed the predators for declining whitetail deer, antelope, and bighorn sheep numbers in and around the park. By eliminating the predators, the NPS thought it could bolster the numbers of these big game animals for sportsmen. Chase counters that the park service was wrong in blaming predators. He argues that the problem was overgrazing by a burgeoning population of elk, a problem exacerbated by fewer and fewer predators.

The park's 1916 annual report credited two special rangers, employed solely for the purpose of killing predators, with successfully shooting or trapping 83 coyotes, 12 wolves, and 4 mountain lions; the 1918 annual report boasts 190 coyotes and 36 wolves. In 1920 another 107 coyotes were taken and 28 wolves were destroyed. Monthly reports from 1922 could not ascertain the exact amount of animals taken because the park service was likely missing some animals killed by the poison bait placed in Yellowstone for predator control; still, the number killed was about 175 coyotes and 15 wolves (McIntyre 1995, 205).

The elimination of wolves in Yellowstone actually began several decades before the NPS took over the region, under the auspices of the U.S. Army. McIntyre cites an army manual for soldiers stationed in the park with the following orders:

> Scouts and noncommissioned officers in charge of stations throughout the park are authorized and directed to kill mountain lions, coyotes, and timber wolves. They will do this themselves, and will not delegate the authority to anyone else. They will report at the end of the month, in writing, the number of such animals killed, and will retain all skins or scalps in their personal possession until directed what to do with them. (McIntyre 1995, 203)

Still, while the U.S. Army managed Yellowstone for thirty-two years, it managed to kill only fourteen wolves. The NPS and the Biological Survey were much more effective in exterminating wolves. From 1918, when the park service took over Yellowstone, to 1926, the agency and the Biological Survey, which it often employed, had killed at least 122 wolves and nearly 1,300 coyotes (Chase 1986, 123). In 1926 the last wolves were destroyed by the park's predator control program. After that, wolves were occasionally reported, but there were not enough animals for a breeding population (McIntyre 1995, 292).

The war against wolves to boost big game populations was equally intensive in Alaska. Wolves there were under siege during the years following World War II. The U.S. Fish and Wildlife Service (USFWS) offered free ammunition to encourage pilots in the Arctic to shoot wolves. It reasoned that fewer wolves meant more caribou for sportsmen and subsistence hunters. This kept resident hunters and the purveyors of the territory's growing outdoor tourist industry happy. Starting in 1948, the USFWS began sending its own employees up in planes to destroy wolves. Working as a two-man team of flier and gunner, they could make substantial kills from the air. Over one particularly fruitful fortnight, three teams succeeded in bringing down 270 Arctic wolves (Laycock 1990, 44). Throughout the 1950s, the federal government carried out a program of poisoning and aerial shooting to control the wolf population.

When Alaska earned statehood in 1959, the wolf control programs were ostensibly stopped as the newly formed Alaska Department of Fish and

Game labeled wolves as big game animals and decided that their control was unimportant in regulating prey populations. There seems to be some question as to when bounties officially ended in Alaska. The Alaska Board of Game claims on its Website that the state legislature ended the bounty system in the late 1960s (Alaska Board of Game 1993). The 1972 Cain Report, however, notes that Alaska spent $46,950 on wolf bounties in 1970 (Cain et al. 1972, 74).

Wolf control was again used to improve herds of caribou and moose for hunters in the early 1990s. In 1993 the Alaska Department of Fish and Game planned to kill 150 wolves to reduce pressure on a herd of caribou to the southeast of Fairbanks (Mestel 1993, 9). Right up until the winter of 1994–95, the department still used snares in its wolf control program. The program ended, however, when the governor ordered the department to stop after pictures of snared wolves made it into the national media (*Economist* 1997, 29).

When plans to increase the Fortymile caribou herd in the east-central portion of Alaska arose, the state chose a more picture-friendly route. In 1997 it opted to spend $200,000 annually to sterilize wolves preying on the herd (*Fairbanks Daily News Miner* 1997b). This followed the advice of a report from the National Academy of Sciences National Research Council. The report, commissioned from the state for $318,000, proposed that the state give more consideration to sterilization and other nonlethal techniques, though it offered no clear-cut rules (*Fairbanks Daily News Miner* 1997a).

In January 2000, an attempt to improve moose herds near McGrath and in the Nelchina basin resulted in the Alaska Board of Game approving a measure to reauthorize predator control to cut the wolf population from fifty-five to twenty in the area, although it was unlikely that the governor would give the necessary consent (Palmer 2000, 53).

The United States is not the only place that wolves have been killed by government agents or by hunters encouraged through government bounties. As mentioned, American animosity toward wolves came partly from Europe. In France, a fifty-year campaign was waged to eliminate wolves from the Alps: They were finally eliminated by 1924. Thanks to reintroduction in 1992, however, the wolf is the subject of controversy in France once more. In April 2000, French shepherds paraded their sheep through the town of Aix-en-Provence, calling for the government to either place wolves in pens or have them killed (Banoun 2000).

Russia bears wolves no goodwill either. In 1998 the Russian Ministry of Agriculture and Food, as well as a majority of Russian governors, initiated a drive to control wolves for the sake of livestock. Hunters could receive a bounty between $100 and $200 for each wolf killed. In a twist of irony, some of the Russian provinces were paying for the bounties out of their environmental protection funds (Barinov 1998, 16).

Canada also has a history of wolf destruction at the hand of government. Gunson (1992) recounts the history of wolf management in Alberta. The province witnessed a decline in wolf numbers from 1860 to 1920 thanks to poisonings, bounties, and a declining prey population of elk, moose, sheep, and deer. Caribou and goat numbers were still strong (Cowan 1947). Wolf numbers grew over the course of the next twenty years, probably due to removal of bounty payments during the 1930s. In the 1950s, a program to eradicate rabies led to wolf reduction once again, dropping the population from an estimated 5,000 before the program to between 500 and 1,000 at the end of the decade. Finally, numbers rose to a new peak in the early 1970s before fur harvest for pelts, mange, and wolves killed by the province in response to depredation complaints sent the numbers back down. Reduction of prey is blamed for a continued decline in the Alberta wolf populations during the 1980s.

Alberta was not alone among the provinces in sponsoring wolf killing. Between 1982 and 1989, the Yukon's Department of Renewable Resources destroyed 454 wolves in order to increase caribou numbers (Killick 1997). In 1992 the department killed another 62 wolves and planned to eliminate 50 more in 1993 until questions of how many remained in the Aishihik region near the Yukon's southern border were raised (Watt 1994, 12).

HAWKS—PRIVATE SECTOR HAS THE EDGE

Although most Americans now probably consider hawks beautiful as they soar through the sky and unleash their trademark cry, this was not always the case. In earlier years, state governments and game associations supported the killing of hawks by placing a bounty on them (Anderson and Leal 1997). The raptors were persecuted as vermin or "chicken hawks" because they preyed on poultry, game birds, and songbirds. Conservationist efforts to protect hawks were even seen as "pro-German" during World War I as well as in the 1930s leading up to World War II because they removed opportunities for young American men to practice shooting at live targets. Even the National Audubon Society supported control of hawks in order to encourage songbirds (Smith 1999, 1–3).

As far back as 1885, hawks joined owls, weasels, and minks as predators with a fifty-cent bounty on their heads. The "Scalp Act" paid out $90,000 for the destruction of 128,571 of these animals during the eighteen months it was in action. Many predatory animals suffered from the antipathy of biologists, wildlife managers, and leaders of the environmental movement. Dunlap (1983, 56) writes:

> William Hornaday, a leader in the fight to protect and preserve wild species, had little charity for the predators. Peregrine falcons, he declared, looked best "in

collections," the Great Horned Owl was an "aerial robber and murderer," and the wolf a "master of cunning and the acme of cruelty"—as well as being a coward. Coopers and Sharp-shinned hawks should be shot on sight. Biologists and wildlife managers shared many of these attitudes. There were few who objected to characterizations (in the *Journal of Mammalogy*) of predators as "criminals" and "murderers," and when Aldo Leopold was calling, in the early 1920s, for the total elimination of large predators from New Mexico, he found much support and no opposition.

In 1929, less than half a century after the Scalp Act, Pennsylvania placed a bounty of $5 per head on goshawks. Given the value of $5 during the Depression, the bounty provided an enticement to shooters. It ended in 1951, but not before large numbers of goshawks and other hawks confused for the goshawk were killed (Smith 1999, 3).

One of the few people to stand up for the hawks in Pennsylvania was a woman named Rosalie Edge. A conservationist and bird watcher, Edge took up the cause of hawks and other nongame species. In 1929 she began her attack on the National Association of Audubon Societies, the U.S. Biological Survey, and state game departments for catering to sportsmen and agricultural interests. Ms. Edge publicly accused these organizations of, with few exceptions, only caring about game birds (Anderson and Leal 1997, 44).

Her efforts did not end there. She acted to protect raptors by buying property well known as a popular migration spot for hawks. Known as Hawk Mountain, the property is located in the Appalachian Mountains of eastern Pennsylvania. It derives its name from the tens of thousands of hawks flying through the area each autumn. Before Rosalie Edge purchased the mountain, it had served as a slaughtering area for hawks by hunters who took hundreds and even thousands of hawks in a single day (Anderson and Leal 1997, 44). Edge leased the 1,398 acres of the mountaintop in 1934 for $500 and purchased it outright in 1935 for $3,500. She hired a guard to patrol the grounds and keep hawk hunters out.

PRAIRIE DOGS AND THE STATES

Basically, every state where prairie dogs live lists them as pests. This includes South Dakota, Texas, New Mexico, Colorado, North Dakota, Wyoming, Montana, and Kansas (Williams 2000, 39).

In South Dakota the state government requires control efforts on private or state property "infested" by pests. According to state statute 38-22-16.1: "The existence of weeds or pests in any amount or quantity upon land is sufficient to determine that such land is infested." The landowner must bear the costs for control on his land. At the same time, if a private landowner requests help with prairie dogs, the South Dakota Department of Agriculture will provide aid under statute 40-36-3.1: "The secretary of game, fish and parks shall establish a program to continue prairie dog control on private lands at the written request and with the cooperation of the participating landowner. The program is to be funded from revenues in the state animal damage control fund." Help occurs as "technical assistance to landowners in the form of directions on control techniques, toxicant distribution and all-terrain vehicles for control operations" (South Dakota Department of Agriculture 2000a). As for prairie dogs on state lands, statute 34A-8-7 states: "The secretaries shall establish and conduct control programs at state expense on private lands that are encroached upon by prairie dogs from contiguous public lands." South Dakota's listing of prairie dogs as pests has even prompted federal authorities to poison them at Badlands National Park (Long 1998, 124).

South Dakota's control efforts include the bait mixing facility at the Pierre Municipal Airport that provides prairie dog poisons to other government agencies and individuals at cost, while also engaging in research on experimental poisonous baits. The facility was originally run by the U.S. Department of the Interior's Bureau of Sports Fisheries and Wildlife, but was turned over to the South Dakota Department of Agriculture in July of 1969. According to the department's Website, "The necessity to insure quality, economically priced rodent baits and maintain a facility capable of producing experimental toxicants for pest control is as important today as it was when the bait station was accepted from the U.S. Department of Interior." The department fears that turning the operation over to a private firm would eliminate the bait program. It writes: "The concern is that because this is such a limited use product the private industry will either give up quality for cost or decide that there is not enough need to justify manufacturing and will simply quit making bait, leaving these agencies without a reliable source of quality bait" (South Dakota Department of Agriculture 2000b, 2).

In Montana, statute 7-22-2207 of the state law defines prairie dogs as rodents along with field mice, several different species of ground squirrels, and pocket gophers. Statute 80-7-1101 then designates that the state department of agriculture is to operate a pest management program that includes the destruction of prairie dogs:

> 80-7-1101. Department to operate vertebrate pest management program. The department may establish and operate organized and systematic programs for the management and suppression of vertebrate pests. Vertebrate pests are defined as . . . prairie dogs . . . when they are injurious to agriculture, other industries, and the public. For this purpose, the department may enter into written agreements with appropriate federal agencies, other state agencies,

counties, associations, corporations, or individuals covering the methods and procedures to be followed in the management and suppression of these vertebrate pests, the extent of supervision to be exercised by the department, and the use and expenditure of funds appropriated, when this cooperation is necessary to promote the management and suppression of vertebrate pests.

Part of Montana's program involves a simple information exchange. According to a 1985 Prairie Dog Control Bulletin printed up by the Environmental Management Division of the Montana Department of Agriculture, "Field demonstrations are available free of charge to inform landowners how, when, and where to control prairie dogs and other field rodent pests." The bulletin also advises that "because of the reproductive capacity of prairie dogs, it is necessary to reduce their numbers by approximately 90 percent if long term control is desired" (Montana Department of Agriculture 1985, 2, 5). Montana, however, has no active poisoning infrastructure like South Dakota and Wyoming. Roemer and Forrest (1996, 357) explain that this may be because federal programs at the beginning of the twentieth century virtually eliminated the prairie dog in the Treasure State, thereby reducing the need to fund control programs.

In Wyoming the prairie dog is a designated pest under the state's Weed & Pest Control Act of 1973. Listed by the act as "detrimental to the general welfare of the state," county weed and pest districts are required to poison prairie dogs (Davitt et al. 1996, 9). Roemer and Forrest (1996, 355) surveyed twenty-three counties in Wyoming; thirteen of them had prairie dog poisoning programs and eleven had data on their programs to provide to the survey. From 1989 through 1992, the counties spent $291,433 on the programs, with private landowners paying an additional $97,267 as part of cost-sharing efforts.

Prairie Dogs and the Feds: The Irony of Success

In February 2000, the USFWS announced that the black-tailed prairie dog merited protection under the Endangered Species Act, but that the prairie dog would have to wait to be listed—the agency was too busy with other species. The USFWS look into listing the prairie dog came at the behest of the National Wildlife Federation and several other environmental groups, which formally requested that prairie dogs be listed as threatened in 1998 (McMillion 2000). Listing the prairie dog would be a 180-degree turn from past federal policies toward the species.

Prairie dogs were among the creatures that Congress mandated the U.S. Biological Survey to destroy in 1914 (Chase 1986, 121–22). Thirteen million acres of prairie dog–inhabited lands were poisoned under federally supervised programs between 1916 and 1920 (Roemer and Forrest 1996, 350). These programs continued over tens of millions of acres in the Midwest through the 1930s (Forrest, Proctor, and Roemer 2000, 2). Between 1937 and 1968, 30,447,355 acres were treated with prairie dog poison by the Biological Survey and subsequently the USFWS (Cain et al. 1972, 140). In a 1928 report co-written by Albert Day, supervisor of the Biological Survey's Predatory Animal and Rodent Control Division in Wyoming, Day noted that prairie dogs were among several creatures the federal agency worked with the state of Wyoming to control (McIntyre 1995, 194). This record of destruction at the hands of the federal government continues today.

The Bureau of Land Management (BLM) has encouraged the recreational shooting of prairie dog populations in certain areas for prairie dog control and as a recreational use of public lands since 1979 (Vosburgh and Irby 1998). In Phillips County, Montana, the BLM's encouragement has come in the form of advertisements in magazines, signs identifying legal shooting areas, and district maps that show prairie dog colony locations (Vosburgh 1996, 26). More direct methods of prairie dog control by the federal government such as poisoning, have declined as a percentage of overall control in the latter half of the century, but it does continue. In the Nebraska National Forest, the Forest Service poisoned 138,000 acres of prairie dog habitat between 1978 and 1992 at a cost of $616,000. More than 17,000 acres were poisoned at the Medicine Bow National Forest in Wyoming between 1989 and 1992. And in the Custer National Forest (which has lands in Montana, North Dakota, and South Dakota), at least 4,600 acres of habitat were poisoned between 1982 and 1992[2] (Roemer and Forrest 1996, 352).

The Forest Service also manages the country's national grasslands. On eleven of the national grasslands in the Great Plains, the agency poisoned 100,000 acres of prairie dog lands between 1985 and 1998 (Forrest, Proctor, and Roemer 2000, 4). As of 1994, the U.S. Department of Agriculture's Animal Damage Control program was conducting research on prairie dog control methods at a center in Denver, Colorado, and manufacturing rodenticides at the Pocatello Supply Depot in Idaho, according to Roemer and Forrest (1996, 354), whose 1996 analysis found substantial modern-day government involvement in prairie dog control.

> We found that there was state and federal involvement in 423,200 ha (1,045,524 ac) of prairie dog control in the northern Great Plains from 1978 through 1992. . . . This estimate does not include hectares poisoned through indirect assistance of state and federal agencies (such as supplying applicants with poison bait), strictly private control efforts, or illegal control on public lands. Of this total, approximately 68,211 ha (168,550 ac) were poisoned on USFS, NPS, and BLM lands during 1978–1992. Documented costs for control during this period exceed $10,000,000, a rough accounting, which in some cases does not include administrative costs or the cost of applicant-supplied labor. (Roemer and Forrest 1996, 356)

WILDLIFE SERVICES—EXTERMINATING "VERMIN" SINCE 1931

Government efforts to destroy predators for the benefit of agriculture today are run under the auspices of the U.S. Department of Agriculture's Wildlife Services program. As noted, the Biological Survey was charged by Congress with the task of "destroying wolves, prairie dogs, and other animals injurious to agriculture and animal husbandry" in 1914. The results of their efforts were often calamitous. Dunlap (1983, 58) notes that in January 1927, a scene right out of the biblical plagues struck Kern County, California. Mice had been breeding in the fields of a nearby dry lakebed and ended up overrunning the countryside. Dunlap (1983, 58) writes, "A slick coating of mice covered the roads; at one factory workers put out poison and then had to bury two tons of dead rodents; and stories circulated in the towns of housewives who had not touched ground for a week, doing their housework by leaping from one piece of furniture to another." One biologist who visited the area blamed the problem on the lack of predators in the area as the Biological Survey had poisoned and shot coyotes in Kern County during 1924 and 1925 and farmers had shot any hawks or owls in the area.

Destruction of certain animals damaging to agriculture gained a more official status with the Animal Damage Control Act of 1931 (General Accounting Office [GAO] 1995, 1). Dunlap (1983, 57) attributes passage of the bill at the time to greater political power by agriculture and public support for predator control. After the 1931 act, animal damage control activities were bounced between federal agencies over the next decades. In 1942, the Biological Survey was absorbed into the USFWS when federal agencies were reorganized (McIntyre 1995, 239). The wool growers were able to keep the predatory control program going strong throughout the 1950s and 1960s; nearly 1.5 million coyotes were destroyed by the program during these two decades alone (Cain et al. 1972, 22). As conservation became the name of the game for the USFWS in the following two decades, Animal Damage Control found itself out of sync with the rest of the agency's goals. As a result, the program was steadily reduced until 1986, when it was transferred to a friendlier home at the U.S. Department of Agriculture [USDA], where it has remained (Satchell 1990, 36). In 1997 the program changed its name from Animal Damage Control to Wildlife Services, no doubt a euphemism to give the effort a more acceptable stature before the public. The agency described the reason for the name change as follows:

> The name Wildlife Services captures the essence of our program's current mission of balancing the needs of humans and wildlife in many different situations. Whether it's working to ensure human health and safety, protecting threatened or endangered species, safeguarding people's property, we are increasingly being asked to utilize our expertise in many areas outside of our traditional role of

livestock protection. Wildlife Services encompasses the diversity of these activities and accurately conveys the wide array of services our program provides.

The new name also reflects our program's vision of "living with wildlife." We recognize the need to take into account a wide range of public interests on wildlife management, even if these interests conflict with one another. We also recognize the need to conduct our activities in a manner that considers wildlife interests while reducing the damage caused by wildlife. Wildlife Services brings our name in line with these key principles. (U.S. Department of Agriculture 1997a)

Many environmental groups refuse to use the new name, arguing that the program does nothing to help wildlife (Swanson 1998), and they have a point. Despite its name, Wildlife Services is in the business of killing species that prey on livestock and crops. In 1998 the program spent nearly $10 million to destroy 88,354 predators, most of which were coyotes (table 6.1).[3]

All told, nearly 100,000 coyotes were killed each year in the early 1990s before dropping back down to around 80,000 at the end of the decade. According to the program's Website, "Most of [Wildlife Services'] efforts are conducted on private land in response to specific requests for assistance" (USDA 1997b). Additionally, the program claims that among different control strategies, "consideration is first given to nonlethal methods." A 1995 GAO report that examined the at-the-time Animal Damage Control program found that, to the contrary, the program actually tended toward the use of lethal methods.

Although written program policies call for field personnel to give preference to nonlethal control methods when practical and effective, field personnel use lethal methods to control livestock predators. ADC program officials told us that nonlethal methods are more appropriately used by livestock operators, have limited effectiveness, and are not practical for field personnel to use. (GAO 1995, 4)

An article in *U.S. News & World Report* further characterized the lethal aspect of the program's history in 1990 when it stated, "Predator-control programs have poisoned vast numbers of Western eagles, killed all the lions east of Texas and the Rocky Mountain states except for a sickly, inbred handful

Table 6.1   Predators Killed by Wildlife Services, 1998

Animal	Killed
Coyote	77,997
Fox	6,809
Bobcat	2,250
Badger	580
Bear	380
Mountain Lion	338
Total	88,354

Source: Predator Conservation Alliance (2000).

Table 6.2   Animals Killed by Animal Damage Control, 1988

Animal	Intentional	Unintentional
Coyote	76,033	17
Skunk	15,239	102
Beaver	9,143	28
Raccoon	5,348	1,117
Opossum	5,329	505
Fox	5,195	1,155
Bobcat	1,163	63
Badger	939	555
Porcupine	799	935
Nutria	612	21
Prairie dog	538	0
Rat/mouse	505	0
Hog (feral)	392	17
Muskrat	323	63
Bear (black)	289	2
Marmot	258	0
Mountain lion	203	4
Russian boar	192	5
Rabbit	186	231
Cat (domestic)	178	104
Ground squirrel	159	24
Dog (domestic)	151	393
Javelina	0	764
Blackbird	4,453,842	1
Pigeon	7,982	0
Egret	6,729	0
Other animals	2,398	342

Source: Satchell (1990).

of Florida panthers, and almost wiped out the grizzly and wolf in the Lower 48 states" (Satchell 1990, 36). The article went on to list every animal killed by Animal Damage Control in 1988: both predator and non, as well as intentionally and accidentally killed (table 6.2). Despite continued controversy surrounding the program, the U.S. Department of Agriculture's Wildlife Services program spent nearly $10 million yet again to control predators that prey on western livestock in fiscal year 2000 (Friends of the Earth 2000, 14).

UNINTENDED CONSEQUENCES: CITES AND THE ESA

Although the above programs by government to destroy species have been intentional, there are also programs meant to help species that have had the unintended consequence of harming them.

CITES, Ivory Trade, and Local Incentives

CITES is one of the oldest international environmental treaties. It was drawn up in 1973, took effect in 1975, and counts the United States among its signatory nations. CITES intends to protect endangered species by banning international trade in their body parts. This assumes that making a product illegal lessens its harvest. It is as flawed as modern drug policy in which illegal activity simply goes underground, thrives, and has even more destructive results in some respects.

It was under CITES that trade restrictions in ivory arose. The African elephant was originally listed under appendix II of CITES in 1978, which led to a 1985 quota system on ivory trade. Between 1979 and 1988, Zimbabwe exported approximately 100 tons of ivory. But according to Mofson (2000, 108), illegal trade in ivory was swamping the legal trade, thanks to poaching and smuggling throughout much of Africa. Elephant populations declined by as much as 50 percent during the 1980s.

In 1989 the elephant moved to appendix I, which banned trade in ivory outright. The hope was that an all-out ban would stop the decline in elephant populations. Simmons and Kreuter (1989, 49) found, however, that poaching has generally been worse in areas where elephant hunting has been banned. A scientific study by 't Sas-Rolfes (2000) offered, at best, mixed results from the trade ban on African elephant ivory. Poaching increased in some countries while it decreased in others. 't Sas-Rolfes went on to note that field enforcement budgets for administering the ban were falling in most range states.

Concurrent with the trade ban on ivory, the Communal Area Management Program for Indigenous Resources (CAMPFIRE) was implemented in Zimbabwe. Under colonial rule, when Zimbabwe was known as Rhodesia, wildlife was made property of the Crown. As a result, rural communities that had been historically dependent on the wild species lost their traditional rights to take wildlife for their benefit, but still faced the wildlife-associated costs. The animals destroyed crops, competed with the indigenous people's livestock, and even killed humans (Child, Ward, and Tavengwa 1997, 6). Such threats to communities continue today. As 't Sas-Rolfes (2000, 77) writes, "In countries such as Kenya and Zimbabwe, expanding elephant populations are increasingly encroaching on areas inhabited by peasant farmers. These animals are a menace to the local people, destroying their crops and threatening their lives." Under such a system of zero benefits and many costs, it is no surprise that poachers appear as heroes to the local people.

Trying to reverse the poor incentives created by Crown rule, the new nation of Zimbabwe implemented the Parks and Wildlife Act in 1975. The program gave private landowners the ability to manage wildlife on their land as well as the right to commercially exploit the animals. Benefits once more accrued to the landowners, and wildlife populations began to grow as game ranchers restocked animals and conserved the ones already there.

Building on the success of this act, Zimbabwe established CAMPFIRE, which gave the same rights to wildlife that private landowners held on their property to the district councils for communal properties, which make up 42 percent of the land in Zimbabwe. CAMPFIRE essentially allocates property rights in wildlife to local communities. This allows the communities to capture some of the returns the animals generate through sport hunting and other wildlife ventures.

As the elephants began to generate income, the communities began to cut back on agriculture that competed with elephants for habitat. In addition, the attitude toward poachers changed. Under CAMPFIRE, one poached elephant means perhaps $33,000 lost in sport hunting fees to a community where the average family of eight subsists on about $150 per year. Thus locals no longer take kindly to poaching (CAMPFIRE Association and African Resources Trust 1998). In fact, many CAMPFIRE communities have hired guards to protect their elephant herds. Problem animals that do destroy crops or knock down fences are given a lot more leeway in their actions, whereas without CAMPFIRE they would have been killed almost immediately. The number of problem elephants shot in CAMPFIRE areas between 1987 and 1992 declined from 156 to 54, and even the number of elephants killed for trophies declined from 203 to 187 (Getz et al. 1999, 1855).

CAMPFIRE has demonstrated overall success. Income that communities earned from wildlife rose from nothing before 1989 to $4.9 million by 1996. These revenues have provided incentives to protect elephants as well as help community development, from drilling wells to building schools. Getz et al. (1999, 1855) found increasing elephant populations under CAMPFIRE. Botswana has initiated a similar program to encourage conservation by its communities. Early signs indicate it, too, is experiencing an increasing elephant population.

Unfortunately the ivory ban stands in the way of progress. It impedes countries from bringing in substantial revenue for further elephant conservation. Kreuter and Simmons (1995, 159) estimate the ivory trade could bring $100 million per year to Africa. Programs like CAMPFIRE have demonstrated to local communities the economic returns of a sustainable harvest; another source for wildlife revenue would reinforce these lessons to communities.

Much of the opposition to removing the ban has come from Western environmental groups that have rallied around the trade ban. Kreuter and Simmons imply that the environmental groups may be self-serving in their efforts. Largely reliant on public donations, they support the trade ban because it became "the most lucrative slogan in the environmental movement's history" (Kreuter and Simmons 1994, 49). Bonner describes how the pressures of funding caused internal conflict for the World Wildlife Fund (WWF). Although conservationists at the WWF knew the ivory ban was bad for elephants, those who provided significant funds to the organization were generally supporters of preservation over sustainable use. Bonner quotes the chairman of the board for the U.S. branch of the WWF as saying, "We're trying to bring our members along on utilization, but our development people, the fund-raisers, are very nervous because there is no question that the great majority of our membership are animal lovers and have difficulty in making the evolution to a more sophisticated understanding of conservation" (quoted in Bonner 1994, 63). Bonner goes on to list donations to environmental groups in the name of saving the elephant.

The good news is that there has been some recognition of the success of CAMPFIRE and the potential that the ivory market could add to elephant conservation. At the 1997 CITES meeting in Harare, Zimbabwe, the parties of CITES approved an experimental sale of ivory stockpiles. In February 1999, Botswana, Namibia, and Zimbabwe sold fifty-five tons of ivory to Japanese buyers. The $5 million in proceeds were applied to elephant conservation efforts and community development. There were some incidents of poaching, but according to the Associated Press, CITES monitors found no connection between recent poaching incidents and the legal sale. As CITES deputy secretary-general Jim Armstrong says, "The experimental trade was a success" (Moulson 2000).

Still there is a long way to go before the harmful CITES ban is removed. Mofson (2000, 111) writes, "It was at the eighth COP [1992 Conference of the Parties to CITES] in Kyoto that a number of underlying tensions in CITES were brought to a head and the dispute over the appendix I listing of the African elephant became the trigger for a larger debate over the appropriate environmental conservation paradigm to be employed by the CITES regime: sustainable use or preservation." This debate over sustainable use or preservation proceeded throughout the 1990s, with the ban in ivory trade continuing and the countries that were doing the most for conservation of elephants, according to population numbers, pushing for a removal of the ban. At the 2000 Conference of the Parties, Zimbabwe and Botswana again tried to get the African elephant downlisted to appendix II in countries where elephant populations were growing, but failed.

The ivory trade harmed elephant populations in the past because local communities had no stake in the animals. No one owned the wildlife. Killing one elephant meant one less destructive beast in addition to ivory available for sale. Since no one owned the creatures, the race was on to poach them. Under the new system elephants are not in danger for the same reason that beef cattle are not threatened. Someone owns the cows, takes care of the cows, and wants to sustain the production of other cows in the future.

Ivory is merely another valuable product that could give lc
ties a reason to steward elephants. And so, for those countrie$
elephant conservation, the ivory trade ban and the governmen⊾ ⌐
are not helping elephant numbers. As Zimbabwe has shown, the key is im-
parting the elephants' economic value to the people who have the greatest
control over their chance at survival. Rowan Martin (2000, 34) examined
when CITES worked and when it failed, and he came to the conclusion that
"CITES should actively seek to encourage sustainable wild harvests. The
banning of all trade, other than from captive breeding programs, does not act
as an incentive to conserve wild populations."

The Endangered Species Act and Preemptive Habitat Destruction

Whereas the ivory trade ban denies benefits to low-income people in southern Africa, the Endangered Species Act imposes costs on private landowners in
the United States—the very people who might otherwise steward wildlife. Thus
any costs to landowners caused by wildlife damage, such as crop depredation,
are compounded by government-imposed restrictions.

Under the ESA, landowners who harbor an endangered species are subject
to land use restrictions on their private property. As Lueck (2000, 87) writes,

> Once a species has been listed, the ESA is in force, so that land that provides
> habitat for a listed species (endangered or threatened) is governed by the regu-
> lations under section 9. A landowner thus finds that a portion of his or her rights
> to the use and income of the land are essentially transferred to the FWS [U.S.
> Fish and Wildlife Service] and to those who can influence FWS through political
> or legal avenues.

One such group using the ESA to influence land management through political means is the Center for Biological Diversity. Robin Silver, a prominent
member of the center recalls that the idea behind the center arose when a friend
said, "We're crazy to sit in trees when there's this incredible law that we can
make people do whatever we want" (Lemann 1999, 106). The law referred to
by Silver's peer was the ESA. Quotes from the Center demonstrate that the organization plans to continue managing others' land via the ESA. Responding to
a USFWS proposal to list the California red-legged frog, Brendan Cummings of
the Center said, "It's the largest proposed critical habitat designation in the history of the state. And it should have a large impact on development projects, assuming it's enforced" (quoted in G. Martin 2000, A15).

The GAO provides an example of how government agencies use the ESA
to impose land-use restrictions and other costs on private landowners:

> A privately owned company in California that produces salt owns land con-
> taining habitat for two protected species—the salt marsh harvest mouse and

California clapper rail (a bird). As a result of a formal consultation with the Service and the Corps, the company was required to modify the dredge-and-fill practices used to maintain its salt ponds to reduce the practices' adverse impacts on the species. Specifically, the Corps' dredging permit directed the company to (1) avoid areas with active nests belonging to the clapper rail, (2) minimize the amount of dredge material deposited in the species' marsh habitat, and (3) reestablish marsh vegetation in areas disturbed by the dredge-and-fill operations. (GAO 1994, 8)

Another instance in which the ESA forced a landowner to manage his land differently in a way that hurt his bottom line occurred in the 1990s. Ben Cone of Pender County, North Carolina, decided to sell some timber on his land. A biologist hired by Cone had determined that there were twenty-nine red-cockaded woodpeckers living in twelve colonies on Mr. Cone's land. Unfortunately the red-cockaded woodpecker is listed as an endangered species under the ESA. Guidelines drawn by the USFWS for compliance with the ESA forced Mr. Cone to limit his harvest to a half-mile radius away from each woodpecker colony, essentially restricting Mr. Cone's use of 1,560 acres of his land (Stroup 1995, 5).

Restrictions like these encourage landowners to manage their land with an eye to the three-S method: shoot, shovel, and shut up (Stroup 1995, 5; Whitman 2000, 31). The person who knows the land and creatures living on it best is the landowner, who is also likely to be the first person to discover an endangered species on the property. But at the risk of losing control over his property to the government and incurring costs that threaten financial survival, the landowner has a strong incentive to kill the species, hide its remains, and tell no one about it.

Not surprisingly, proof of shoot, shovel, and shut up is hard to come by. Still there is evidence of a somewhat less dramatic reaction created by the ESA—preemptive habitat destruction.

Lueck and Michael (1999) discovered preemptive habitat destruction as it relates to the red-cockaded woodpecker in North Carolina. They studied how the proximity of red-cockaded woodpeckers to private timberlands altered harvest patterns. They found that landowners, fearing federal control of their land made perfectly legal decisions to make their lands less hospitable to red-cockaded woodpeckers, before the birds showed up on their land, by cutting down timber earlier than they might without woodpeckers nearby. Because the woodpeckers prefer older-aged stands, quicker harvests keep the forest young and unappealing to the birds.

Using Forest Service data, Lueck and Michael found that the average age of harvested trees on industry-owned land decreases from nearly sixty years, if there are no red-cockaded woodpecker colonies nearby, to thirty-six years if there are 25 colonies within twenty-five miles of the logging site, and to sixteen years if there are 437 colonies (the densest population in the state) within twenty-five miles. They concluded that their findings tend to validate the concerns of some environmentalists who have noted that red-cockaded woodpecker populations have been declining on private lands during the periods in which the species has been listed on the ESA.

In addition to providing an incentive for preemptive habitat destruction, the ESA provides little incentive to those who want to help endangered species. Dayton Hyde, owner of a 6,000-acre ranch in Oregon, worked to build habitat for fish and wildlife. He created wetlands on 25 percent of his pasturelands. He built a lake. He even formed an organization with the goal of improving the wildlife habitat of private lands. Unfortunately for Hyde, the Endangered Species Act made the beauty he had created a liability in his pocketbook. Hyde's ranch was habitat for endangered bald eagles and a rare species of algae that grows in only six isolated parts of the world. According to Hyde, "Federal regulators had the authority to shut me down anytime, without compensating me" (quoted in Anderson and Leal 1997, 110). Hyde adds that many landowners are afraid to help wildlife because of the ESA and other land-use regulations, such as zoning.

More than half of the endangered or threatened species in the United States have at least four-fifths of their habitat on nonfederal lands; 78 percent of listed species in 1993 had some or all of their habitat on private lands (GAO 1994). Clearly, private landowners wield the most power in wildlife protection or destruction. Unfortunately the ESA is encouraging them to choose the latter.

With the incentives of the ESA, it is little wonder that the act's recovery rate has been so abysmal. As of February 28, 2001, there were 1,244 species listed as threatened or endangered under the ESA, with many more proposed. Among those listed, 736 were plants and 508 were animals (USFWS 2001). In a 1997 analysis, Gordon, Lacy, and Streeter (1997, 365) looked at the record of the 27 species that had been delisted since the 1973 act's inception. Seven species were removed because they became extinct. Another 14 never warranted listing in the first place due to data errors. Of the remaining 6 delisted species, recovery was most likely attributed to other reasons. The ESA could take credit for none of the recoveries, though it might deserve some of the blame for the extinctions.

CONCLUSION

Government is not wildlife's best friend or steward. It has carried out policies since colonial America with the intention of eliminating certain species. Bounties and government-funded extermination programs zeroed in on the complete removal of hawks and wolves. Centuries later, programs continue to target disfavored species, such as prairie dogs, for removal. While some groups fight to list the prairie dog under the ESA, government agencies continue to poison the animals. It is also clear from CITES and the ESA that even when the intentions of government policy are good, the desired results do not necessarily follow. The perverse incentives created by CITES and the ESA result in the unintended consequence of further destroying animals already on the brink of extinction.

Government is not the savior of wildlife. The all-or-nothing institutional setup of government-managed wildlife leans toward an end game in which the answer is too few of one species, such as wolves, or too many of another, such as elk in Yellowstone National Park. It offers neither the most efficient biologically sound nor the most just system of management. The premise that committees in Congress, mandating policy to federal agencies, will come up with the best protection for wildlife, while at the same time balancing a diverse array of interests, is naive. Whether ordering the extinction or salvation of a species, political decision makers have a dreadful record of wildlife management.

NOTES

1. An English trading company that evolved into a theocracy, organized in 1629 as the Governor and Company of the Massachusetts Bay in New England.

2. These figures include retreatment of areas where prairie dogs have appeared again over different years.

3. This tally also includes foxes, bobcats, badgers, bears, and mountain lions.

REFERENCES

Alaska Board of Game. 1993. Wolf Conservation and Management Policy for Alaska. June 29. Online: www.state.ak.us/local/akpages/FISH.GAME/wildlife/geninfo/ game/wolf-pol.htm (cited: May 12, 2000).

Anderson, Terry L., and Donald R. Leal. 1997. *Enviro-Capitalists: Doing Good While Doing Well*. Lanham, MD: Rowman & Littlefield.

Banoun, Jean-Charles. 2000. French Shepherds Protest Wolves. April 2. *AP Online*. Document ID: EB20000402030000038. Online: gilawilderness.com/local/wolffrench.htm (cited: March 19, 2001).

Barinov, Dmitry. 1998. Wolf War: Control of Wolves and Rewards for Hunters in Russia. *Current Digest of the Post-Soviet Press*, September 9.

Bonner, Raymond. 1994. Western Conservation Groups and the Ivory Band Wagon. In *Elephants and Whales: Resources for Whom?* ed. Milton M. R. Freeman and Urs P. Kreuter. Basel, Switzerland: Gordon and Breach, 59–72.

Cain, Stanley, John A. Kadlec, Durward L. Allen, Richard A. Cooley, Maurice G. Hornocker, A. Starker Leopold, and Frederick H. Wagner. 1972. *Predator Control 1971: Report to the Council on Environmental Quality and the Department of the Interior.* Advisory Committee on Predator Control. Washington, DC, January.

CAMPFIRE Association and African Resources Trust. 1998. *Sharing the Land: People and Elephants in Rural Zimbabwe.* Fact sheet. Harare, Zimbabwe: African Resources Trust.

Chase, Alston. 1986. *Playing God in Yellowstone: The Destruction of America's First National Park.* Orlando, FL: Harcourt Brace Jovanovich.

Child, Brian, Simon Ward, and Tawona Tavengwa. 1997. *Zimbabwe's CAMPFIRE Program: Natural Resource Management by the People.* Environmental Issues Series No. 2. Harare, Zimbabwe: IUCN-ROSA.

Cowan, Ian M. 1947. The Timber Wolf in the Rocky Mountain National Parks of Canada. *Canadian Journal of Research* 25(5): 139–74.

Davitt, Kim, Renee Grandi, Carla Neasel, and Tom Skeele. 1996. *Conserving Prairie Dog Ecosystems on the Northern Plains.* Bozeman, MT: Predator Project.

Dunlap, Thomas R. 1983. The Coyote Itself: Ecologists and the Value of Predators, 1900–1972. *Environmental Review* 7(1): 54–70.

Economist. 1997. Horribly Ensnared: Alaska's Wolves. September 6.

Fairbanks Daily News Miner. 1997a. Panel Suggests Alternatives to Wolf Control. October 26.

———. 1997b. State to Sterilize, Relocate Wolves. November 16.

Forrest, Steven C., Jonathon D. Proctor, and David Roemer. 2000. *Poisoning and Prairie Dogs: Federal Policies and Prairie Dog Ecosystem Conservation.* Bozeman, MT: Predator Control Alliance and Hyalite Consulting, March.

Friends of the Earth. 2000. Green Scissors 2000. January 20. Online: www.foe.org/eco/scissors2000 (cited: May 15, 2001).

General Accounting Office. 1994. *Endangered Species Act: Information on Species Protection on Nonfederal Lands.* GAO/RCED-95-16. Washington, DC.

———. 1995. *Animal Damage Control: Efforts to Protect Livestock from Predators.* GAO/RCED-96-3. Washington, DC.

Getz, Wayne M., Louise Fortmann, David Cumming, Johan du Toit, Jodi Hilty, Rowan Martin, Michael Murphree, Norman Owen-Smith, Anthony M. Starfield, and Michael I. Westphal. 1999. Sustaining Natural and Human Capital: Villagers and Scientists. *Science* 283(5409): 1855–56.

Gordon, Robert E., James K. Lacy, and James R. Streeter. 1997. Conservation under the Endangered Species Act. *Environment International* 23(3): 359–419.

Gunson, John R. 1992. Historical and Present Management of Wolves in Alberta. *Wildlife Society Bulletin* 20(3): 330–39.

Killick, Adam. 1997. No Wolf Kill. *Yukon News,* December 17.

Kreuter, Urs P., and Randy T. Simmons. 1994. Economics, Politics and Controversy over African Elephant Conservation. In *Elephants and Whales: Resources for Whom?* ed. Milton M. R. Freeman and Urs P. Kreuter. Basel, Switzerland: Gordon and Breach, 39–58.

———. 1995. Who Owns the Elephants? The Political Economy of Saving the African Elephant. In *Wildlife in the Marketplace,* ed. Terry L. Anderson and Peter J. Hill. Lanham, MD: Rowman & Littlefield, 147–65.

Laycock, George. 1990. How to Kill a Wolf: Laws to the Contrary, "Mechanical Hawks" Decimate Alaskan Packs. *Audubon*, November.

Lemann, Nicholas. 1999. No People Allowed. *New Yorker*, November 22.

Long, Michael E. 1998. The Vanishing Prairie Dog. *National Geographic*, April.

Lueck, Dean. 2000. The Law and Politics of Federal Wildlife Preservation. In *Political Environmentalism*, ed. Terry L. Anderson. Stanford, CA: Hoover Institution Press, 61–119.

Lueck, Dean, and Jeffrey Michael. 1999. Preemptive Habitat Destruction under the Endangered Species Act. Department of Agricultural Economics and Economics, Montana State University, Bozeman, MT.

Martin, Glen. 2000. Habitat for Twain's Fabled Frog May Receive Federal Protection. *San Francisco Chronicle*, September 9.

Martin, Rowan B. 2000. When CITES Works and When It Doesn't. In *Endangered Species Threatened Convention: The Past, Present, and Future of CITES*, ed. Jon Hutton and Barnabas Dickson. London: Earthscan Publications, 29–37.

McIntyre, Rick. 1995. *War against the Wolf: America's Campaign to Exterminate the Wolf*. Stillwater, MN: Voyageur Press.

McMillion, Scott. 2000. Black-tailed Prairie Dogs at Risk. *Bozeman Daily Chronicle*, February 4.

Mestel, Rosie. 1993. Alaska Revives Big Bad Plan to Kill Wolves. *New Scientist* 138(1879): 9.

Mofson, Phyllis. 2000. Zimbabwe and CITES: Influencing the International Regime. In *Endangered Species Threatened Convention: The Past, Present and Future of CITES*, ed. Jon Hutton and Barnabas Dickson. London: Earthscan Publications, 107–22.

Montana Department of Agriculture. 1985. *Prairie Dog Control Bulletin*. Helena.

Moulson, Geir. 2000. Experimental Ivory Sale Succeeded without Poaching. *Associated Press*, March 29.

Palmer, Les. 2000. Wolf Control Approved . . . Or Maybe Not. *Alaska*, May 1.

Predator Conservation Alliance. 2000. *Wildlife "Services"? A Presentation and Analysis of the USDA Wildlife Services Program's Expenditures and Kill Figures and Kill Figures for Fiscal Year 1998*. Bozeman, MT.

Roemer, David M., and Steven C. Forrest. 1996. Prairie Dog Poisoning in Northern Great Plains: An Analysis of Programs and Policies. *Environmental Management* 20(3): 349–59.

Satchell, Michael. 1990. Uncle Sam's War on Wildlife. *U.S. News & World Report*, February 5.

Simmons, Randy T., and Urs P. Kreuter. 1989. Herd Mentality: Banning Ivory Sales Is No Way to Save the Elephant. *Policy Review* 50: 46–49.

Smith, Robert J. 1999. *Hawk Mountain Sanctuary Association*. Private Conservation Case Study. Washington DC: Center for Private Conservation, April 1.

South Dakota Department of Agriculture. 2000a. Prairie Dog Management in South Dakota. Online: www.state.sd.us/doa/das/pd_mngt.htm (cited: April 28, 2000).

———. 2000b. SD DOA Bait Mixing Facility. Online: www.state.sd.us/doa/das/hp-bait.htm (cited: April 28, 2000).

Stroup, Richard L. 1995. The Endangered Species Act: Making Innocent Species the Enemy. *PERC Policy Series*, PS-3. Bozeman, MT: PERC, April.

Swanson, Doug J. 1998. Despite Name Change, Agency Can't Shed Killer Image. *Washington Post*, November 4.

't Sas-Rolfes, Michael. 2000. Assessing CITES: Four Case Studies. In *Endangered Species Threatened Convention: The Past, Present, and Future of CITES*, ed. Jon Hutton and Barnabas Dickson. London: Earthscan Publications, 69–87.

U.S. Department of Agriculture. 1997a. Wildlife Services. Online: www.aphis.usda. gov:80/adc/ (cited: February 28, 2000).

———. 1997b. Wildlife Services. December. Online: www.aphis.usda.gov/oa/pubs/ wsgen.html (cited: February 28, 2000).

U.S. Fish and Wildlife Service. 2001. Summary of Listed Species. February 28. Online: ecos.fws.gov/tess/html/boxscore.html (cited: March 12, 2000).

Vosburgh, T. C. 1996. Impacts of Recreational Shooting on Prairie Dog Colonies. Master's thesis. Fish and Wildlife Management, Montana State University, Bozeman.

Vosburgh, T. C., and Lynn R. Irby. 1998. Effects of Recreational Shooting on Prairie Dog Colonies. *Journal of Wildlife Management* 62(1): 363–72.

Wagner, Frederic H. 1988. *Predator Control and the Sheep Industry*. Claremont, CA: Regina Books.

Watt, Eric. 1994. Yukon Wolf Kill: The Wildlife Hot Seat. *Canadian Geographic*, January-February.

Whitman, David. 2000. The Return of the Grizzly. *Atlantic Monthly*, September.

Williams, Ted. 2000. The Prairie Dog Wars: Is the Prairie Dog a Grass-Eating Varmint That Threatens Cattle, or a Vital Keystone Species? The Federal Government Must Soon Decide. *Mother Jones*, January.

Wooley, Charlie. 2000. Gray Wolf Recovery in the Upper Great Lakes States. In *State of the Great Lakes 1999 Annual Report*. Lansing: Michigan Department of Environmental Quality, April, 48–50.

7

The Untouchables: America's National Forests

Holly Lippke Fretwell

The USDA Forest Service (USDAFS) is espousing a return to custodial husbandry. A vaguely defined concept of ecosystem management is taking hold and eliminating many uses of our national forest lands. Draconian reductions in timber harvest and expanding de facto wilderness come at great cost to forest health, forest users, and timber communities. Although highly motivated special interest groups gain the right to lock up national forests to fit their specifications, taxpayers pay the price through shrinking recreational access and returns on the valuable assets, wasteful government spending, and poor land stewardship.

From a long history as custodian of the land and provider of multiple uses, the Forest Service has digressed to a nebulous agenda of ecosystem management. With no change in legislation, the agency shifted the mission for land managers. The number one goal of national forest managers is to protect and restore watershed health. At the same time they allegedly promote the sustainability of ecosystems by ensuring their health, diversity, and productivity (Fedkiw 1996, 276). Existing legislation continues to mandate the provision of sustainable production and multiple uses, but this new ambiguous environmental agenda accomplishes none of these.

The Forest Service manages 192 million acres of federal land—an area the size of Texas and Louisiana combined. Rapidly growing restrictions already cover one-third of it, and more and more land is being harbored under limited use: 35.2 million acres are managed under wilderness statute, 19 million acres are under the Northwest Forest Plan for the protection of old-growth species and the spotted owl, 3.4 million acres are designated national monuments, 1.2 million acres are protected as wild and scenic rivers, and 1.2 million acres are game refuge and wildlife preserves (USDAFS 2000). In addition, the Roadless Area Conservation Rule, promulgated by the Clinton administration, restricts logging and road building in previously inventoried roadless areas not designated as wilderness encompassing 58.5 million acres of national forests (USDAFS 2001b, 3245). This effectively removes 37 percent of the remaining nonwilderness areas from multiple use and hamstrings public land managers from taking an active role in ensuring forest health.

Now more than ever our national forests are in need of more, not less, management to reduce the risk of catastrophic wildfire. Nearly a century of fire suppression and past management practices have changed the structure of many forests (Fretwell 1999). Without fire to suppress undergrowth, some federal forests have become as much as 82 percent denser than they were in 1928 (Western Communities for Safe and Healthy Forests 1997, 3); they have lost the habitat and forage they once provided for wildlife and are less resilient to disease, insect infestation, and wildfire.

Management of our national forests is not cheap. Whether for commodity production, recreation, wilderness, or healthy ecosystems, the Forest Service spends nearly $3.5 billion annually, most paid for by tax dollars (U.S. Department of Agriculture 2000). But Americans are not getting sound fiscal or environmental management.

CONFLICTING MISSIONS

Forest reserves, now the national forests, were designated under the Organic Act of 1897. Under the act federal management is intended to preserve and protect the forest, to secure favorable water flows, and to furnish a continuous supply of timber for the use and necessities of the people in the United States. Subsequent legislation has complicated this mission.

During the past thirty years, more than 200 new regulations have been passed that impede managers from responding promptly to changing forest conditions. The Clean Air Act, Endangered Species Act, the Federal Land and Management Policy Act, the Multiple Use and Sustained Yield Act, the National Forest Management Act, the National Environmental Policy Act (NEPA), and the Public Range and Improvement Act, among others, have the express goal of protecting the environment and providing for multiple uses. But in some cases they have the opposite effect. Public comment periods and citizen appeals allowed under NEPA can result in lengthy delays to land management decisions that are critical to forest health. For example, insect infestations require immediate action by forest managers, but they face lengthy delays from regulations resulting in irreparable damage to millions of acres of national forest land (Fretwell 1999, 4).

Quintessentially, the national forests were to be managed equally for all uses, none of which are to preclude future productivity and use. But in the

1990s, an administrative directive of ecosystem management emerged with a guiding principle of management for sustainable ecosystems over production and use.

A Wealth of Resources

National forests have many valuable uses. Three-quarters of the lands are classified as productive for timber harvest. Productive timberlands are those capable of producing more than twenty cubic feet of timber per acre per year. The national forests grow 30 percent of the nation's standing timber inventory and have supplied as much as 20 percent of U.S. softwood. But they provide much more than just wood products.

They claim to be the largest supplier of public outdoor recreation, reporting 859 million visitors in 1996 (USDAFS 1999, 63). The agency manages more than 23,000 facilities including campgrounds, visitor centers, picnic areas, boat ramps, trailheads (with 133,000 miles of trails), and 380,000 miles of authorized roads. About 60 percent of the nation's downhill ski areas utilize national forest lands, providing entertainment for 31 million recreationists.

The forests contain more than 200,000 miles of fishable streams including 4,400 miles of Wild and Scenic Rivers. The national forests contain habitat for numerous fish and wildlife species including 283 species listed as endangered or threatened. Flora and fauna sweep across the forests and grasslands. There are some 2 million acres of lakes, ponds, and reservoirs. The national forests occupy the headwaters of most rivers in the West and provide water to about 900 cities and communities (USDAFS 1998b). The value of water from these lands is estimated to exceed $3.7 billion per year (Dombeck 2000).

Other resources include rangelands that provide forage for 9 million head of livestock per month and millions of acres of potentially valuable mineral deposits. National forest lands host the largest coal mine in the United States and produce much of the nation's phosphate and lead. Energy and minerals extracted from the national forests are valued at more than $4 billion each year (USDAFS 1998b; 1999). The Forest Service also provides access for pipelines, telephone lines, highways, and communications.

Because national forests provide marketed and nonmarketed goods (hunting and bird watching, for example) to the public, their valuation is somewhat speculative. Estimates are in excess of $100 billion (O'Toole 1997, 5).

The End of the Rainbow

With 35,000 full-time employees, the Forest Service has the largest budget of all federal land agencies. In 1998 it received $3.4 billion but generated only $788 million in revenues to cover less than one-fourth its budget (USDAFS 1999, table 52). Fortified with valuable resources, one would expect the return on the assets to be a pot of gold. Though the agency generates revenues from the sale of timber, livestock grazing, minerals, oil and gas, and some recreational activities, it is not required to cover costs or generate a profit. Moreover, the majority of revenues collected are returned to the general treasury and are not linked by Congress to the budget.

There is one important exception, however. A portion of receipts from timber and grazing remain with the agency for unappropriated expenditure. As a result, even though legislated to provide equally for multiple use, timber and grazing have been used by Forest Service management to enhance budgets. Prior to the 1990s, managers often emphasized these activities at the expense of environmental amenities (Hyde 1981; O'Toole 1999, 92). Retention of a portion of timber and grazing receipts also provides an important source of funds that are used for restoration including reforestation, stand improvement, habitat enhancement, stream restoration, trail and road maintenance, facility construction, and so on (General Accounting Office [GAO] 1998, 16–19).[1] These activities ensure that forest health and infrastructure are properly maintained.

Unfortunately, without incentive to maximize Forest Service asset values or keep costs low, there is little prospect for sound fiscal management. Between 1974 and 1978 more than one-half of our national forests did not recover the costs of timber management and reforestation from timber sales (Fedkiw 1996, 220). That trend continues more than twenty years later. According to the agency, 70 percent of the national forests in 1997 did not recover costs from the timber program, for a combined loss of $88 million (USDAFS 1998a, 6). Critics argue that the timber sale accounting system (TSPIRS) is an inaccurate measure and actual losses are even greater (O'Toole 1999, S-1; McKetta 1994, 10).

The Pot of Gold

Although critics claim that below-cost timber sales are the result of harvesting lands not economically viable for timber production, agency inefficiencies appear to be the more likely reason. A 1995 study comparing state trust and national forest timber sale programs in Montana from 1988 to 1992 supports this argument. State forests generated $2 for every dollar spent on timber sales, whereas adjacent national forest timber sales yielded only $.50 in revenue for each dollar spent (Leal 1995, 6). A later study reveals that these results are no fluke. Combined results from Montana, Washington, Idaho, and Oregon show the numbers are even more dramatic: The national forest average yield in 1996 was $.93 in timber revenues for each dollar spent on the timber sales program. State-managed forests yielded $7.42 in revenue for each dollar in costs—an eightfold performance margin for the state-managed lands.[2]

It might be thought that the states' lower costs are the result of skimping on environmental protection, but in fact, just the opposite appears to be true. Evaluations carried out by independent audit teams (which include state, federal, and industry experts and representatives from environmental groups) show that environmental protection and economic performance go hand in hand. State forests rated higher than the national forests in mitigating the impacts from logging and protecting watersheds (Leal 1995, 11).

The states' superior environmental and economic performances are the result of their clear incentive to maximize the long-term value of forest assets while keeping costs low. Law for most western states mandates that state forests be managed to provide returns to help support the public schools and other state institutions. In contrast, national forests are mandated to "achieve quality land management under the multiple-use, sustained yield concept to meet the diverse needs of the people" (USDAFS 1998b, 11). This vague goal provides no real direction for Forest Service management. Almost any set of environmental or economic outcomes is consistent with this mandate. Almost any degree of economic waste or deteriorating forest ecology can be asserted to fulfill the congressional directive.

Budgetary Incentives

Under the current funding system, the prosperity of the Forest Service as an agency is tied to a budget that it augments in various ways. Budgets are escalated through increased staff and construction projects—one reason for the massive road system that is long enough to reach the moon. Most roads are permanent, costing about $50,000 per average mile of road built. They are constructed with high specifications for safety and environmental stewardship. In comparison, state timber roads cost between $4,000 and $8,000 per mile built and are obliterated after harvest and regeneration (Leal 1995, 9). The construction, reconstruction, and maintenance of federal timber roads are funded through appropriations and provide for timber harvest, resource management, and public access.

This interdisciplinary provision of services is another facet of below-cost sales. Timber harvest and management provide a variety of amenities including roads that are used 99 percent of the time by recreationists. In fact, between 1994 and 1996, recreationists received greater financial benefits from national forest management than all other users. Recreation management cost the Forest Service $315 million more per average year than the revenues it generated compared with $245 million lost by timber management and $25 million lost by grazing activities (Fretwell 1998).

Under the new ecosystem approach to management, road construction has been temporarily halted and timber harvest reduced to a trickle. Timber output from the national forests has declined 75 percent, from 12.6 billion board-feet in 1988 to 3.2 billion board-feet in 1998. Timber receipts have similarly declined from an inflation-adjusted $1.8 billion to around $500 million (USDAFS 1999, table 52). But costs of the timber program have not reciprocally declined. A result of increased regulations, less harvest, and smaller tree size, timber program costs have increased from $75 per thousand board-feet offered for sale to $182 (O'Toole 1999). Though timber output has fallen, the overall (constant dollar) agency budget has continued to hover around $3.5 billion annually since 1988 (Office of Management and Budget 1999; see fig. 7.1).

The Forest Service budget request for 2001 was $3.6 billion, up from $3.4 billion in 2000 (USDA 2000). This budget promises to offer 3.2 billion board-feet of timber and 8.2 million animal unit months of grazing allotments. An animal unit month is the amount of forage needed for one animal unit—one cow and calf, one horse, or five sheep or goats—for one month. Nearly all other outputs are left unquantified. Even recreation visits are left uncounted and have not been reported since 1996. Under the new planning regulations, levels of goods and services provided are not enumerated, and the forest plan will no longer specify a time period for achieving goals and objectives (Fedkiw 1996, 202). This means it is nearly impossible to calculate the cost per unit of output for most agency activities. It is therefore even more difficult to ensure agency accountability to the taxpaying public and their representatives in Congress.

Though the ecosystem approach has swung the pendulum from timber interests to environmental ones, without institutional reform there will be no real change in management and no reason to presume that forest ecology will benefit. Fiscal responsibility is taking a backseat to poorly defined ecosystems that are far more difficult to measure than physical outputs such as timber and grazing allotments.

As long as Congress continues to fund the agency's budget, and the majority of its receipts are sent to the general treasury, there will be little incentive for cost control or concern for asset values. Although most revenues are returned to the general treasury, those retained will continue to be exploited. Though harvest is down and use restrictions up, managers still have more incentive to harvest so they can retain and spend the revenues than they do to manage for ecological concerns. The new budget with ambiguous goals only allows more abuse.

"POLITICAL" SCIENCE

The real tragedy of federal management is poor resource stewardship. One-third of the national forest system is at known risk of catastrophic wildfire

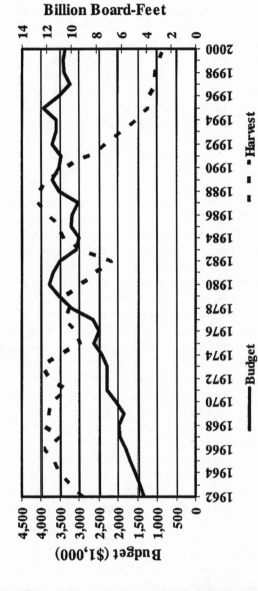

Figure 7.1   Forest Service Budgets High, Harvests Low. Note: Annual budget data presented in 1999 dollars. Sources: Budget data: Office of Management and Budget (1999). Harvest data: Jim Culbert, budget assistant, U.S. Forest Service, Washington, DC, by fax; USDA Forest Service (2001a,b).

(GAO 2000, 14). More than 6 million acres of federal forests are loaded with dead and dying trees in the Blue Mountains of eastern Oregon and Washington from insects and disease. Wildlife habitat is diminishing, and hundreds of thousands of miles of roads in desperate need of repair are left unmaintained, causing erosion problems that damage streams, water quality, and fish habitat.

The problem is not too much commodity production and too little wilderness protection, or the converse. It is not the result of inept managers. The key problem is the perverse incentives and the procedural requirements that prevent managers from responding to the resources under their care. The institutional rules have not changed for nearly a century and will not change without fundamental reforms in the public policy that controls national forest management.

Political Fire

Created under the premise of scientific management, since its beginning the Forest Service has been unable to respond to resource management using available scientific information. For nearly a century it has suppressed fire across the federal landscape as though it were a cancer. Yet as early as 1920 there was strong evidence showing the fire dependence of many forest types (Nelson 2000, 99). The understanding of the ecological role of fire in landscapes was so insurmountable by the 1960s that many national parks adjusted policy, allowing some fires to burn and prescribing others.

The public perception of the Forest Service, however, was based on the Smokey Bear campaign, the most popular advertising campaign in the 1940s. To change this perception would be to lose faith in the prevailing "scientific management" questioning the legitimacy of the agency. But the mainstay of science used in its management is "political" science. Ashley Schiff, a Forest Service historian, noted more than 40 years ago that the "internal culture of the Forest Service was antagonistic to the generation and use of sound scientific information" (quoted in Nelson 2000, 98).

It was not until 1979 that the agency recognized the need for a more comprehensive fire policy, adopting a small prescribed burn policy. Even then fire suppression was based on the "10 A.M. policy"; put it out by ten o'clock the following morning. All the while, the ecological systems of many forests are being substantially altered.

In the absence of frequent fire, once open savannahs of ponderosa pine on the national forests of the interior West have turned into dense stands of fir and pine. Competition for sunlight, moisture, and soil nutrients leaves these areas susceptible to disease, insect outbreaks, and intense wildfire. By the Forest Service's own accounting, more than 39 million acres in the West are reported in this high-risk condition (GAO 1999, 29). Another 18 million acres are ecological systems in which periodic fire should be a normal part of the process (Nelson 2000, 19).

Nearly a century of fire suppression, however, is much more to the agency than just a public relations issue or a peculiar view of forest management. Again, there are budgetary incentives at play. Fire suppression provides a significantly enhanced budget. In inflation-adjusted dollars, fire protection and firefighting expenditures have expanded from about $225 million in 1970 to more than $1 billion in 2000, a figure the Forest Service projects will increase another $19 million every year into the future (USDAFS 1995, 26; Nelson 2000, 35).

Outside interests depend on firefighting funds as well. Missoula, Montana, is a firefighting depot that supplies the needs for regional fire crews. A high fire year can bring millions of dollars into the economy as well as fill the pockets of the crews. Responding to fire within its borders alone, the Lolo National Forest, just outside Missoula, spent more than $9 million on firefighting in 1994, a high fire year, compared with only $900,000 in 1993, a wet summer (*High Country News*, September 15, 1997).

Even with expenditures of $1 billion a year, it is becoming increasingly difficult to squelch wildfire. Jack Ward Thomas, previous chief of the Forest Service, commented that once a forest fire "reaches a large size, putting it out is a joke" (quoted in Nelson 2000, 36). After spending $120 million and risking the lives of 25,000 firefighters, then superintendent of Yellowstone Bob Barbee said of the 1988 fires, "It was ultimately uncontrollable no matter what you did" (quoted in Fretwell 1999, 8). The Yellowstone fire burned almost unhampered by firefighting efforts, only to be snuffed out by seasonal rain and snow.

This facade of wildfire suppression clashes with science and policy goals. The century-old fire suppression philosophy has fostered the accumulation of fuels and biomass in many forest types frequented by fire. To deal with it, federal policy now advocates prescribed burns. So while one federal manager is fighting fire, another is lighting it.

This dire ecological state sometimes places both the lighter and then the fighter on the same fire line. This was the tragedy of Los Alamos in the spring of 2000. The Cerro Grande prescribed fire was set to remove excess brush and reduce wildfire hazard in Bandelier National Monument. A load of fuels and bad weather empowered the burn into a ravaging inferno that consumed 47,000 acres, eating up 260 homes and threatening the Los Alamos National Laboratory. Sadly this was not the first nor will it be the last wildfire, prescribed or not, to take out home, life, and property. In Arizona's Tonto National Forest, six firefighters lost their lives in 1990 when a wildfire overran their crew. In 1991 the Oakland–Berkeley Hills fire killed twenty-five people and damaged or destroyed 3,000 structures, causing more than $1.5 billion in damage. In 1994 more than 14,400 fires were fought on 1.5

million acres accompanied by the tragic loss of twenty-eight lives (Fedkiw 1996, 234). At a cost exceeding $1 billion for firefighting, the fires of 2000 raged across more than 7 million acres, taking 852 structures.

The paradox is that to correct the travesty of past federal fire management requires the "unnatural" act of vigorous management by man. Thinning and prescribed burns are proven remedies for many forests to reduce the risk of high-intensity fires and return the forest to a more resilient state. But the projected cost of cleaning up this mess is no small tally. Costs for reducing fuels on high-risk areas are estimated to be about $725 million annually, or $12 billion over the next fifteen years (GAO 1999, 41). Unfortunately, proven remedies may not be forthcoming even given sufficient funding.

More than 200 regulations, perverse incentives, and administrative barriers limit managers' ability to respond to the forest resources. Public comment periods and citizen appeals allowed under NEPA often result in lengthy delays to land management decisions. For example, harvests to reduce insect infestations have been delayed by regulations, resulting in irreparable damage to millions of acres of national forest land (Fretwell 1999, 10). Federal air quality standards under the Clean Air Act may prohibit prescribed burns that exceed minimum emissions standards.[3]

Equally disturbing are the incentives provided. Managers are rewarded for the number of acres on which fuels are reduced, not the priority of the lands treated. To "treat" an area previously harvested can be done at lower cost with fewer objections than a higher-priority treatment in a dense, less accessible area. Likewise the timber sales management program, increasingly being used to improve forest health, relies heavily on revenues to fund many of its activities. As a result, its achievement measures are related to volume of timber offered for sale, which encourages a focus on commercial harvest rather than a reduction of accumulated fuels in high-risk forest areas.

In addition, statutorily defined contracting procedures for commercial timber sales and service contracts do not facilitate fuel reduction needs. They are not conducive to the long-term removal of large volumes of low-value material that must be removed to reduce fuel loads. In 1998 only six of twenty-three projects proposed by the Forest Service to demonstrate fuel-reduction strategies were allowed to proceed under existing statutory authority. The Forest Service has been authorized, under FY 1999 Omnibus Consolidated and Emergency Supplemental Appropriations Act, to enter into twenty-eight demonstration project contracts in which the value of material may be retained by the contractor and may exceed the current statutory limit of $10,000. Under demonstration project contracts the remaining seventeen projects could proceed (GAO 1999, 45).

Meanwhile a subverted notion of logging has become the driving force for an ever-increasing land base restricted from timber removal. All these barriers reduce the effectiveness of the agency to respond to the critical and changing conditions of the national forests, leaving millions of acres at extreme risk of wildfire and many others continuing to accumulate fuels.

Habitat Mutation

Concordant with the changing structure of the forest is the alteration of wildlife habitat. Increased forest density and a move toward older stands limit both the availability of forage for wildlife and the diversity of habitat. Elk are disappearing from the Clearwater National Forest in Idaho that was once considered a mecca for wildlife. Much of the Clearwater basin burned in the great fires of 1910 that were the impetus for the fire-suppression policies adopted by the Forest Service. Since then, the forest has been managed in the absence of fire, resulting in an even-aged stand of dense fir. Without the openings and meadows historically created by fire, the elk have nowhere to graze. The dense thicket of undergrowth blocks the sunlight and prevents the growth of essential forage. Over time, elk and other wildlife have virtually disappeared from the forest ecosystem (Fretwell 1999, 22). Other areas in this forest have been so ravaged by timber harvest that stream sedimentation has become too great for fish habitat (Wilkinson 1998, 192).

Hardwood forest stands in the Cherokee National Forest in Tennessee have grown too old to nest the golden-winged warbler. During the 1999 breeding season the warbler was missing. These birds require very young stands of northern hardwood forest, intermixed with herbaceous cover. Controversy over logging has so restricted harvest that the youngest stands are now too old for warbler habitat. The birds have moved to adjacent private lands where timber harvest continues. Other species are also at risk. The majority of upland game species, including quail, grouse, deer, rabbit, and turkey, require young forests with forest edge and openings (McCabe 1999, 1–2).

Flagstaff, Arizona, surrounded by 100,000 acres of national forest, was once known as Antelope Springs. The ponderosa pine forests surrounding the community were open, parklike savannahs providing abundant browse for antelope and other wildlife. Today these animals are seldom seen. A century of fire suppression, grazing, and historical logging practices allowed the pines to become too dense to walk through. Without sunlight reaching the forest floor, there are no grasses or forage for wildlife. Catastrophic fire is inevitable. It consumes about 1,500 acres each year, threatening wildlife habitat, community health, property, and livelihood. Perhaps unique to the Southwest, many areas that burned as many as fifty years ago remain unforested. "There is no greater threat to the goshawk and Mexican spotted owl than catastrophic fire," says Taylor McKinnon of the Grand Canyon trust. "More are lost to fire than anything in the past five years."[4]

Many years ago wildfire burned through the forests randomly re-creating small forest openings and providing forage for wildlife. But wildfire today takes a different form. Merely allowing fire to play its role now can be cata-strophic. As the density of the forests has risen, so has the accumulation of biomass fueling what were once frequent ground fires into crown fires. In ponderosa pine forests, for example, fires of the past would clear the under-brush with little damage to the fire-resistant pine. Other forest types, like the lodgepole pine, are fire-dependent species that require stand-replacing fires for regeneration. Today's fires are often so large and intense they take with them every living thing, leaving little refuge for wildlife.

Past Sins

With a look at Forest Service timber practices during the 1960s and 1970s, it is no wonder that logging restrictions today hamper proper management. Some areas of national forest harvest and road building are unjustified by nearly any definition. Others have been so ravaged they have become known as the "industrial forests" and their managers the "timber beasts." The Bitterroot National Forest in western Montana provides a case in point. It is here that an overemphasis on timber by the Forest Service was brought to light from coast to coast.

The Bitterroot National Forest contains steep mountains with rugged ter-rain. The slopes are carpeted with ponderosa and lodgepole pines; they are pocketed with high mountain lakes and surrounded by snowy peaks. In the 1960s and 1970s, aggressive timber harvests clearcut large swaths of land that were crisscrossed by logging roads. Called timber mining, it was an area with poor prospect for regeneration—it was more extractive than renewable. Re-generation costs alone were estimated to be at least thirty-five times more ex-pensive than the value of the timber (Bolle et al. 1970, 19). The cut-over slopes were terraced with bulldozed trenches to mechanically plant seedlings and reduce competition from other vegetation.

The town of Missoula below did not stand idly by to watch the devasta-tion. Citizen objections came in many forms. Conservation groups defied the Forest Service actions. Even local loggers took a stand, realizing that the ex-cessive harvest would put them out of business rather than entertain the in-dustry for years to come. "The timber stands in our area are being ruined for the next three generations," said Ernie Townsend of Darby, Montana, a third-generation logger (quoted in Burk 1970, 11).

Although state timberlands in Montana meet similar protest, there is no timber mining and fewer frivolous delays. Mandated to provide a contin-uous flow of revenue to help support the public school system, the forests are managed for long-term interest. They must generate revenues in ex-cess of costs forever. To reduce future profitability of the land would be unsustainable and in direct conflict with the perpetual nature of the trust doctrine. There is a direct relationship between perpetual revenue production and the perpetual capacity to produce it (Souder and Fairfax 1996, 281).

Objections to national forest timber plans, however, were echoed across the nation. In the Bridger Wilderness in Wyoming it was argued that the Forest Service harvest was poorly planned and was destroying the aesthetics of the area. Demonstrators petitioned logging on the Willamette National Forest in Oregon. The secretary of agriculture directed a committee to report on the abuses of Forest Service timber harvest in Idaho and Montana. It was becoming clear that the agency was building timber roads and harvesting without "commensurate consideration" of other forest uses as required by the Multiple-Use and Sustained Yield Act (Burk 1970, 6–8). The Bitterroot and similar forests were the epitome of single-use management.

Resource production goals of an agency managed from Washington, D.C., were given priority over land management considerations that would make more sense at the local level (see Bolle et al. 1970). Though social and legislative emphasis took a multiple-use approach to natural resources, the federal appropriations process encouraged timber harvest. Forest plans estimated the maximum volume of timber that could be sold without subverting other forest values. Known as the "allowable sales quantity" (ASQ), the measure was intended to be a ceiling instead of the yearly target that it became. Many foresters, among others, claim that ASQs were exaggerated volumes that could only be ecologically sustainable at levels one-half to three-quarters of those given (Wilkinson 1998, 29). Congress rewarded the agency with funding for all programs if these "targets" were met. Foresters refusing to achieve timber quotas dictated by Washington were often harassed and transferred to desk jobs (Wilkinson 1998, 29). Facing such political incentives, most managers strived to meet performance targets regardless of the productivity of the forest and the dollar or ecological costs.

The allowable sales quantity on most forests has since been reduced. And public input has a much greater impact on agency decisions. Many regulations have been installed that require environmental concerns commensurate with timber planning. Ecosystem management, the agency claims, has moved away from ecologically damaging production. But the institutional structure of the Forest Service has *not* changed, nor have the incentives that uphold it.

FORESTS BEHIND BARS

The transposing political environment, as witnessed by the Northwest Forest Plan, is moving Forest Service management to a realm of hands-off management. In response to the 1990 listing of the northern spotted owl as an endangered species, 24 million acres of land managed by the Forest Service and Bureau of Land Management have been set aside under the Northwest Forest Plan. Timber harvests on federal lands in Oregon and Washington have fallen from about 5 billion board-feet per year to 300 million board-feet. Similarly, the hands-off approach is emphasized under the Roadless Area Conservation Rule that prohibits road construction and restricts logging on 58.5 million acres of national forest land. These examples parallel the ecosystem management approach to wilderness management—for preservation and protection in their existing condition, unimpaired and untrammeled by man.[5] But human intervention has already significantly affected the condition of these lands through a century of recreation use, fire suppression, and timber harvest. Like the scientific management approach that was unable to use scientific evidence for management decisions, the ecosystem approach appears uninterested in managing for ecological function. Both philosophies are congruous, fostering management response to political incentives.

Without real institutional reform there is no reason to believe the ecological integrity of the national forest system will be better managed under the ecosystem approach. Current policies of walking away and letting nature take its course may in fact be more damaging to the environmental amenities and the ecology of the forest than an active management program.

Because of the fuel buildup and other deteriorating conditions in many old-growth forests, to let them be may mean to let them die. Chad Oliver, professor of silviculture and forest ecology at the University of Washington, says that by leaving these old-growth forests to nature, "we have no assurance that forest set-asides will actually grow older; there is a greater probability they will burn up or blow down first" (quoted in Nelson 2000, 55).

The late-seral reserve in the Shasta-Trinity National Forest in northern California provides a striking example. Reserved to provide habitat for late-seral species such as the spotted owl, the forest has become known as the Valley of Death. Wrought with disease and insects, the giant trees are crashing to the forest floor. Each lost tree thins the overstory, which reduces the closed canopy and changes the habitat. Managers are unable to respond because of a maze of regulation that is only exasperated by the forest's reserve status under the Northwest Forest Plan. The area of tree mortality is expanding at a rate of more than 300 additional acres each year.[6]

Elsewhere a disaster is waiting to happen in the Lake Tahoe basin of the Sierra. Surrounding the beauty of one of the clearest, deepest lakes in the world is a tinderbox forest of dead and dying trees. In the sequence of fire suppression, tree competition, and drought, the Lake Tahoe National Forest has become ravaged with bark beetles and disease. Ironically forest management practices have put at risk the very qualities they were supposed to save. Environmental regulations have delayed management actions and restricted timber harvests and forest treatments. In the meantime tree mortality reaches 80 percent in many overstocked stands (Fretwell 2000, 14).

Contrary to public perception (Webster 1999, 1), active forest management is not synonymous with environmental destruction. Look at Mount St. Helens in Washington after the violent volcanic eruption in 1980. The explosion destroyed 150,000 acres of forest land in western Washington, leaving Weyerhaeuser Company with 68,000 acres of burned, fallen trees smothered under ash. A hand from man salvaged the timber and applied extensive restoration. A healthy forest now towers forty-five feet above abundant fish and wildlife habitat. Adjacent to company land sits the federally owned Mount St. Helens National Monument. Preserved to document the natural restoration process, twenty years later trees are beginning to sprout again (Fretwell 1999, 28–29).

With already one-third of the national forests relegated to limited use, the roadless rule brings the tally of untouchable land to more than 100 million acres (an area the size of California) or one-half of the land managed by the Forest Service. But by locking the public out of the forest we are not getting healthier forests, we are losing their productivity for man and beast and reducing their pristine value and our enjoyment of them.

Ecosystem Management: More Malpractice

Under the guidance of so-called ecosystem management there is no guarantee that we will get management that is ecologically inclined. An ecosystem is not a living thing defined by natural boundaries and health issues. Arthur Tansley, the British plant ecologist who coined the term in 1935, says that ecosystems are no more than mental constructs of areas that are "included as parts of larger ones and overlap, interlock, and interact with one another" (quoted in Fitzsimmons 1999, 25). These constructs help focus areas of research.

To direct land management under an ecosystem approach is to make management arbitrary. The Congressional Research Service reports that there is little agreement about the goals of ecosystem management. "[R]arely has a term of public discourse gone so directly from obscurity to meaningless without any intervening period of coherence," says Michael Bean of Environmental Defense. Jack Ward Thomas, former chief of the Forest Service says, "I promise you I can do anything you want to do by saying it is ecosystem management" (quoted in Fitzsimmons 1999, 2).

It's just such management philosophy, covered by a green cloak, that reinforces authority to manage without accountability. With no outputs there is no accountability. There is no timber or livestock heads to count, no miles of roads or trails to construct. Rather the approach applies to alleged outcomes: the restoration of watersheds and ecosystems. But the achievement of such goals is impossible to measure without a clear definition of what they are and their current condition. That is, we are not in a "virgin" state of nature. We begin with lands subject to a century of active management, good or bad. Merely counting acres of land treated or dollars spent only encourages more perverse treatment.

The former manager of the Bitterroot National Forest in Montana acknowledges the misguided motivations from the current system of appropriations and target performance measures. She wanted to treat an unroaded area that has a high biomass accumulation. Selective harvest and brush removal could provide openings for wildlife, encourage forage, and reduce the dense structure of the forest, returning its resiliency. But public appeals make active management in remote areas a near impossibility. Despite the additional costs of appeals and litigation, it is also more expensive to negotiate sales in remote regions. To meet target goals, most resources are dedicated to treating more acres at the least cost. This is likely not the greatest priority for ecological and health concerns.[7] It virtually eliminates active management in low-access areas and encourages large cuts capable of producing high timber volume. What proves to be the most efficient use of resources to the manager may in fact be harmful to the resource, even under ecosystem management.

Neither scientific nor ecosystem management will alone provide the fundamentals necessary to achieve an improved ecological state in our forests. The management name has changed but the incentives have not. "We are altering the way we cut more out of social concerns than environmental concerns," says Steve Petro, a forester on the Clearwater National Forest (quoted in Wilkinson 1998, 203). Managers must still respond to Congress for annual budgets, and the majority of revenues retained are still provided by timber harvest. The increasing regulations and set-asides are only making it more difficult for land managers to respond to the conditions of the lands under their care.

Forest Dissidents

Short of institutional reform, there will be little chance of improving ecological and economic management on national forests. Rather the Forest Service will be forced to respond to those who control the purse strings—politicians and powerful special interests. Jeff DeBonis, once a timber sale planner now a self-proclaimed whistle-blower of the Forest Service, makes clear how perverse agency management is in his statement that "[these agencies] no longer serve the public trust—[they] have lost sight of their original missions. These agencies have turned into instruments of mismanagement, instruments of political pork barrels, instruments of environmental destruction, and instruments of repression against ethical employees." This mismanagement, he says, is politically tied; "rule by tyranny has become an accepted part of the Forest Service's process of decision making" (quoted in Wilkinson 1998, 18, 21).

Nez Perce National Forest supervisor Tom Kovalicky is another dissident of agency political mismanagement in the Forest Service. He refused to raise harvest levels on the Nez Perce to meet targets set in Washington, claiming it was impossible to do so without breaking environmental laws. Hired to manage the forest for ecological health, he was continually harassed by upper management to increase the ante on timber harvest. Though such dissidents are few, Forest Service surveys have found that personnel from all grades agree that bureaucratic values—organization loyalty and target achievements—are better rewarded than professional competence and careful land stewardship (Kennedy and Quigley 1998, 120).

The facts remain that high harvest levels on the national forests from the 1960s to the 1980s were unsustainable. Even former chief of the Forest Service Max Peterson was quoted in 1989 as saying, "Anybody could have figured out on the back of an envelope that the rate of timber harvest cannot be sustained" (quoted in Wilkinson 1998, 54). Budgets were at stake and targets, provided in forest plans, were the goals to be reached.

Though the influential power of the timber industry on Forest Service actions has given way to environmental interests, it is unlikely that the Forest Service will stop cutting trees in areas where it makes little sense to do so. Without institutional reform the incentives are unlikely to change. This is one area in which groups on all sides agree. Melinda Pierce, public lands lobbyist for the Sierra Club says "it will require sweeping structural reform" to get "real change in the Forest Service" (quoted in Wilkinson 1998, 54).

WHITHER THE FOREST SERVICE

Whether timber companies or environmental groups, special interest efforts continue to drive the direction of national forest management. In the past, commodity interests played the dominant role, resulting in high levels of timber harvest. Environmental groups have since gained control. Today nonuse has replaced multiple use, and taxpayers are footing the bill.

The changing of the guard was spurred by rising environmental awareness. This environmental cognizance and influence made timber production a public relations issue for the Forest Service. Though the pendulum has swung, decisions are still devoid of opportunity costs. The result is a move from too much timber harvest to too little. Timber that was once harvested with little regard to other environmental amenities is now left standing without regard to the economic or ecological costs. The Pacific Northwest, for example, has the most productive softwood forests in the United States (Powell et al. 1993, 7). One acre of timber harvest there requires as much as four or more acres for similar harvest levels elsewhere.[8] To restrict harvest on 20 million acres in the Pacific Northwest may cost 80 million acres of timber cut in another place. Without a relative value on these lands and their multiple assets, it is easy to lock them up with no regard to the consequences of hands-off management. Meanwhile, forest managers are forced to strive to meet politically set targets to ensure subsequent budgets rather than care for the forest resources.

Political targets set on Capitol Hill for harvest, prescribed burns, restoration, or ecosystem health do not guarantee good stewardship. Like the historical timber targets, if prescribed burns and silvicultural treatments begin to drive budgets, we will likely see an overemphasis of these activities without regard to their fiscal or environmental costs. A treatment of thinning and prescribed burn in an overly dense ponderosa pine forest with historical fire frequency of 5 to 25 years could be ecologically devastating to a lodgepole pine forest with a natural fire cycle of 50 to 300 years. Only by changing the incentives and allowing managers to respond to the conditions of the forests rather than the political climate will we see good long-term stewardship on our federal lands.

Prospects for national forest management remain dim with current budgetary incentives. Under the current set of political constraints, it would be absurd to expect the Forest Service to react any differently. A twenty-year veteran biologist of the Forest Service, Sandy Knight says that "while some staffers are trying to push the agency toward responsible, science-based management, the incentive system pulls them in the other direction" (quoted in *High Country News*, March 30, 1998). The current incentives do not provide for good land stewardship or sustainable production.

CONCLUSION

Federal land management is clearly dysfunctional and harmful to the health of national forests. Managers must respond to a multitude of demands that are contrary to their goal of healthy ecosystems.

Meanwhile, private timberlands exhibit generally healthy, vigorous forests (Clark and Sampson 1995, 2). Private landowners who grow trees for commercial harvest have a long-term commitment to the value of the timber and a strong incentive to manage for a productive forest. Port Blakely Tree Farms of Seattle, Washington, is a prime example. In the timber business since 1864, the company can attribute much of its longevity to careful management of the resource. Similarly, Weyerhaeuser, Boise Cascade, and International Paper Companies have owned private tree farms for many years. They have a clear incentive to maintain the value of the land.

Though the values from recreation, watersheds, and habitat protection may be slighted if land managers cannot capture their worth, many of these assets have entered the private calculus of forest management. Recreation and user fees generate profits and motivate landowners to provide recreational facilities. For years the International Paper company (IP) has provided land for recreation use in Arkansas, Louisiana, and Texas. But it wasn't until 1980, when they began charging user fees, that recreation was a function of the harvest formula. With recreation revenues representing 25 percent of regional profits, there was incentive to manage the forests for recreation and wildlife as well as timber. Rather than clearcut huge swaths of land, the size of timber cuts has been reduced and perimeters made irregular, corridors of trees are maintained between harvest areas for wildlife production, and harvests are restricted in riparian areas (Fretwell 1999, 18).

In addition, many conservation groups and land trusts have made their desires a reality through fee simple ownership of forests. The Nature Conservancy, the National Audubon Society, and numerous other conservation and land trusts purchase land and management agreements solely for the purpose of wildlife habitat and ecosystem preservation. The Nature Conservancy's Washo Reserve in South Carolina provides habitat for the endangered red-cockaded woodpecker (Fretwell 1999, 22). The Nature Conservancy owns and manages more than 4 million acres of land for the preservation and protection of rare and endangered species and habitats.[9] Unfortunately many conservation groups spend all or a portion of their resources encouraging more federal landownership, regardless of the government's poor stewardship track record (see Fretwell 2000).

The management of our federal lands is hampered by politics. Land managers respond to the incentives they are provided, which ties them to congressional whim. As politicians respond to the special interest of the day, so too must federal land managers. Whether providing timber for industry or wilderness for wild lands advocates, the science is being surpassed for political clout and public opinion is overrun by special interests. A group of political operatives benefits with management that fits its agenda, whereas taxpayers foot the bill through budgets, revenues, and lost resources.

Central planning of forest lands is no better than central planning of wheat lands in the USSR—it is costly, inefficient, and an environmental mess. Only through institutional reform that changes the incentives for Forest Service managers will we get beyond the status quo. Harnessing markets, so the relative value of the various land uses becomes known, would ensure that lands valued most for conservation purposes are properly cared for. Those providing high timber productivity would be sustainably harvested, ensuring future timber values. By providing incentives that encourage managers to protect asset values while constraining costs, the Forest Service could be held fiscally and ecologically accountable.

NOTES

1. The Knutson-Vandenberg Act of 1930 and amendments (16 USC 576-576b) en-sure that a portion of timber sale receipts is retained by the agency for forest restora-tion, all salvage sale receipts are retained to cover the direct costs of sale preparation and harvest of salvage timber, and 10 percent of the National Forest Fund is retained for trails and road maintenance.

2. See also Fretwell (1998, 6). Data compiled from USDA Forest Service (1998b); Beth Ann Christensen, accountant, and Bob Burke, scaling supervisor, Idaho Depart-ment of Lands, Boise, telephone and written communication; Montana Department of Natural Resources (1996); Pat Flowers, bureau chief, Forest Management, Montana Trust Land Division, Helena, written and telephone communication; Faye Pitts, ac-countant, and Dan Korgan, business section, Oregon Division of State Lands, Salem, telephone and written communication; and Washington Department of Natural Re-sources (1996).

3. Per telephone interviews, September 13, 1998, Colin Hardy, research forester, Rocky Mountain Research Station, Missoula Fire Lab, USDA Forest Service, and Ann Acheson, ecologist, Region 1, Regional Office, USDA Forest Service Missoula, Mon-tana, agree that new EPA air quality standards may prohibit some prescribed burns, though there are few historical burns that have surpassed twenty-four-hour limita-tions. Most prescribed burns, they say, are upheld by the appearance of smoke and public uproar.

4. Taylor McKinnon, program associate, Grand Canyon Trust, Flagstaff, AZ, tele-phone communication, November 2, 2000.

5. The Wilderness Act of 1964.

6. Nancy Ingelsbee, Klamath Alliance for Resources and the Environment, Yreka, CA, written communication, January 12, 1999. See also Fretwell (1999).

7. Cathy Stewart, Bitterroot National Forest manager and silviculturist, Missoula, MT, personal interviews, October 6 and 13, 1998.

8. Bruce Lippke, director for the Center for International Trade in Forest Products, telephone interview, August 10, 2000.

9. Jon Schwedler, member relations assistant, The Nature Conservancy, telephone interview, September, 27, 1999.

REFERENCES

Bolle, Arnold W., W. Leslie Pengelly, Robert F. Wambach, Gordon Browder, Thomas Payne, and Richard E. Shannon. 1970. *A University View of the Forest Service*. Uni-versity of Montana Report on the Bitterroot National Forest. Washington, DC: Gov-ernment Printing Office.

Burk, Dale A. 1970. *The Clearcut Crisis: Controversy in the Bitterroot*. Great Falls, MT: Jursnick Printing.

Clark, Lance R., and R. Neil Sampson. 1995. *Forest Ecosystem Health in the Inland West: A Science Policy Reader*. Washington, DC: American Forests, Forest Policy Center.

Dombeck, Mike. 2000. The State of the Forest Extending Our Land Ethic. March 27, 2000. Online: www.fs.fed.us/intro/speech/20000328.htm (cited: April 27, 2000).

Fedkiw, John. 1996. *Managing Multiple Uses on National Forests, 1905–1995.* Washington, DC: USDA Forest Service.

Fitzsimmons, Allan K. 1999. *Defending Illusions: Federal Protection of Ecosystems.* Lanham, MD: Rowman & Littlefield.

Fretwell, Holly Lippke. 1998. The Price We Pay. *Public Lands.* Bozeman, MT: PERC, August.

———. 1999. Forests: Do We Get What We Pay For? *Public Lands II.* Bozeman, MT: PERC, August.

———. 2000. Federal Estate: Is Bigger Better? *Public Lands III.* Bozeman, MT: PERC, May.

General Accounting Office. 1998. *Forest Service: Distribution of Timber Sales Receipts, Fiscal Years 1995 through 1997.* GAO/AIMD-99-24. Washington, DC, November.

———. 1999. *Western National Forests.* GAO/RCED-99-65. Washington, DC, April.

———. 2000. *Forest Service Roadless Areas.* GAO-01-47. Washington, DC, November.

Hyde, William F. 1981. Compounding Clear-cuts: The Social Failures of Public Timber Management in the Rockies. In *Bureaucracy vs. Environment: The Environmental Costs of Bureaucratic Governance*, ed. John Baden and Richard L. Stroup. Ann Arbor: University of Michigan Press, 186–202.

Kennedy, James J., and Thomas M. Quigley. 1998. Evolution of USDA Forest Service Organizational Culture and Adaptation Issues in Embracing an Ecosystem Management Paradigm. *Landscape and Urban Planning* 40: 113–22.

Leal, Donald R. 1995. Turning a Profit on Public Forests. *PERC Policy Series*, PS-4. Bozeman, MT: PERC, September.

McCabe, Richard E. 1999. *Outdoor News Bulletin.* Washington, DC: Wildlife Management Institute, October 29.

McKetta, Charles W. 1994. *Socio-Economic Implications of a Below Cost Timber Program on the Wallowa-Whitman National Forest.* Moscow, ID: McKetta and Associates, February 9.

Montana Department of Natural Resources. 1996. *Annual Report.* Helena.

Nelson, Robert H. 2000. *A Burning Issue: A Case for Abolishing the U.S. Forest Service.* Lanham, MD: Rowman & Littlefield.

Office of Management and Budget. 1999. *Budget of the U.S. Government Fiscal Year 2000.* Washington, DC.

O'Toole, Randal. 1988. *Reforming the Forest Service.* Washington, DC: Island Press.

———. 1997. Run Them Like Businesses: Natural Resource Agencies in an Era of Federal Limits. July. Online: http://www.ti.org/~rot/business.html (cited: May 15, 2001).

———. 1999. Forest Service Responds to Accountability Issue by Becoming Less Accountable. *Subsidies Anonymous #39: Forest Service 2001 Budget.* Portland, OR: Thoreau Institute.

Powell, Douglas S., Joanne L. Faulkner, David R. Darr, Zhiliang Zhu, and Douglas MacCleery. 1993. *Forest Resources of the United States, 1992.* General Technical Report RM-234. Fort Collins, CO: USDA Forest Service, Rocky Mountain Forest and Range Experiment Station, September.

Souder, Jon A., and Sally K. Fairfax. 1996. *State Trust Lands: History, Management, & Sustainable Use*. Lawrence: University Press of Kansas.

U.S. Department of Agriculture. 2000. *USDA FY 2001 Budget Summary Outlays*. Washington, DC.

USDA Forest Service. 1995. *Fire Economics Assessment Report*. Washington, DC, September 1.

————. 1998a. *National Summary Forest Management Program Annual Report Fiscal Year 1997*. Washington, DC: USDA, July.

————. 1998b. *FY 1998 Budget Explanatory Notes for the Committee on Appropriations*. Washington, DC: USDA.

————. 1999. *1998 Report of the Forest Service*. Washington, DC: USDA, May.

————. 2000. *Land Areas of the National Forest System 1999*. Washington, DC: USDA, March.

————. 2001a. Quarterly Sold and Harvest Reports. Updated January 11, 2001. Online: http://www.fs.fed.us/land/fm/ (cited: March 21, 2001).

————. 2001b. Special Areas; Roadless Area Conservation: Final Rule. *Federal Register*, 36 CFR 294, January 12.

Washington Department of Natural Resources. 1996. *Annual Report*. Olympia.

Webster, Henry H. 1999. Some Sources of Persistent Error in Thinking about Resources. *Forestry Chronicle*, January/February.

Western Communities for Safe and Healthy Forests. 1997. *Media Resource Guide: The Lake Tahoe Presidential Event*. Sacramento, CA.

Wilkinson, Todd. 1998. *Science under Siege: The Politician's War on Nature and Truth*. Boulder, CO: Johnson Printing.

8

Banking on Disaster: The World Bank and Environmental Destruction

Matthew Brown

By the rubbish in our wake, and the noble noise we make,
Be sure, be sure, we're going to do some splendid things!

—"Road-Song of the Bandar-Log,"
The Jungle Book (Kipling 1964, 72)

In his 1893 fable *The Jungle Book*, set deep in the heart of India, Rudyard Kipling tells of a group of monkeys, the Bandar-Log, who are obsessed with getting the attention of their forest companions by becoming more like people. Through their rhetoric and tenacity they planned to prove their superiority. Their prisoner, the "man cub" Mowgli, was told how foolish he was to wish to leave them. Who could desire to leave such enlightenment? "We are great. . . . We are wonderful. . . . We all say so, and so it must be true," the Bandar-Log extolled. Their strange actions puzzled Mowgli, who thought the monkeys must be suffering from *dewanee*—"the madness" (Kipling 1964, 59).

A century later it probably seemed to the inhabitants of the same region of central India that *dewanee* had struck again. In the forests of India, where Kipling set *The Jungle Book*, begins India's fifth longest river, the Narmada. Here, and in countless other places around the world, the "noble noise" of the Bandar-Log has been replaced with that of the World Bank.

Since its founding in 1944, the World Bank has lent hundreds of billions of dollars in an attempt to spark economic development and eliminate poverty in Third World countries. But despite its lofty ambitions, the bank has become the target of critics, who decry not only its failure to alleviate poverty but also the environmental destruction that has become commonplace in the projects it finances. One of the most controversial of those projects was the decades-long plan to dam the Narmada River in central India. The saga of this project reveals much about World Bank operations, so it is reviewed in some detail. Other bank-generated catastrophes will be covered more briefly to illustrate that their environmental and economic blights are global in nature and continue today.

THE SARDAR SAROVAR DAM

With a population of 1 billion people and a per capita income of $430, India is one of the world's largest, and poorest, countries. Since the country gained independence from Great Britain in 1947, it has received more than $50 billion in development assistance, much of it from the World Bank (Kamath 1992, 1). Favorite projects of the Indian government and the bank have been the construction of big dams.

India's first prime minister, Jawaharlal Nehru, asserted the dams were India's "secular temples," and the key to industrialization (Morse and Berger 1992, 3). He extolled to the villagers displaced by the Hirakud Dam to accept their circumstance patriotically: "If you are to suffer, you should suffer in the interest of the country" (Roy 1999, 7). Many of India's poorest citizens have been doing so for years. Estimates of the number of Indians coercively removed from their homes to make way for dam projects since the country gained independence have ranged from 11 to 20 million (Caufield 1996, 11), with some as high as 40 million (Roy 1999, 17).

The Sardar Sarovar Dam is the culmination of plans that began in the 1940s to harness the water of the Narmada River, which flows through three Indian states—Gujarat, Madhya Pradesh, and Maharashtra—before flowing into the Arabian Sea on India's western coast. The purpose of the project is to carry drinking water to drought-plagued regions of Gujarat and irrigation water to Gujarat and the state of Rajasthan. To accomplish this goal, a dam as tall as a forty-five-story building and 4,000 feet wide was to be built across the Narmada River. It would direct almost 10 million acre-feet of water from the Narmada through a canal system for distribution. The canal system would be one of the largest in the world with a total length of 75,000 kilometers, requiring 85,000 hectares of land to complete (Morse and Berger 1992, 201). Additionally, given the tremendous volume of water that flows through the Narmada during monsoon season, a total of 30 major dams (including Sardar Sarovar), 135 medium-size dams, and 3,000 small dams are required on the Narmada River to complete the project (Caufield 1996, 8).

In 1961 with 2,000 villagers displaced from the construction zone, Nehru laid the first stones for the Sardar Sarovar Dam, but almost immediately the project was plagued by controversy. In 1969 the government of India created the Narmada Water Dispute Tribunal to settle the issue of who would receive the benefits of the dam. The project languished for a decade while a negotiated settlement was worked out. With the dispute finally resolved in the late 1970s, the government of India set about trying to secure funding for the project from the World Bank. In 1985 after several years of negotiations the bank entered into a $450 million loan agreement with India's government and the three Narmada states (Caufield 1996, 10; Morse and Berger 1992).

Construction of the dam Nehru had envisioned did not begin in earnest until 1987—twenty-seven years after the first villagers had been forced from their homes (Morse and Berger 1992, 5). Just as the political and financial roadblocks appeared to have been cleared, however, the real problems began for Sardar Sarovar. In the decades since the project had been proposed, many in the environmental movement had become suspicious of big dam projects and the promises governments and the World Bank made about them. Their challenges to the Sardar Sarovar Dam ultimately revealed not just the inherent flaws of the project, but of the World Bank's entire development assistance program.

Financing Disaster

Since independence, more than 3,000 dam projects had been started in India. Of those, the majority were never finished or had failed to provide their promised benefits. In the half century that the World Bank had been funneling money to India in the name of national development, as many as 40 million of India's citizens had been forcibly relocated, theoretically for their own good. Millions of these, however, failed to obtain a standard of living similar to the even modest ones they enjoyed before relocation: In the words of the World Bank, they have not been rehabilitated, and many had become beggars in India's crowded urban centers (Caufield 1996, 11–12, 16).

The World Bank has been directly involved in the financing of many such human tragedies in India. Between 1978 and 1990 it provided funding for thirty-two projects that expelled at least 600,000 Indians from their homes (Rich 1994, 252). Despite the massive investment in dam and affiliated water projects, India continued to be plagued by chronic water shortages. Hundreds of millions of Indians still lack access to safe drinking water and basic sanitation, and devastating droughts and floods continue. In 1986, after decades of unfulfilled promises, Indian prime minister Rajiv Gandhi conceded that "we can safely say that almost no benefit has come to the people from these projects. . . . The people have got nothing back, no irrigation, no water, no increase in production, no help in their daily life" (quoted in Caufield 1996, 16).

Given this poor track record, and under increasing pressure from environmentalists and citizens groups such as Narmada Bachao Andolan (the

Save Narmada Movement), the World Bank, in 1991, took the unprecedented step of allowing an independent commission to review the Sardar Sarovar project and its own involvement (Caufield 1996, 24). The team was chaired by former congressman and administrator of the United Nations Development Program, Bradford Morse. For nine months they assessed the bank's and India's efforts to "resettle and rehabilitate" the people displaced by, and "ameliorate the environmental impact" of, the Sardar Sarovar Dam. The commission's report presents the project as a potential, and in some cases already-realized, human and environmental disaster. It concluded that there were fundamental failures in the implementation of the flawed project, that it was not possible to achieve for affected persons resettlement and rehabilitation . . . under prevailing circumstances, and that the bank and Indian government had not "properly considered or adequately addressed," the environmental impact associated with the construction of Sardar Sarovar (Morse and Berger 1992, xi–xii).

In terms of the project's enormous human toll, the review found that inadequate measures had been taken by the bank to ensure rehabilitation of the 100,000 people estimated to be forced out of their homes for the submergence zone, and the additional 140,000 families that would be affected by the canal system. In fact, in addition to the poor planning for refugees that *had* been anticipated, the commission viewed the estimate of how many people would be displaced as conservatively small, further calling into question the likelihood that they would be properly rehabilitated. The situation was so bad, they concluded, that the disregard shown for relocation issues "offends recognized norms of human rights" (Morse and Berger 1992, xx, 4).

Despite these abuses, however, the most troubling aspect of the bank's involvement in the unfolding human tragedy was that it was fully aware of the potential problems big dams presented, had strict policies spelling out how to prevent such problems, and ignored virtually all the warning signs and their own policies in this regard. Indeed, its behavior was so egregious, the report of the review dedicates an entire chapter to describing in detail the bank's own policies toward human resettlement that existed *prior* to the agreement to fund Sardar Sarovar. In the following chapter it spells out in equal detail how these policies were blatantly disregarded.

Good Policies, Bad Deeds

Over the years the World Bank's development programs proved so destructive that the organization was led to adopt a series of increasingly detailed regulations for dealing with people displaced by bank projects. As early as 1980 it had instituted a policy titled Social Issues Associated with Involuntary Resettlement in Bank Financed Projects, which stated that displaced peoples should be provided means to achieve, if not exceed, "their previous standard of living," and that plans to ensure this happens "should be clarified before, and agreed upon during, the loan negotiations" (Morse and Berger 1992, 23). In 1982 the bank expanded its official concern for displaced peoples by addressing specifically the issue of tribal people displaced by the institution's projects. Of the three states where people were to be heavily affected by Sardar Sarovar, in two—Gujarat and Maharashtra—almost all the inhabitants are "tribals" and in Madhya Pradesh almost 40 percent are. According to one estimate, almost 58 percent of the displaced in the case of Sardar Sarovar are *adivasi* (indigenous people), whereas only 8 percent of the entire Indian population is so designated. The "ethnic 'otherness'" of the groups, it is argued, has made it easier for the government and World Bank to ignore their plight (Roy 1999, 7 n1, 18–19).

The World Bank acknowledged in its 1982 policy that "tribal people are more likely to be harmed than helped by development projects that are intended for beneficiaries other than themselves," and that it would fund projects only when the borrowing government supports and can implement mitigative measures (Morse and Berger 1992, 26–27). Despite these noble-sounding policies, however, the bank proceeded on Sardar Sarovar with little actual regard for the human toll the project threatened to extract.

The review discovered that the government of India had failed to meet World Bank requirements to develop a realistic resettlement plan and that the bank knew as much. Despite the fact that four missions had evaluated Sardar Sarovar between 1982 and 1983, they failed to take account of the impact the project would have on local inhabitants. The review concluded, "From the very beginning . . . the Bank failed to implement its own policy," and in fact seemed unconcerned with India's flagrant disregard for its policy. "Having recognized the governments' [sic] failure to conform to the Bank's requirements, the Bank relaxed these requirements." The report said that the bank demonstrated a "readiness to accept whatever India offered, and to disregard [its] own requirements and expertise" (Morse and Berger 1992, 42, 45, 47).

This behavior is not uncommon, the review found. Despite the fact that the World Bank had funded hundreds of similar projects around the world since 1970, resulting in the displacement of millions of civilians, it has failed to learn from its mistakes. In case after case, it ignores problems that are brought to its attention. Violations are noted, demands are made, and then forgotten. "The problems besetting the Sardar Sarovar Projects are more the rule than the exception to resettlement operations supported by the Bank in India" (Morse and Berger 1992, 53), the review lamented.

In addition to the human toll of Sardar Sarovar, the project also threatened severe environmental destruction. Here again the bank allowed the project to proceed in violation of its own policies. As early as 1984 it had in place a policy that required environmental concerns to be addressed during the "early stages of a project." And in 1983 the Indian Department of Environment failed to give Sardar Sarovar clearance because of noncompliance with Indian environmental laws. Despite this fact, the bank went ahead with the loan agreement in 1985 after its Staff Appraisal report failed to point out that Indian regulators had still failed to give environmental approval. Proceeding without an environmental plan, the bank's own Back-to-Office report from October 1988 observed, "it is evident that many of the environmental components of the project are in disarray" (Morse and Berger 1992, 218, 227).

The effect of Sardar Sarovar on the environment could be devastating. The World Bank's own *Environmental Assessment Sourcebook* recognizes that "large dam projects cause irrevocable environmental changes," and have "health, navigation and ecological consequence" (quoted in Morse and Berger 1992, 239–40). Despite these potentially devastating effects, the Sardar Sarovar review found that environmental concerns were not considered when determining the "location, design, and operation of the dam" (Morse and Berger 1992, 244).

In addition to the 37,000 hectares of land to be submerged by the dam's 200-kilometer-long reservoir, the project also poses serious environmental concerns to the command area (the area of the canal system), and the downstream area. In its attempt to assess the environmental impact of the dam downstream the review noted that "in all our expectations we have been disappointed." Although there was one study of the dam's impact on fisheries under way during the review's work, those results were expected to be "about a decade later than necessary for proper planning and design" (Morse and Berger 1992, 241, 277, 281). The review eventually concluded the food web of the river would not be sustainable in the long run given the dam's design.

In the command area no specifics existed about how water would be supplied to urban or rural areas, despite this being the primary purpose of the canal system. In fact the project was so heavy on goals and light on detail that 200 of the villages listed to be beneficiaries of the project were uninhabited. The bank had required that environmental concerns in the command area be addressed in a work plan by the end of 1985, but they still had not been by the time the review went to press in 1992. The review concluded that "the Bank, in sanctioning deficient fulfillment of negotiated obligations, has demonstrated its unwillingness to enforce conditions required by its own environmental policies." Proceeding as it did with such disregard "will almost certainly result in a long series of [environmental] crises, which will have to be dealt with one after the other" (Morse and Berger 1992, 297, 228, 293).

Finally, the review concluded that the World Bank had also ignored the health risks Sardar Sarovar posed. As early as 1985 bank staff had recognized that the dam could result in an increase in water-borne diseases, including malaria, schistosomiasis, and filaria. One report described the project areas as "ideal breeding sites" and "death traps" for malaria. In fact after construction began, the rate of malaria increased sixfold, but standard malaria control measures were ignored (quoted in Morse and Berger 1992, 327). This blatant disregard for public health was evidenced by the bank's failure to consult with India's Ministry of Health, and despite what the review termed "a century of well-known historical examples" (Morse and Berger 1992, 328) of the dangers similar projects posed, including many where the bank was involved, several in India itself.

At the heart of the Sardar Sarovar project's problem, the review concluded, "was an eagerness on the part of the Bank and India to get on with the job" (Morse and Berger 1992, 354). To this end, environmental quality and public health were sacrificed. But such an "eagerness" on the bank's part to push through development projects was not unique to Sardar Sarovar and is an inherent side effect of its institutional structure and evolution.

LENDING AT ANY COST

The World Bank group is composed of five entities: the International Bank for Reconstruction and Development, the International Development Association, the International Finance Corporation, the Multilateral Investment Guarantee Agency, and the International Center for the Settlement of Investment Disputes. The organization was created at the Bretton Woods Conference in July 1944, as part of the Allied effort to reconstruct the global economic order after World War II. The World Bank, and its sister institution the International Monetary Fund (IMF), were envisioned by the architects of Bretton Woods as the safeguards of the world economy—the IMF would help countries maintain their exchange rates, and the bank would provide the capital and expertise to help the war-ravaged nations of Europe and the Third World develop industrial economies.

The two programs represented the newfound faith of industrial countries, such as the United States and Britain, in technocratic economic policies—a visible helping hand to the invisible hand of the free market. The chief architect of the IMF and the World Bank was John Maynard Keynes, the prominent British economist and central figure of Bretton Woods. "In general, it will be the duty of the Bank, by wise and prudent lending, to promote a policy of expansion of the world's economy. . . ," Keynes writes. "By 'expansion' we should mean the increase of resources and production in real terms, in physical quantity, accompanied by a corresponding increase in purchasing power" (quoted in Rich 1994, 55). Hopeful that the new order would remove the specter of economic depression and global conflict, Keynes foresaw that the "nightmare, in which most of us here present have spent too much of our lives, will be over. The brotherhood of man will have become more than a phrase" (quoted in Rich 1994, 49).

With the European economy rebounding quickly from the war's devastating effects, the World Bank had to look to the Third World for projects to finance. It was believed that what prohibited economic growth in these countries was a lack of investment capital. If the bank could provide this, and the necessary expertise on how to apply the capital, it was believed, poor countries would rapidly industrialize. It raises money for lending by selling bonds to pension funds and other investors and by contributions from national governments. Although relying on the private sector for a portion of its funds provides some discipline, if it is to maintain its AAA credit rating, its support from national governments, such as the United States, allows it to behave in ways that private lenders would avoid.

As the bank looked around the Third World, it encountered an embarrassing problem for an organization that was supposed to lend money for development: There were few projects in need of funding. As Pres. Eugene Black informed the United Nations in 1950, there was a lack of "bankable" projects resulting not from a "lack of money but the lack of well-prepared and well-planned projects ready for immediate execution" (quoted in Rich 1994, 68). The World Bank realized that it would have to take a more active role in the planning and execution of projects if it was to justify its existence.

The Best and the Brightest

When former Defense Secretary Robert McNamara took over as head of the World Bank in 1968, the organization provided slightly less than $1 billion a year in loans to the Third World. By the time McNamara left the bank in 1981 it lent more than $12 billion per year, a sixfold increase after inflation. This increase was accompanied by a ballooning of staff from 1,574 employees to 5,201 in the same time (Rich 1994, 81).

McNamara was aware of the need for the bank to be seen to be doing something—anything—and his zeal for expansion led to what has been termed a "pressure to lend." Bank staffers were encouraged to neglect concerns about the impacts of their projects and focus instead on moving money. Despite its grandiose statements about helping the poor, emphasis within the group was actually on helping the bank lend more money (Rich 1994, 73).

Despite the increased pressure to lend during the McNamara years, however, the problems besetting the bank—namely a lack of sound projects—were more obvious than ever. In response, under McNamara's direction, it began to push large, expensive projects that often required a series of loans from the World Bank. This emphasis on big projects led to not only more dams and power plants but also more intensive agriculture programs in areas that had typically been left undisturbed by development. As Bruce Rich (1994, 95), an expert on the World Bank's environmental record, charges, "The proliferation of land settlement projects in the McNamara years increasingly resembled a war against the earth's rapidly dwindling tropical forests."

Increasing the destructiveness of these projects was adoption of a one-size-fits-all policy. In the bank's bigger-is-better mentality there was little room for local concerns. According to one researcher who studied the programs in India, the bank demonstrated a "disregard of the heterogeneity of local ecological and institutional considerations" (quoted in Rich 1994, 90). This disregard is not unique to India but prevalent wherever the bank is active. And it often occurs despite objections from the organization's advisers.

A study of the World Bank's decades-long involvement in Cote d'Ivoire revealed that its spending on public health, education, and housing benefited mainly the nation's wealthy elite while actually decreasing the well-being of the poor. The situation is all the more disturbing considering that staff members often warned of such potential and real problems. The institutional structure of the bank, however, ensured that the staff that actually negotiated the loans cared only about moving the money, whereas the professional analysts who uncovered the problems had little influence in the decision-making process. For extending the loans the staffers were rewarded with larger budgets and a greater likelihood of promotion. The success or failure of the schemes they implemented was seldom noted (Wick and Shaw 1998, 17). Despite best intentions and thousands of highly trained development experts, in country after country the well-being of the poor and the environment was sacrificed for the well-being of the bank's bureaucracy.

Easy Money

Early on in its lending bonanza, the World Bank was aware that Third World governments would encounter difficulty repaying their loans. These worries were further increased by the prospect of net-negative transfers—Third World countries, which already had difficulty meeting their financial obligations, paying back more in principal and interest than they received in new loans. It was an embarrassing prospect for the bank (Rich 1994, 79), but an obvious solution presented itself: Increase the amount of money lent to the Third World.

This plan worked fairly well until 1982, when Mexico announced that it was unable to make its debt payments. The ensuing Third World debt crisis led to a revolution in policy. Faced with the prospect of borrowers defaulting on their debts, the World Bank, along with the IMF, engaged in a new

program of structural adjustment loans. The loans, designed to help countries reform their economies and place more emphasis on earning foreign
exchange, allowed the bank to continue to move money—now at an even
greater pace—while ensuring that the Third World could continue to make
its debt payments (Rich 1994). In effect, structural adjustment loans made a
quick round-trip journey from bank headquarters in Washington, D.C., to
Third World capitals and back to Washington in the form of payments on
past debts.

While temporarily solving the problem of looming defaults, structural
adjustment loans, in addition to being decried as an international Ponzi
scheme, have been attacked for their effect on the environment and resource base of Third World countries. In many of these nations, services to
the poor were slashed and wages dropped as governments struggled to
meet the demands of the bank and IMF. At the same time, governments
dramatically increased activities such as deforestation to earn the demanded increased foreign exchange, which encouraged the conversion of
forests and other undisturbed lands to produce export crops such as coffee. In addition to destroying countless acres of land, the programs led directly to the collapse of commodity prices as supply surged, further frus-
trating the bank's effort at poverty reduction. Oxfam accused the programs
of "dramatically worsen[ing] the plight of the poor," in much of Africa
(quoted in Rich 1994, 187).

The World Bank's penchant for lending has also led to a disregard for its
own charter, which directs it to fund only projects in countries that could not
otherwise gain access to loans through international capital markets (Lerrick
1999). But the need to move money and its desire to ensure that loans are
paid back has led the organization to greatly expand its scope. In November
1998, Congress established the International Financial Institution Advisory
Commission (IFIAC) to make recommendations about U.S. policy toward the
World Bank and other institutions such as the International Monetary Fund.
The commission, chaired by economist Allan Meltzer, concluded in its March
2000 report that "seventy percent of World Bank non-aid resources flow to
eleven countries that enjoy substantial access to private resource flows" (U.S.
Senate 2000, 6). The commission pointed out that although the bank criti-
cizes private lenders for directing most of their loans to only a dozen developing countries, it actually follows much the same policy, with 145 of the
poorest member countries dividing only 30 percent of bank loans.

The most favored of the World Bank's recipients is China, which in the
1990s received a full 12 percent of the bank's resources (U.S. Senate 2000,
31), despite having ready access to international capital markets. The World
Bank has been charged with overstating the amount of money China needs
to borrow for its energy sector. Capable of meeting 80 percent of its investment needs domestically, and with numerous Western financiers eager to tap

into the tremendous Chinese market, "the Chinese power sector is hardly out with a begging bowl" (Hampton 1999, 27).

Underlying the bank's seemingly irrational actions is what its own 1992 review, known as the Wapenhans Report, characterized as a lending culture. Eight years later Congress's independent commission concurred with the Wapenhans Report, finding that "incentives to lend for lending's sake are built into the structure of the Banks" (the World Bank as well as the other regional development banks such as the USAID). The fact that unlike private lenders there are no penalties to executives for lending to bad projects, and that the World Bank reviews only 5 percent of projects after money has been lent, leads to as many as 60 percent of the projects failing to reach sustainable results as determined even by bank standards (U.S. Senate 2000, 37–38).

Such behavior was likened by one employee as similar to that which resulted under the incentives of the Communist system. Such systems have been described as encouraging "'conspicuous production,' in which activities are performed not for their final output but for the sake of activity itself" (Steele 1998, 1–2). "We are like a Soviet factory. The push is to maximize lending . . . pressures to lend are enormous and a lot of people spend sleepless nights wondering how they can unload projects" (quoted in Georgia 1999, 12). Plants in the former Soviet Union were infamous for conspicuous production. If a factory was ordered to meet a production quota for a certain tonnage of nails, it would produce very large, heavy, and largely useless nails. Whereas if the quota demanded a large number of individual nails, the factory would produce enormous quantities of small, and again largely useless nails. As with the World Bank, rewards have been based on quantity. Such incentives lead to an equally low quality of output, be it in industrial goods in the Soviet Union or development projects financed by the World Bank.

EMPIRE BUILDERS

Making the World Bank's drive to lend more money difficult is the fact that it is working with a limited customer base (Rich 1994, 79). This has meant that unlike traditional lenders it has to keep going back to the same few customers in order to keep moving money. One way to get around this problem was for the bank to create demand for its projects within developing countries. It did this through a process dubbed "institution building." It provided the funding to establish government agencies within developing countries, agencies that would then borrow money from the organization for development projects.

Because they received most of their funding from the bank, the agencies were relatively free from oversight by governments in their own countries (Rich 1994, 74–75). Their relationship developed into one of mutual advantage—the bank had a ready customer base in the new agencies, and the agencies had a virtually guaranteed source of funding. Given the bank's lack of interest in project quality, the new agencies faced very little accountability if they used the loans wastefully. Both bureaucracies thrived in the arrangements; "instead of detached economics' [sic] calling the shots, everything was seen through rose-colored glasses by bureaucrats and borrowers out to build empires" (Adams 1994).

Often such agencies were created in countries with already weak traditions in the rule of law, and the creation of agencies relatively free from oversight contributed to the disregard for the human and natural environment characteristic of World Bank projects. "The people who are most affected are often the poor, the illiterate, the voiceless, and powerless in their own national societies" (Rich 1994, xi).

One of the most notorious examples of a government agency established by the World Bank is in Thailand. Early on, as a condition of future loans, it began insisting that the government of Thailand establish a national power agency. This led to the development of Thailand's Electricity Generating Authority (EGAT), which has received more than $700 million in loans (Sharma and Imhof 1999). From the start, EGAT's history has been one of environmental destruction and disregard for human well-being. The World Bank provided its first loan for a hydroelectric dam in Thailand in 1964. The Bhumibol Dam, which evicted more than 3,000 people from their homes, promised to bring much needed electricity and drinking water to the affected families. But according to one resident, a former Thai military officer, even twenty-seven years after they were forced from their homes, "We still don't have electricity or water despite the fact that [their home] is only 1 kilometer from the reservoir and 36 kilometers from the power plant at Bhumibol" (Rich 1994, 9–10).

Bhumibol was only one of many destructive dams the World Bank financed for EGAT. Most have failed to even approach the projected benefits stated at the time of construction. Of nine major dams in Thailand that are supposed to provide irrigation, only 42 percent of the intended benefits have been realized (Rich 1994, 12).

One of the most destructive projects built by EGAT was the Pak Mun Dam in northwest Thailand. Despite widespread protests by locals and Thai environmental groups, the bank and EGAT insisted that the project was sound, although EGAT denied access to its environmental assessments of the dam. A leading expert on the Mekong River's fish, University of California professor Walt Rainboth, who was presented with a leaked copy of the report, concluded, "Based on the importance of the project and the capacity for irreversible damage, the report is *criminal*. If something like this were submitted to Congress in order to solicit funds, its fraudulent nature would deserve criminal indictment" (quoted in Rich 1994, 11–12). The project was further objected to by public health experts, who warned of dramatic risks from schistosomiasis.

A 1999 study of the Pak Mun Dam project concluded that there was no evidence that planners ever took into account the effect the dam would have on the local population, disregarding policies about resettlement that had been in place since the 1980s (Sharma and Imhof 1999). The number of households displaced by the dam was seven times greater than the bank or EGAT had asserted earlier; 3,000 of the affected families have yet to receive compensation (*Probe Alert* 1999). The river's fish populations have also suffered from the dam. In one example of the disregard EGAT and the bank have for the environmental impact of their projects, a Nordic-style fish ladder was constructed to allow fish to pass through the dam. But the designers overlooked one problem: The ladders, which are used to help salmon, were of no use on the Mun River because the local fish species don't jump like salmon and thus couldn't utilize the ladder or pass through the dam.

Despite its alleged benefits and its massive human and environmental disruption, the Pak Mun Dam still only provides enough electricity to power one Bangkok shopping mall.

Despots on the Dole

The World Bank's support of quasi-independent agencies in developing countries, such as Thailand, and its insistence on lending at all cost, has fostered an atmosphere of unaccountability both internally and in the governments it funds. In the case of EGAT, deals were often struck between the power agency and the World Bank before they were presented to the Thai government. Part of the problem stems from the bank's charter, which states that its employees "owe their duty entirely to the Bank and to no other authority" (quoted in Adams 1991, 67). In its technocratic zeal it has thus largely ignored policies that harm individuals or political freedom in the Third World.

As lending to Third World governments increased, each government became more and more detached from the reality of its own country's economic circumstances. Under such circumstances governments are no longer accountable to their citizenry. They are free to pursue projects that in the absence of World Bank funding would be both politically and financially unfeasible. Chinese activist Fang Lizhi has promoted the end of foreign aid to China for this very reason, arguing, "We must make our government realize that it is economically dependent on its citizens" (quoted in Adams 1991, 179). Such a lack of dependence has allowed the dictatorships common in the Third World to use World Bank funding to support their various tyrannical agendas, creating a situation environmentalist Patricia Adams calls "despots on the dole" (Adams 1991, 124).

This funding has allowed despots to thrive at the expense of the populace and the environment in countries all over the world. One common result is rampant bribery and kickbacks on projects involving bank money. In India one businessman anonymously characterized the situation with a local bank-funded irrigation project this way:

The World Bank has given [a] loan to this Madurai town to improve the water supply. Within a month the money was used by the politicians to sink 100 borewells of which 50 percent of the amount went as [a] bribe. After a couple of years the World Bank once again gave [a] loan to improve the water facility. Once again, another 100 borewells were sunk right next to the old 100 borewells which were not in use. The same thing was repeated again. The corrupt politicians always use the World Bank loan since they can take up any project, whether they are required or not, just to get bribes from the project. They need not raise the tax to meet the project expense. The loan has to be repaid only by future taxes by which time these rascals won't be there. (quoted in Kamath 1992, 11)

Such corruption is common almost everywhere the World Bank operates. According to economist and president of The Free Africa Foundation, George Ayittey, such induced irresponsibility has left the African continent "littered with a multitude of black elephants [basilicas, grandiose monuments, grand conference halls, and show airports]." Yet the people of Africa continue to be mired in poverty, the victims of what he dubs pirate states "hijacked by a phalanx of kleptocrats" (Ayittey 1999, 3–4) whose sole purpose is acquiring World Bank funding for their own enrichment. Although the bank has funneled billions into Africa, its lack of interest in project quality has allowed these kleptocrats to flourish while the general population suffers setbacks to their already abysmal standards of living. Projects like the Kariba Dam on the Zambezi River have led to the forcible eviction of countless poor and the destruction of wildlife habitat, and has encouraged, through structural adjustment programs, the introduction of unsustainable and environmentally damaging agricultural programs. Despite a tenfold increase in foreign aid between 1970 and 1988, incomes in Africa decreased (Adams 1991, 182). In the end, Ayittey concludes, Africa is left with "institutional decay, crumbling infrastructure and environmental degradation" (Ayittey 1999, 4).

In Indonesia, loans led to one of the greatest human and environmental tragedies of recent times. A program of massive social engineering and resettlement, known as Indonesia Transmigration, was carried out by the Suharto regime with World Bank funding. Between 1976 and 1986 it lent approximately $1 billion to the Indonesian government to finance the resettlement and agricultural development of many of the country's most environmentally pristine islands. Most of the migrants were from Indonesia's crowded inner islands, like Java and Bali, whereas the receiving islands were the outer, sparsely populated Borneo, Irian Jaya, and Sumatra. In addition to being home to some of the most important rainforests in the world, these islands are also populated primarily by non-Javanese cultures. According to estimates of the number of people transplanted by transmigration, the World Bank is responsible for at least 4 million itself (Rich 1994, 34–36). Its justification for this massive relocation scheme was shaky, relying primarily on "unquantifiable economic and social benefits" (Adams 1991, 32). But even these dubious results, for the most part, were never realized. Many of the settlers had to abandon their new homes because of the terrible soil quality (Rich 1994, 36), and others found themselves in areas that lacked access to water half the year (Adams 1991, 31). Given the lack of benefits from relocation, most would have been better off receiving a cash handout and staying in their original location. At a cost of $7,000 to move a single family through transmigration, that same sum could have kept them above the poverty level for approximately thirteen years—more than half of those who resettled could not even achieve this modest level and 20 percent were even worse off, living below subsistence (Rich 1994, 36–37). But Indonesia pursued the program for what many observers believed were political reasons. The outer islands were home to non-Javanese populations opposed to the Suharto regime. By transplanting his preferred ethnic group to the troublesome regions, Suharto hoped to quell such resistance with World Bank support.

Matching Indonesia Transmigration's human toll was its environmental devastation. The receiving outer islands were home to 10 percent of the world's remaining tropical rainforests. And to make way for the growing of cacao, palm oil, and coffee, the program led to the clearing of between 40,000 to 50,000 square kilometers of those forests, as well as the conversion of 35,000 square kilometers of wetlands. Most of this was for naught, because although the outer islands are home to some of the most diverse and pristine ecosystems in the world, they also contain soil perfectly suited to *prevent* successful cultivation. Bruce Rich has concluded that the resettled areas "were beset by environmental calamities of biblical dimensions: acidic peat soils, flooding, paltry agricultural yields, and plagues of insects, rats, and wild boars" (Rich 1994, 36).

Long-Term Losers

Given the environmentally destructive nature of bank-funded programs like Indonesia Transmigration, supporters of its policies have little to rest their case on. One common belief is that although destructive in the short term, its programs are necessary in order to make the transition to First World status and achieve a higher quality of life. Thus, Third World countries face a tradeoff, it is argued, between near-term environmental quality and long-term prosperity and quality of life. But this choice has proven to be false. The bank's environmental toll has not been met in most places with economic success. This failure to achieve development, despite development being the main objective, means that poor countries face not only prolonged economic stagnation subsidized by First World taxpayers, but also continued, and in some cases hastened, environmental deterioration.

Increasing evidence suggests that economic growth is important for the realization of improvements in the natural and human environment. Whereas some environmental deterioration is common during the initial stages of the transition to an advanced economy, measures of environmental quality and quality of life, such as air particulates, water quality, sanitation, forestation rates, and life expectancy all improve as countries become wealthier and can afford cleaner production processes and better health care (Brown and Shaw 1999; Goklany 2001). Additionally, even among poor countries, the rate at which their economy grows can dramatically reduce the environmental problems associated with development (Norton 1998).

By supporting despots on the dole and African kleptocrats, the World Bank has helped destroy or prevent the development of indigenous markets in Third World countries. It has undermined the rule of law and the protection of private property rights, all of which are essential if those countries are going to grow wealthier. Recent reviews of the effect development assistance has had on the Third World show that neither per capita assistance nor aid as a percentage of the gross domestic product can be shown to promote economic growth—in some cases the relationship is actually negative. In recent years development assistance from the First World has increased to countries whose economic freedom has declined; this continues the bank's long trend of propping up dictatorships and rogue states. Ian Vasquez found that in the 1980s and 1990s development experts actually knew the negative impacts such policies would have and continued them anyway: "They were increasing aid flows despite widespread acknowledgment that such action would not promote development and would likely inhibit it" (Vasquez 1998, 276, 279).

CONCLUSION

In the wake of the public relations disaster and political turmoil that followed the Sardar Sarovar report by the Morse Commission, the bank canceled the remaining $170 million of the $450 million it had promised India for the project. And many heralded the event as the beginning of a new era of environmental responsibility at the World Bank. Throughout the 1990s it increased its funding and rhetoric on environmental causes and tried to establish itself as the center of the global movement for sustainable development. Following protests by environmentalists at the bank's April 2000 meetings in Washington, D.C., the *Washington Post* (2000, A24) criticized the protestors as anachronisms failing to acknowledge all the improvements it has made.

But the changes in the bank's policies are largely meaningless. Although it canceled loans to Sardar Sarovar and claims to scrutinize projects much more closely now, it fails to realize that money is fungible. Shortly after the Sardar Sarovar disaster, it announced eight new loans to India of more than $2 billion (Caufield 1996, 28), far more than those it canceled, and half of these had no directly stated purpose (Adams 1994). By continuing to fund irresponsible governments who are not financially dependent on their own citizenry, and are not subject to the discipline of private sector lenders, the bank allows destructive schemes to continue despite its well-intentioned rhetoric.

And although its proclamations about protecting the environment have increased in recent years, earth-friendly promises are nothing new, and neither is its blatant disregard for such policies. In 1972 bank president Robert McNamara informed the UN that each project underwent "careful in-house studies" to ensure environmental protection. He failed to mention, however, that the staff supposedly conducting these reviews was composed of only one person (Rich 1994, 82, 111–12). Although that staff has ballooned in recent years, its effectiveness is still questionable. The incentives to lend are still present, as confirmed by the IFIAC, and the bank has been accused of increasing aid for regimes where opposition to projects is not tolerated—China has replaced India as a favored recipient, receiving more than $3 billion for dam projects since the mid-1980s (Roy 1999, 30). And to quell criticism from environmental groups, the bank has started funding many of them itself. With their well-being attached to the organization, many have become noticeably less critical in the past few years (Sheehan 2000). So although the bank has mastered the public relations of environmentalism, its actions continue to defy its lofty goals.

Given such a record it is unlikely that the Third World will see much improvement any time soon as they continue to act as outlets for the World Bank's conspicuous production. But from its institutional perspective, this situation is perversely encouraging. If the Third World did develop economically, the bank would lose its raison d'être. Such an occurrence is unlikely though. It seems the Third World will continue to bank on disaster, human, economic, and environmental. And the World Bank will continue to sing the "Road-Song of the Bandar-Log":

Dreaming of deeds that we mean to do,
All complete, in a minute or two—
Something noble and grand and good,
Won by merely wishing we could. (Kipling 1964, 71)

REFERENCES

Adams, Patricia. 1991. *Odious Debts: Loose Lending, Corruption, and the Third World's Environmental Legacy.* London: Earthscan.

———. 1994. The World Bank's Finances: An International S&L Crisis. *Cato Policy Analysis* 215. Online: www.cato.org/pubs/pas/pa-215.html (cited: November 1, 2000).

Ayittey, George B. N. 1999. The Effectiveness of World Bank and African Development Bank Programs of Africa. Study prepared for the International Financial Institution Advisory Commission of U.S. Senate Committee on Banking, Housing, and Urban Affairs, Washington, DC, October.

Brown, Matthew, and Jane S. Shaw. 1999. Prosperity and the Environment. *PERC Reports*, Bozeman, MT: PERC, February.

Caufield, Catherine. 1996. *Masters of Illusion*. New York: Henry Holt and Company.

Georgia, Paul. 1999. Stop Banking on Failure. *UpDate*, November.

Goklany, Indur M. 2001. Economic Growth and the State of Humanity. *PERC Policy Series*, PS-21. Bozeman, MT: PERC.

Hampton, Kate. 1999. Smokescreen. *New Internationalist*, December.

Kamath, Shyam J. 1992. Foreign Aid and India: Financing the Leviathan State. *Policy Analysis* 170. Washington, DC: Cato Institute. Online: www.cato.org/pubs/pas/pa170.html.

Kipling, Rudyard. 1964 [1893]. *The Jungle Book*. Garden City: Doubleday & Company.

Lerrick, Adam. 1999. Wither the World Bank? Study prepared for the International Financial Institution Advisory Commission of U.S. Senate Committee on Banking, Housing, and Urban Affairs, Washington, DC, October.

Morse, Bradford, and Thomas R. Berger. 1992. *Sardar Sarovar: Report of the Independent Review*. Ottawa, ON: Resource Futures International.

Norton, Seth. 1998. Property Rights, the Environment, and Economic Well-Being. In *Who Owns the Environment*, ed. Peter J. Hill and Roger E. Meiners. Lanham, MD: Rowman & Littlefield, 37–54.

Probe Alert. 1999. Villagers Occupy World Bank Dam Site to Demand Compensation. Probe International, June. Online: www.probeinternational.org/probeint/probealerts/pa99june.html (cited: November 1, 2000).

Rich, Bruce. 1994. *Mortgaging the Earth*. Boston: Beacon Press.

Roy, Arundhati. 1999. *The Cost of Living*. New York: Modern Library.

Sharma, Shefali, and Aviva Imhof. 1999. The Struggle for the Mun River: The World Bank's Involvement in the Pak Mun Dam, Thailand. International Rivers Network, December. Online: www.irn.org/programs/pakmun/rep.01toc.shtml (cited: November 1, 2000).

Sheehan, James M. 2000. The Greening of the World Bank: A Lesson in Bureaucratic Survival. *Foreign Policy Briefing* 56. Washington, DC: Cato Institute.

Steele, Charles. 1998. EPA Planning of Superfund Activities: The Problems of Allocation without Markets. Working paper 98-11. Bozeman, MT: PERC.

U.S. Senate Committee on Banking, Housing, and Urban Affairs. 2000. *Final Report of the International Financial Institution Advisory Commission*. 107th Cong., 2nd sess, March.

Vasquez, Ian. 1998. Official Assistance, Economic Freedom, and Policy Change: Is Foreign Aid Like Champagne? *Cato Journal* 18(2): 275–86.

Washington Post. 2000. Evolution at the World Bank. May 1.

Wick, Pascal, and Jane S. Shaw. 1998. The Cote d'Ivoire's Troubled Economy: Why World Bank Intervention Failed. *Cato Journal* 18(1): 11–20.

9

All Play and No Pay: The Adverse Effects of Welfare Recreation

J. Bishop Grewell

"Our national parks are being overused, over-loved.
They're being loved to death." (quoted in Hebert 1999)

—Sen. Harry Reid (D-Nev.)

Commodity development has been rolled back on federal lands.[1] Now environmentalists have turned their attention to public recreation. Two reports in 1999—one from the Wilderness Society and one from the National Parks and Conservation Association (NPCA)—listed ecosystems considered endangered by the organizations. The Wilderness Society report cited fifteen environmental areas in the United States and the NPCA designated ten U.S. national park areas of concern (NPCA 1999b; Wilderness Society 1999). The striking thing about the reports is an increased focus on the damage caused to environmental lands by recreational use. The NPCA noted problems from recreation in half of their listed areas; the Wilderness Society cited similar problems in four of the fifteen sites studied.

The irony with recreation is that in the past environmental activists have tended to ignore the economics. Not so, however, with commodity development. Environmentalists have fondly pointed out that grazing and timber harvesting on federal lands lose money, and indeed they do. Grazing lost an average of $66 million per year from 1994 to 1996, and timber harvesting lost about $290 million per year over the same period. Yet the largest loser for federal lands is recreation, which lost more than $355 million annually during the same three-year stint (Fretwell 1998, 1).

The rise in recreational budgets continued in fiscal year 2001. Recreational spending by the Bureau of Land Management rose nearly $11 billion, for a 21 percent increase over fiscal year 2000 (U.S. Department of the Interior, Bureau of Land Management 2001, III–79). The Forest Service added over $25 million more in funding for recreational activities, for a 13 percent increase over fiscal year 2000 (U.S. Department of Agriculture, Forest Service 2001, 6–1).

Recreational activities used to be overlooked by environmentalists as a cause of environmental damage, because they had bigger fish to fry and because the "user" is the public. With grazing, logging, mining, and commercial providers of recreation, such as ski resorts, the user is private enterprise. It was easier to vilify these users when making their case before the public. But with the recent success of shutting down commodity development, it appears the environmental movement is willing to venture into the politically tenuous waters of public recreation. As NPCA's Rocky Mountain regional director Mark Peterson states, "We need to recognize that tourism can be as environmentally destructive as mining and logging" (Tennesen 1998, 29). For that, environmentalists need to strengthen their economic case.

This chapter discusses how recreation, as offered by federal land agencies, encourages overuse of resources and poor recreational services. To illustrate the harm it causes I focus on our national parks. In addition, I demonstrate how market-driven recreation coupled with the business requirement of linking revenues with costs can improve the management of recreation and the natural resources that support it. Finally, I examine the arguments against the "commercialization" of recreation.

WHAT IS WELFARE RECREATION? HOW DOES IT CAUSE HARM?

In a competitive market free of government interference, the amount of recreation provided is determined by the interaction of buyers and sellers freely dictating how much they will consume and produce. In the long run, there is neither a shortage nor an oversupply of recreation. If there is a shortage, the price will rise, encouraging a greater supply of recreational services. If too many recreational services are provided, the price will fall, encouraging a smaller supply. When the federal government enters the game, however, the corrective forces of the market are impeded. Price signals no longer convey the amount of recreation that consumers are willing to pay producers.

This situation is possible because the federal government does not need to consider the full costs of providing too much or too little of a good or service. Because activities are largely financed out of taxes, it can charge less than the cost of providing a service, and keep operating. In the case of recreation on federal lands, we have what might be called "welfare recreation," because the government often charges substantially less than would be charged in the marketplace.[2] Under this scenario, site managers have no way of telling how much recreation should be produced, because government-distorted prices do not reflect consumer demands. In addition, with prices set far below market prices, the quantity of recreation demanded escalates. In short, the incentives created by welfare recreation intensify recreational pressures on federal lands.

These pressures manifest themselves in different ways, such as multiple visits beyond what a recreationist would have made at the market price and visits from people who would not visit otherwise. Such pressures increase the likelihood of damage to the environment. In the case of national parks, assets worth hundreds of billions of dollars—including infrastructure like roads, visitor centers, and sewage systems as well as natural resource assets such as wildlife, habitat, and water and air quality—suffer from abuse and overuse. Anderson and Leal (1991, 76) sum up the harms from welfare recreation on federal lands this way: "Zero or token fees result in crowding, abuse of resources, and reduced incentives for the private sector to provide similar activities. The move to higher recreational user fees eliminates fiscal problems caused by subsidized recreation. . . ."

Another major problem that stems from welfare recreation is the failure to link costs with revenues. Just raising the price of recreation will not solve all the problems. For much of the twentieth century, most of the proceeds from user fees have gone to the federal treasury instead of the facility or agency collecting the fees. This leaves managers with little discretionary funds for site upkeep and recreational provision. Instead they must turn to politicians to supply the funds. Since politicians control the purse strings, they decide which projects are funded and which are not. As discussed later, the pet projects of politicians often take priority over resource protection and facility upkeep.

THE HARMS OF WELFARE RECREATION TO NATIONAL PARKS

From 1960 to 1998, the U.S. population increased by nearly 50 percent, and visitation to national parks shot up by more than 260 percent. The rise in park demand is a function of more than just population growth. Anderson and Leal (2001, 59) identify another critical factor: "Since World War II, incomes for United States citizens have been rising dramatically, increasing the willingness of Americans to pay more for outdoor opportunities."

Unfortunately park visitors are not paying most of the higher costs from higher park utilization, because park fees have been kept too low. When adjusted for inflation, fees taken in at park entrances declined during the twentieth century. Consider that in 1997 the fee for Yellowstone's annual vehicle pass was $40. Visitors paid more in real terms, $133, for entry into Yellowstone in 1916 (Leal and Fretwell 1997, 3). On the one hand, by not linking the revenues from fees to the costs of managing recreational and environmental assets, park managers have neither the wherewithal nor the incentive to provide the things that give visitors a quality experience, such as maintained roads, sewage systems, and a well-preserved environment. On the other hand, users have been given an incentive to recreate more, because of artificially low fees.

As a result, taxpayers and federal lands are bearing the costs of the increased recreation through higher taxes and declining infrastructure. With recreation provided below market and below cost, it is not surprising that there is increased use and abuse of our national parks. The problem is manifest by recent evidence that the National Park Service (NPS) has not kept up with the growing need for maintenance caused by the additional wear and tear from overcrowding. A severe maintenance backlog of basic infrastructure has built up in our national parks and other federal sites. According to the NPS, it will cost an estimated $3.54 billion to fix backlogged problems at national parks, monuments, and wilderness areas (Janofsky 1999).

Congress took one step in the right direction to solve the problem of welfare recreation. The fee demonstration program, which was authorized in 1996, allowed four federal agencies including the NPS to charge higher or new fees at selected sites. At least 80 percent of the increased revenue from this program must be spent at the facility where it is collected; the remainder is spent at the agency's discretion (Fretwell 1999b, 10). Allowing most of the fees to remain at their collection sites links revenues with costs and sensitizes site managers to recreational demands and the costs of provision.

The initial results of the fee demonstration program have been encouraging. Such improvements, as noted by Fretwell (1999b, 13), include:

- Natural Bridges National Monument in Utah, which is managed by the NPS, used fees to rebuild 5,000 feet of deteriorating trails. The monument had not had a trails maintenance and repair program in more than thirteen years; it now has a trails maintenance crew of five.
- Fees helped Grand Teton National Park survey wildlife in the park and monitor water quality.
- At the Forest Service's Mount St. Helens National Monument, fees kept open three visitor centers that otherwise might have been closed. Other funds at Mount St. Helens were used for plowing snow to provide early access to the monument's popular Windy Ridge and Lava Canyon areas.

Unfortunately fees from the program remain a small part of the park service's overall budget, which means congressional appropriations still provide the lion's share of the agency's financing. In 1999 the outlays of the park service budget were $1.86 billion, whereas the fee demonstration program brought in $141.4 million in receipts.[3] The program provided only about 8 percent of the total park service budget. This means Congress, the administration, and, therefore, politics are still controlling the purse strings, and that means there is a long way to go to end welfare recreation on federal lands. Maintenance backlogs are not the only result of welfare recreation. Increased congestion, direct damage to the environment from overuse, and increased pollution also occur.

Trash and Sewage

The oldest, and perhaps, most recognizable of the national parks is Yellowstone. Yellowstone's attractiveness as a tourist destination causes it to suffer some of the greatest threats from welfare recreation, sewage disposal among them.

Alan Sumerski, the assistant chief of maintenance at Yellowstone, remarks that the park's broken water lines have been "strained beyond reason by the growing use of bathing facilities and toilets" (McMillion 1999a, 9). Malfunctions in the sewage system at Old Faithful caused by old age and increased use have led to spills into pristine streams near the park's most popular tourist attraction. Another decaying sewer system has led to sewage spilling into Yellowstone Lake.

In 1999 the Wyoming Department of Environmental Quality issued a citation to the NPS for violating water quality laws; it was the second such instance in two years. The violation arose because the park service needed to siphon sewage from one of the sewage ponds at the Fishing Bridge treatment plant into a nearby meadow in order to keep the pond from failing (Milstein 1999b). The park service has identified 142 water and sewer problems needing $30 million worth of repairs (Moen 1999).

The sewage problem stems, in part, from the failure to link revenues with rising costs. Park attendance more than doubled between 1960 and 1998, rising from just under 1.5 million visitors annually to more than 3.1 million (NPS 1999, 9). Those 3.1 million visitors produce 270 million gallons of waste, using up to eighteen rolls of toilet paper per toilet daily (Moen 1999). Yet when visitors enter Yellowstone's gates, they do not pay a high enough fee to cover the costs of keeping the park in good condition for public use. In recent years, fees covered less than one-quarter of the park's operating costs. According to an NPCA report on Yellowstone's sewage problem, the park's budget has climbed less than 3 percent since 1980, whereas the number of visitors to the park has climbed by nearly 40 percent (NPCA 1999c). Using NPS figures and adjusting for inflation, I found Yellowstone's budget to have increased by 25 percent between 1980 and 1998, whereas visitation increased by 56 percent (fig. 9.1). In either case, there is a substantial disparity between visitor growth and budget growth. As a result, it comes as little surprise that there is a $30 million backlog in sewer repairs at Yellowstone. As

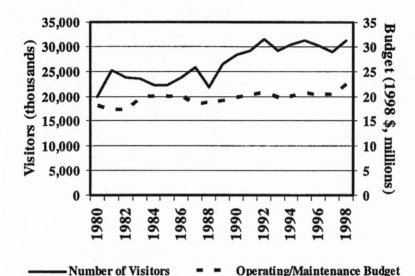

——— Number of Visitors   ▪ ▪ Operating/Maintenance Budget

Figure 9.1   Yellowstone National Park, 1980 to 1998. Sources: Budget data: Jack
O'Brian, Freedom of Information Act officer, National Park Service, Intermountain Region, Denver, CO, by written correspondence, September 16 and 27, 1999. Visitation
data: National Park Service (1999).

Tom Brokaw stated on *NBC Nightly News* (August 3, 1999), Yellowstone is
"strained to the breaking point by its popularity."

The park's sewage repair backlog is not the only sewage problem needing attention at a national park. Everglades National Park needs an updated
water treatment center that will cost $20 million, and Grand Canyon National
Park suffers from the same need at a price tag of $15 million (Janofsky 1999).
Until welfare recreation ends, these sewage problems in our national parks
will persist.

It is important to understand that the sewage problem in Yellowstone and
the other national parks only partially results from visitors not paying the full
cost of their recreational activity. On the other side of the coin, because park
managers are not required to balance their revenues against their costs and
politicians control the purse strings, funding is not properly allocated to real
maintenance needs. Even if the NPS took in greater revenues from visitors by
charging higher user fees, politics can and often does override park needs.

Consider the employee housing situation at parks like Yosemite. New employee housing was built at an average cost of $580,000 per unit in 1997. This
housing came in at two to four times the average construction rate for nearby
local housing. Despite spending a small fortune, the new housing accommodated fewer than 60 of the park's 5,000 employees, leaving some to dwell
in tent-cabins without running water (Fretwell 1999b, 4). The unnecessarily

high building costs no doubt led to fewer accommodations and more employees stuck out in the cold.

Unneeded ventures like the $1 million outhouse built in Glacier National Park in 1998 provide another example (Pound 1997). The park had other pressing needs, such as road repair, but politicians diverted funds to the outhouse. With park managers still receiving most of their funds from the federal treasury, additional funds from user fees may not be enough to offset political interference by Congress.

If national park managers were required to pay all costs out of revenues from fees and had no spending orders from Congress, then the above problems would be mitigated. Services that paid their way would be the rule instead of the exception. And what projects tend to pay their way? Those that bring visitors back year after year, such as upkeep of infrastructure and protection of natural resources. For Congress, oversight should focus on efficiency of park operation, environmental quality, and other like-minded goals instead of mandates for gold-plated outhouses.

Environmental Assets

In the national parks of Utah and all along the Colorado Plateau, the soil is covered with a thin black crust of cyanobacteria. Cyanobacteria, known as blue-green algae, provide many functions in arid desert regions. According to the National Park Service, it provides three basic services to vascular plants. First, it fixates nitrogen, converting the atmospheric gas into a form plants can use. As nitrogen levels are often low in deserts, thus limiting plant productivity, this is an important function. Second, cyanobacteria store water, which is essential to plants in desert regions. Third, the black crust contributes to organic matter in the region, often representing up to 80 percent of living groundcover. The cyanobacteria provide an important function to the entire desert ecosystem by stabilizing the ground against wind and water erosion (Belnap 1999).

Despite all of the strength that they provide to the soil, cyanobacteria cannot stand up to human traffic. The brittle crust is destroyed when the full weight of a human body is applied. Tourists who leave the trails and walk onto the crust can cause significant damage. Harmed areas often take fifty years or longer to recover (Fretwell 1999a, 20). And so, the NPS marks areas of heavy traffic with signs to stay on the trail.

Yet wear and tear from heavy traffic combined with deficient funding for trail repair and maintenance have worn away trails, making it difficult for hikers to know where they can travel with a minimal impact on the crust. The lack of trail maintenance harms the sensitive soil. The same can be said for backcountry hikers in the region. If hikers paid adequate fees and those fees went directly to maintenance upkeep, harm could be avoided.

Cyanobacteria are not the only creatures damaged from foot traffic. Where hikers or bikers create trails, plant life is destroyed. This happens throughout natural landscapes and national parks. The importance of maintaining trails becomes paramount for minimizing the environmental impact of hikers on parklands. Again, to maintain trails, recreationists should pay the cost of their activities.

With trails, linking costs with revenues is as important as making sure that visitors pay for their activity. Knowing that the natural environment keeps visitors returning year after year, park managers who rely upon visitor revenue for their funding must keep the environment in tiptop shape.

Leal and Fretwell (1997, 20–25) underscore this point with their comparison of Big Bend National Park in Texas and its nearby neighbor the Big Bend Ranch State Park. The national park is not forced to balance its revenues and costs, and therefore faces serious deterioration of facilities and trails. It makes no deliberate efforts to control where visitors tread in order to limit the impact on sensitive areas of the park. The state park, in contrast, has divided Big Bend Ranch into zones where visitor activity is strictly controlled at any given time. Environmentally sensitive areas are monitored for the impacts of public use in order to reroute visitors and minimize wear and tear. This is done because the park managers must rely on returning visitors and those who prize environmental protection to pay their salaries. A poor environment means fewer tourists. When the incentives of environmental asset managers are consistent with their personal preference to protect the environment, the results are better than when managers must respond to shifting political interests in Washington.

Congestion: People, Cars, and Congestion Pricing

Many of the problems from welfare recreation boil down to one thing: congestion (too many people in one area at one time). In 1999 game wardens from Tanzania visited Yellowstone National Park. "Too many people. Too many vehicles," commented one warden. Another said, "It's like a city. How can a tourist enjoy with so many vehicles around?" (McMillion 1999b). Anderson and Leal (1991, 62) write, "As with any good, low or zero fees for federally controlled resources increase the demand and result in overcrowding and diminished quality." Problems from overcrowding result in reduced quality of a visit to a desirable locale and reduced environmental quality.

On the convenience side, roads are run down in the parks. Some of the most traveled roads in Yellowstone have not had major improvements in nearly sixty-five years. Potholes along these routes have gotten bad enough to break car axles (Janofsky 1999). In 1998 Yellowstone's Dunraven Pass was in such poor shape that it was closed to traffic until it could be repaved.

High concentrations of visitors lead to traffic jams, and id/ pollution emissions. On summer evenings at the Yavapai / the Grand Canyon National Park, the parking lot is reg\ many visitors to drive away in frustration (T. Watson 1999). Too man., tors using the facilities at one time is also a large reason for overflowing sewage systems. Built for a lower capacity, they cannot process sewage fast enough to keep up with the crowds.

Congestion was addressed in a 1999 General Accounting Office (GAO) report analyzing the success of the fee demonstration program. The report suggested that the park service needed to experiment more with different pricing structures based on use. According to the report,

> The Park Service has done little to experiment with different pricing structures. Visitors generally pay the same fee whether they are visiting during a peak period (such as a weekend in the summer) or an off-peak period (such as midweek during the winter) or whether they are staying for several hours or several days. A more innovative fee system would make fees more equitable for visitors and might change visitation patterns somewhat to enhance economic efficiency and reduce overcrowding and its effects on parks' resources. Furthermore, according to the four agencies, reducing visitation during peak periods can lower the costs of operating recreation sites by reducing (1) the staff needed to operate a site, (2) the size of facilities, (3) the need for maintenance and future capital investments and (4) the extent of damage to a site's resources. (GAO 1999, 4)

Some argue that recreational use does not commit the egregious harms that traditional commodity extraction does because it does not extract a resource. Congestion illustrates the flaw in this thinking. One reason that recreationists visit areas of natural beauty is to get away from civilization. Recreational users extract a resource by taking up a given space at a specific time. The difference between four people in a meadow and forty affects a visitor's enjoyment of nature.

The problem of too few parking spaces in the Grand Canyon viewing area is a prime example of a valuable space resource being allocated by first-come, first-served with no restriction on length of stay. Long lines and scenic views filled with not-so-scenic crowds of people lessen the outdoors experience for everyone. Despite the GAO's acknowledgment of the benefits of congestion pricing—which would bring the price charged more in line with the actual cost of recreating—the NPS is instead looking at expensive tram systems for Yosemite and the Grand Canyon as well as direct rationing, in which reservations are required for use of parts of the park system.

Plans to reduce the crowding at Yosemite have been under consideration since the General Management Plan began in 1980. According to the National Park Service's original report, "Increasing automobile traffic is the single greatest threat to enjoyment of the natural and scenic qualities of Yosemite"

.PS 1980). Four million people now visit the park annually, double the number in 1980. Under the preferred alternative for the Final Yosemite Valley Plan (the primary planning document for carrying out the goals of the General Management Plan), the following solutions were proposed to handle congestion: Overnight accommodations will be reduced by approximately 16 percent (that includes a 5 percent *increase* in camping units); day-use parking spaces in the Yosemite Valley will be reduced by about 65 percent, leaving only 550 spaces at Yosemite Village; and shuttles, biking, and hiking will provide transportation in the park (NPS 2000, 2-259 through 2-273). Eventually the planners hope to create a transit system to allow for complete removal of all private vehicles from the valley. In addition, restricting the numbers of visitors per day through a reservation system was considered (NPS 1980).

A simpler and less expensive plan to the problem of intensive use would be congestion pricing—not currently one of the options under the Yosemite Valley Plan. Congestion pricing is the reason movie matinees are cheaper than evening shows, telephone calls are less expensive on weekends, hotels have different rates during winter and summer, and airline tickets are priced differently for different days and times of the year. By raising the price at peak hours when their service is in its highest demand, companies reduce the traffic and give greater priority to those with greater demand. Congestion pricing affords everyone the option to visit Yosemite. Those who place a lower value on their trip to Yosemite can postpone their visit to the off-peak season and pay less. By applying a congestion pricing scheme, Yosemite would raise more funding, cut down on congestion, and allow visiting travelers the freedom to drive through the park. At the same time, the extra funds could be put back into enhancing the park by improving wildlife management and hiking trails instead of spending federal tax dollars on building an expensive transportation system that will benefit a fraction of the taxpayers forced to contribute to it.

Overcrowding of national parks, forests, rivers, and other recreational areas harms the environment. It leads to degradation of the wilderness, its environmental amenities, and the recreational experience by stretching the resources beyond their capacity. Yosemite even suffers from overcrowding and environmental damage due to underpricing the right to climb the world-class rock, El Capitan. Rock climber Peter Anderson observes that raw human waste and a high density of climbers have degraded the famous landmark.[4] Congestion pricing could go a long way to ending these problems.

According to the NPS, "During peak visitation periods the noise, smell, glare, and congestion associated with motor vehicles can overwhelm the resource-related visitor experience" (NPS 2000, 1–11). Increased traffic is harmful to wildlife crossing the roadways. Gridlock caused by too many visitors in one place leads to stop-and-go traffic and idling engines, both of which produce air pollution. But like the problems of inconvenience, these environmental harms could be handled by using price structures that reflect the varying demands of park use.

Vandalism and Litter

One park on the NPCA list of Parks in Jeopardy is the Chaco Culture National Historic Park. Among the threats to Chaco according to the NPCA are "inadequate funds for preservation and maintenance, tourism impacts, vandalism and looting" (NPCA 1999a). Vandalism and looting are problems that have yet to be tackled. Not surprisingly, these are also linked to welfare recreation privileges.

With increased recreational users visiting an area, there is a need for an equal increase in law enforcement. In 1989 Yellowstone National Park reached its peak staffing year. Since then, with more visitors and fewer staff, the park has experienced a significant rise in wildlife poaching, thefts, weapons charges, and violations by snowmobile drivers (Janofsky 1999). The cost of extra enforcement is not being considered in the recreational price users pay, and thus there are no funds to hire the appropriate staff.

The *New York Times* reports that criminal deterrence is an unexpected benefit of a user fee program, which attempts to align a park's revenue with the costs imposed on it. The article points out that "since Glen Canyon National Recreation Area started charging fees at the Lone Rock Campground in Utah, documented cases of assault, rape, and drunken driving dropped abruptly, according to a Park Service report, as gang activity decreased and more families began visiting" (Cushman 1999). Gene Zimmerman, forest supervisor for the San Bernardino National Forest, found the same thing from the Forest Service's user fee program, the Adventure Pass. "The anecdotal information is that the Adventure Pass is slowing vandalism in the park" (Sleeth 1999).

These stories are not surprising to private enterprises that offer recreation, such as the North Maine Woods and International Paper (IP). These two operations used to offer recreation opportunities for nothing or next to it. Littering, arson, vandalism, and damage from off-road vehicle use ended the free lunch. The two organizations began charging for recreational use on their lands. Both found that user fees reduced littering, vandalism, and criminal activity. Funds from fees helped provide the support staff to enforce rules on their land, and no doubt the higher fees discouraged vandals from entering the recreational areas in the first place. When damage did occur, fees helped to pay for the cleanup (Anderson and Leal 1991, 69; 1997, 5).

COMMERCIAL ACTIVITY VS. RECREATION: IGNORING THE ECONOMICS OF NATURE

An argument often made against forcing recreationists to pay their way is that it commercializes nature. The Website for Free Our Forests attacks the fee demonstration program. "Fee demo has nothing to do with stewardship of public lands. It is, in fact, the beginning of an attempt by corporate America to privatize and commercialize our public lands" (Free Our Forests 2001). The group also contends, "Our public lands are our heritage and our birthright. We own these lands. They are not a recreational commodity." The Sierra Club writes, "Fee Demo is designed to commercialize these lands—to extract whatever the market can bear and to encourage development of recreational facilities" (Sierra Club 1999). Scott Silver, executive director of Wild Wilderness, compares the difference between free and fee to prostitution: Fees are like the "difference between romantic love and paid sex. It changes the experience totally. It can't be wild if it's not free" (K. Watson 1999).

All of these arguments ignore the economics of recreation. Although the environmental groups and the recreational groups are asserting that pricing is bad, the latter wants unlimited free access and most of the former wants limits on "free" access. The former apparently has little regard for the havoc wreaked on natural resources from wide-open recreation, whereas the latter ignores the problem of inadequate upkeep in tax-supported federal sites.

Does charging recreationists for the costs of their activity commercialize nature? More important, is this a bad thing or even a new thing? Recent debate over allowing companies into Yellowstone National Park to bioprospect provides an interesting anecdote for contrasting recreation and other commercial activity in park areas. Microorganisms that live in the thermal areas of Yellowstone—thermophiles as they are often called—carry unique genetic material that may unleash the secrets to better beer brewing, safer bleach, or new perfumes. One product derived from a Yellowstone thermophile created a $200 million per year industry that replicates genetic material for DNA fingerprinting (Warrick 1998).

The park service recognized that Yellowstone could be receiving significant revenue if it took royalties from bioprospecting. It worked out a deal with the Diversa Corporation from San Diego to do just that. But a few environmentalists were upset and claimed that this could lead to massive resource extraction from the park. The activists sued and successfully got the deal postponed (Milstein 1999a). One of them, Mike Bader, executive director of the Alliance for the Wild Rockies, equated the Diversa deal to "a modern day gold rush." Yet according to David Barna, chief of public affairs for the park service, "Tourists on the boardwalks probably carry more [of] these thermophiles home on our sneakers than the researchers take out" (McMillion 1999c).

The activists' primary worry was that the park was heading down a dangerous path to commercialization. In his decision halting the Diversa deal until an environmental impact statement had been completed, Justice Royce C. Lamberth wrote, "Although parkgoers may be willing to forgive the trespass of their national parkland when the goals of that trespass are scientific and educational, commercial exploitation of that same parkland may reasonably be perceived as injurious" (Milstein 1999a). These worries over commercialization of our national parks are at the heart of the problem. People are unwilling to recognize that the parks already are commercialized. Recreation *is* commercial activity. Dan Janzen (1998, 40), a professor of biology at the University of Pennsylvania and a scientific adviser to the Guanacaste Conservation Area in Costa Rica, puts it this way: "The very nature-oriented tourism industry that thrives in our national parks has been conducting commercial development of biodiversity and ecosystem in, and downstream from, national parks since the first train tracks were laid to Yellowstone's front door more than 100 years ago." In fact, the formation of Yellowstone National Park stems from the commercial drive of the Northern Pacific Railroad (Anderson and Hill 1996).

Recreationists, like any other customer of a commercial venture, need to pay their share of the cost. If they do not, it is the health of the resource, nature, that will suffer. What is not mentioned by activists like Silver who compare user fees to prostitution is that unlike in free love where both parties receive benefits, a plan of free recreation affords the recreationist a benefit, but the environment just gets screwed.

CONCLUSION

Recreation is not the problem, *welfare* recreation is. Recreation coupled with user fees can be quite helpful to the environment by providing funds to maintain habitat and animals and by sensitizing users and suppliers to the values of nature and the costs of protecting those values. Programs to improve habitat for wildlife on IP lands didn't really take off until IP biologist Tom Bourland began to show that wildlife could pay its way through recreation. As Bourland puts it:

> Because the status of wildlife affected the bottom line, the landowners bent over backwards to provide habitat for whitetail deer, wild turkey, fox, squirrel, and bobwhite quail, as well as endangered bald eagles and red-cockaded woodpeckers. They left corridors of trees 100 yards wide between harvested areas through which wildlife could travel safely. They left clumps of trees uncut while younger stands next to them grew, thus creating greater age diversity. They reduced the size of cut areas and made their perimeters more irregular and therefore more attractive to a greater variety of wildlife. They did not harvest large strips of trees and shrubs along either side of streams, and they planted food plots. (quoted in Anderson and Leal 1997, 7)

Throughout the western United States, state game agencies have begun building on the recreational activity of fee hunting in order to preserve habitat.

By allowing landowners to make a profit from wildlife, the game agencies are providing another source of income to stave off development (Leal and Grewell 1999). Ecotourism is used by groups like The Nature Conservancy and the National Audubon Society to pay for ecological preservation on their lands. The Greater Yellowstone Coalition (1998, 22) offers up farm and ranch tourism as a way to protect open space. These are all examples of recreation in a commercial form helping to protect the environment. And in each of these cases, the groups involved must consider the costs of their activities versus the benefits, something that our public lands do not as yet have to do.

Recreation is not a benign activity. It imposes harms and costs on the environment. It extracts resources, not only physical ones like worn-down trails and damaged wildlife, but also more abstract ones like the nature experience of an uncrowded area. Raising the price is not enough: Revenue from fees must be put in park managers' hands so they can manage the resource without the political hand of Congress interfering with resource management. When costs are paid for by recreationists, they call the tune for better services and facility upkeep. Market-driven recreation can help preserve an environmental area by raising its value beyond that of alternate uses such as mining or grazing, and can even turn a profit. The idea of free recreational use on federal lands is a nice but utopian one. It is not practical, and it will not help protect the environmental resources on our federal lands. Commercializing recreation by way of fees may change the experience—some even claim may harm it. But ignoring that recreation is a commercial activity in itself ignores a golden opportunity to manage our lands in a way that protects the environment.

NOTES

1. See chapter 7 (Fretwell 2002) of this volume.

2. Two issues of welfare recreation, which I will not address here, are justice and the driving out of competitive private efforts. On the justice side, should taxpayers who never or seldom use the recreational amenities be forced to pay for their provision? The question becomes even more intriguing when one considers that those who benefit most from the provision of welfare recreation are the upper- and middle-class members of society who can afford trips to recreational areas. On the competition side, charging a price below that of a market price does not allow the private sector to provide recreation and environmental amenities on an equal footing. See Fretwell (1999b, 6–10). This is not beneficial to the environment, because the brunt of meeting recreational demand falls on the public sector, thereby resulting in more stress on public lands.

3. The fee demonstration numbers were taken from the Department of the Interior's 1999 report to Congress on the Recreational Fee Demonstration Program (U.S. Department of the Interior and the U.S. Department of Agriculture 2000). The budget

outlays were taken from the Public Budget Database. Total receipts taken in by the National Park Service were $150.8 million (Office of Management and Budget 2000).
   4. Personal interview with El Capitan rock climber Peter Anderson, August 8, 1999.

REFERENCES

Anderson, Terry L., and P. J. Hill. 1996. Appropriable Rents from Yellowstone: A Case of Incomplete Contracting. *Economic Inquiry* 34 (July): 506–18.

Anderson, Terry L., and Donald R. Leal. 1991. *Free Market Environmentalism.* San Francisco, CA: Pacific Research Institute for Public Policy.

———. 1997. *Enviro-Capitalists: Doing Good While Doing Well.* Lanham, MD: Rowman & Littlefield.

———. 2001. *Free Market Environmentalism,* rev. ed. New York: Palgrave.

Belnap, Jayne. 1999. Cryptobiotic Soil Crust. April 15. Online: www.nps.gov/seug/resource/ecology/cryptos.htm (cited: March 7, 2001).

Cushman, John H., Jr. 1999. Priorities in the National Parks. *New York Times,* July 26.

Free Our Forests. 2001. Why Is the Recreational Fee Demonstration Program Wrong? Let Us Count the Ways. Online: www.freeourforests.org/whywrong.htm (cited: March 21, 2001).

Fretwell, Holly Lippke. 1998. The Price We Pay. *Public Lands.* Bozeman, MT: PERC, August.

———. 1999a. Forests: Do We Get What We Pay For? *Public Lands II.* Bozeman, MT: PERC, July.

———. 1999b. Paying to Play: The Fee Demonstration Program. *PERC Policy Series,* PS-17. Bozeman, MT: PERC.

———. 2002. The Untouchables: America's National Forests. Chapter 7 this volume.

General Accounting Office. 1999. *Recreation Fees: Demonstration Has Increased Revenues, but Impact on Park Service Backlog Is Uncertain.* GAO-RCED-99-101. Washington, DC.

Greater Yellowstone Coalition. 1998. *Incentives for Conserving Open Lands in Greater Yellowstone.* Bozeman, MT.

Hebert, H. Josef. 1999. Neglecting National Parks. *Associated Press,* April 20. Online: http://www.abcnews.go.com/sections/science/DailyNews/parks990420.html (cited: March 18, 2001).

Janofsky, Michael. 1999. National Parks, Strained by Record Crowds, Face a Crisis. *New York Times,* July 25.

Janzen, Dan. 1998. Bioprospecting and Public-Private Benefit Sharing in the U.S. National Parks. *Environmental Forum* (July/August): 38–45.

Leal, Donald R., and Holly Lippke Fretwell. 1997. Back to the Future to Save Our Parks. *PERC Policy Series,* PS-10. Bozeman, MT: PERC.

Leal, Donald R., and J. Bishop Grewell. 1999. *Hunting for Habitat: A Practical Guide to State-Landowner Partnerships.* Bozeman, MT: PERC.

McMillion, Scott. 1999a. Panel Earmarks Funds for Yellowstone Park Sewer Improvements. *Bozeman Daily Chronicle,* June 25.

———. 1999b. An African Perspective: Game Wardens from Tanzania Tour the First National Park. *Bozeman Daily Chronicle,* August 8.

———. 1999c. Judge Nixes Yellowstone's Microbe Deal. *Bozeman Daily Chronicle*, March 26.

Milstein, Michael. 1999a. Judge Disallows Yellowstone's Microbe Agreement. *Billings Gazette*, March 26.

———. 1999b. Park Sewage Overflows. *Billings Gazette*, July 12.

Moen, Bob. 1999. Geyser of Effluent Strains Yellowstone's Budget, Environment. *Los Angeles Times*, July 11.

National Parks and Conservation Association. 1999a. *Parks in Jeopardy: NPCA's 1999 List of 10 Most Endangered National Parks*. Crumbling Treasures: Chaco Culture National Historical Park. Online: www.npca.org/readaboutit/tt_chaco.html (cited: July 30, 1999).

———. 1999b. Parks in Jeopardy: NPCA's 1999 List of 10 Most Endangered National Parks. Introduction. Online: www.npca.org/readaboutit/tt_introduction.html (cited: July 30, 1999).

———. 1999c. Parks in Jeopardy: NPCA's 1999 List of 10 Most Endangered National Parks. Muddying the Waters: Yellowstone National Park. Online: www.npca.org/readaboutit/tt_yellowstone.html (cited: July 30, 1999).

National Park Service. 1980. General Management Plan for Yosemite National Park. Preface and introduction. September. Online: www.nps.gov/yose/planning/gmp/intro80.html (cited: March 7, 2001).

———. 1999. Recreation Visits: Decade Files in PDF Format. June 24. Online: www2.nature.nps.gov/stats/decadepdfs.htm (cited: August 2, 2000).

———. 2000. Yosemite Valley Plan. November. Online: www.nps.gov/yose/planning/yvp/seis/pdf/Volume_IA.pdf (cited: March 7, 2001).

Office of Management and Budget. 2000. Budget of the United States Government: Fiscal Year 2000. Online: www.access.gpo.gov/usbudget/fy2000/other.html (cited: March 18, 2001).

Pound, Edward T. 1997. Panel Chair Raps Park Service on $1M Outhouse: Congressman Wants Explanation. *USA Today*, December 18.

Sierra Club Yodeler. 1999. The Corporate Takeover of Nature. Online: tamalpais.sierraclub.org/chapters/sanfranciscobay/yodeler/199905/corporate.html (cited: August 20, 2000).

Sleeth, Peter. 1999. Saving Mount Hood from Our Loving Soles. *Oregonian*, February 21.

Tennesen, Michael. 1998. The Road Less Traveled. *National Parks*, May–June.

U.S. Department of Agriculture, Forest Service. 2001. FY 2002 Budget Justification. Online: www.fs.fed.us/database/budgetoffice/NFS_2.pdf (cited: November 28, 2001).

U.S. Department of the Interior, Bureau of Land Management. 2001. Budget Justifications and Annual Performance Plan 2002. Online: www.blm.gov/budget/2002just.html (cited: November 28, 2001).

U.S. Department of the Interior and the U.S. Department of Agriculture. 2000. *Recreational Fee Demonstration Program Progress Report to Congress Fiscal Year 1999*. Washington, DC: National Park Service, Fish and Wildlife Service, Bureau of Land Management, and Forest Service, January 31.

Warrick, Joby. 1998. Yellowstone: A Gold Mine of Microbes. *Washington Post*, July 12.

Watson, Keri. 1999. The Wayward West. *High Country News*, August 30.

Watson, Tracy. 1999. Visitors' Cars Not Welcome. *USA Today*, August 20.

Wilderness Society. 1999. Putting Conservation First. Online: www.wilderness.org/newsroom/15most_1999/15most_report.pdf (cited: March 7, 2001).

10

Castles in the Sand: The Army Corps of Engineers and Federal Beach Replenishment

Clay J. Landry

No federal agency has more influence on our nation's beaches than the U.S. Army Corps of Engineers (USACE). Few people probably think of the corps during a typical day at the beach, yet the agency is largely responsible for hundreds of the sandy stretches that buffer coastal communities. Ironically the agency is also responsible for the demise of some beaches. Each year it spends millions to fight the forces of nature that erode, shift, and ultimately reshape the coastline. These efforts are carried out without a clear understanding of the costs, benefits, and ecological effects of shoreline protection.

Shoreline erosion is a serious problem for much of the nation's coastline. The corps estimated in 1972 that 40 percent of the country's shoreline experienced significant erosion (Morris 1992, 122). More recent predictions estimate that over the next sixty years, erosion will claim one out of four houses within 500 feet of the shoreline (Heinz Center 2000, 1). To fight against the pounding waves of erosion, the corps initially armored beaches with jetties and sea walls. That armoring, however, exacerbated the problem in many places by blocking the natural drift of sand. Beach replenishment or nourishment has become the latest weapon against the forces of nature. Replenishment involves using large barges to suck sand off of the ocean floor and pump it onto nearby beaches. This approach has become a compromise between armoring or retreating from the coastline.

In recent years the federal shoreline protection program and beach replenishment have come under increasing scrutiny. Most funding for replenishment projects comes from federal taxes, yet the recreational and storm protection benefits provided by artificial beaches are enjoyed by a select few. Supporters of federal shoreline protection believe that sand replenishment is worth every penny. They claim that without the program damages to coastal properties could reach as high as $530 million a year (Heinz Center 2000, 11). They also argue that public funding is essential because without it the cost of replenishment projects is far too expensive for most coastal property owners and local communities. Critics see replenishment as a waste of taxpayer money to subsidize private shoreline property. Others question the real benefit of beach replenishment when compared with untold environmental damages.

This chapter examines the corps shoreline protection program by looking at the overall cost to taxpayers and the environmental uncertainties associated with replenishment. It begins with a review of the agency's evolution into shoreline protection and beach replenishment. It also examines how expenditures for replenishment projects have steadily increased since its first project. The allocation of those funds among coastal communities, as well as the cost of various types of replenishment projects, are discussed, followed by a review of beach replenishment environmental issues. Finally, privately funded beach protection methods are presented. These projects illustrate that property owners and communities do invest in beach replenishment when given the right incentives.

HISTORY AND BACKGROUND

For more than 200 years, the Army Corps of Engineers has helped defend our country's shores from foreign invaders and marauders. Shortly after its creation in 1779, it went to work fortifying the nation's shores by building military installations. It built numerous harbors and forts, including Fort Henry, where Francis Scott Key wrote the "Star Spangled Banner." That focus changed dramatically during the first part of the twentieth century. The agency's new mission was to defend the nation's beaches from nature.

Corps evolution into coastal protection was incremental. Policies and programs governing coastal protection have been driven primarily by disaster. "Over the past sixty years the federal government has lurched from one approach to another, according to the conventional wisdom of the movement and the whims of congressional appropriations process" (Platt et al. 1992, 12).

Until the 1930s, the corps and the federal government viewed beaches as a problem for the states. At that time the agency's primary duties consisted of dredging, jetty construction, and other activities related to shipping and waterway commerce. The federal government left beach protection to the states. Congress also took a dim view of using federal taxpayer money to protect private shoreline property. The American Shore and Beach Preservation, the nation's first beach lobby group, however, played a significant role in changing that view. It pressured Congress to deploy the corps, arguing that beaches were a national concern because beach visitors came from other states.

Congress agreed, and in 1930 it passed the Rivers and Harbors Act, commissioning the corps to fight beach erosion (Shallant 1994, 147). Physical devices such as jetties and sea walls were built to trap sand and halt erosion. These structures, however, pushed erosion problems onto neighboring areas by blocking sand movement. The approach appeared to be successful at first because most coasts were undeveloped. There was little concern if neighboring beaches eroded as long as buildings or property was not threatened. The strategy became problematic as coastal development grew. Landowners and communities began complaining about erosion and pointed to jetties and sea walls as the culprit. That realization marked a change in the way the corps approached beach erosion. It turned to temporary, nonstructural fixes such as pumping sand, to deal with the problem.

The nation's first beach replenishment project began in 1922 on Coney Island (National Research Council [NRC] 1995, 11). The project was funded and carried out primarily by beachfront property owners (the corps did not start pumping sand until the 1950s). The first significant federal replenishment project occurred in 1962, after a storm devastated beachfront property up and down the eastern seaboard. The damage was so severe in New Jersey that Congress called on the corps to help restore the state's beaches.

Pumping sand has become the leading method for slowing coastal erosion and repairing storm damage. Since the 1950s, more than 1,300 replenishment projects on nearly 400 beaches have been recorded (Trembanis, Pilkey, and Valverde 1999, 329). The majority of these projects were sponsored by the federal government, with the Army Corps of Engineers taking the lead. The agency has made its mark on America's beaches, but the success of these efforts is mixed at best.

GROWING THE CORPS

In the fall of 2000, the *Washington Post* broke a story of corruption and greed that reached the highest ranks of the Army Corps of Engineers (Grunwald 2000). The *Post* exposed a covert operation engineered by top brass to increase their budget and power. The operation, dubbed Grow the Corps, outlined ways to funnel more money into coffers by lobbying Congress and faking feasibility studies. For those familiar with the corps, the story came as no surprise. The agency has a long track record of lobbying Congress for special projects. As far back as the 1800s, critics have linked its waste and corruption with Congress (Shallant 1994, 5). This time, however, corps officials were caught red-handed with a detailed plan for expanding the agency's budget.

Federal funding of beach replenishment projects has grown substantially under the direction of the corps. Although there is significant variability from year to year, the general trend of funding has been upward. Overall, federal funding for replenishment has increased from $5 million in 1950 to about $60 million in 1990 (USACE 1996, iv-12). Officially the corps takes a neutral position in the debate over replenishment appropriations. The agency claims that it responds to requests by local and state governments. Cost and feasibility studies are undertaken once a local sponsor has applied for a project. That position is difficult to believe in light of the *Washington Post* discovery. In fact, the agency has taken an active role in developing projects, with officials openly encouraging and assisting local and state governments and developers in lobbying for projects. The American Littoral Society, an environmental group, claims the corps has tried to encourage a number of New Jersey towns to apply for replenishment projects. As a result, New Jersey has some of the region's most replenished beaches (Trembanis, Pilkey, and Valverde 1999, 331).

Based on recent congressional action, the replenishment program will continue to grow. The 1999 Water Resources Development Act, the primary piece of legislation for financing corps activities, funded a dozen new beach projects. More than 100 shore protection and beach replenishment projects are at various planning stages, most with fifty-year commitments. An ongoing replenishment project in New Jersey represents the escalation in the agency's efforts. The project will provide 100-foot-wide beaches along all 127 miles of the state's coast. When complete, it will be the largest replenishment project in the nation's history at a cost of more than $9 billion over the next fifty years (Stein et al. 2000, 25). At least 65 percent of the cost will be paid by federal taxpayers. If fully funded, the estimated $5.6 billion in federal cost share for New Jersey alone would exceed the total federal expenditure on all replenishment projects ever.

BEACH REPLENISHMENT COST AND EXPENDITURES

Funding beach replenishment has become a central issue in the debate over coastal development. The controversy centers on who should pay and, more fundamentally, whether it is worth the expense. Ironically no one is certain how much money has been spent on beach replenishment. Corps records on replenishment projects are incomplete, but the agency attempted to estimate the cost of its program in a review of major projects since 1956 (USACE 1996). The report was prepared at the request of the Office of Management and Budget and during a time when the Clinton administration was considering various reforms for federal funding of shoreline protection.

The corps estimated that more than $1.4 billion has been spent on beach replenishment (USACE 1996, viii). Officials are quick to point out that the average annual cost of replenishment is $35 million and that this is a relatively small amount of taxpayer money when compared with other subsidy programs. Replenishment advocates such as James Houston, the agency's chief engineer, believe that this is a small price to pay for beach protection (Houston 1995, 21). Orrin Pilkey of Duke University, an ardent critic of federal replenishment, contends that the actual cost of the projects is understated. He and several other colleagues estimated total expenditures to be closer to $2 or $3 billion, with current annual expenditures of more than $100 million (Trembanis, Pilkey, and Valverde 1999, 337).

Some wonder why the corps does not maintain cost records (Trembanis, Pilkey, and Valverde 1999), but the corps counters that there is no funding in place for such information (USACE 1996, 104). The lack of information and data gaps work to the agency's advantage. Without performance and expenditure information, it is able to make exaggerated claims about the durability and cost-effectiveness of beach projects (Pilkey and Dixon 1996, 78); it also contends that its projects have performed as predicted and that costs were within expected budgets. By its own admission, however, the lack of data makes it difficult to assess (USACE 1996, 106).

The 1996 corps review found that most projects finish on time and on budget. But the review showed that cost overruns are more common for larger projects. The overruns averaged 24 percent for projects that cost between $10 and $50 million and 5 percent for projects greater than $50 million (USACE 1996, iv-19), but even these estimates are questionable because the agency is notorious for underreporting. For example, in a 1994 report, it claimed that a replenishment project on Carolina Beach, North Carolina, had budget overruns of about 100 percent. Yet an investigation of the project showed that the project's actual cost was severely underreported with overruns closer to 1,300 percent over original estimates presented to Congress (Pilkey and Dixon 1996, 89).

Tracking corps expenditures is difficult because of the various ways the agency can fund replenishment projects. There are five different funding sources for replenishment projects: flood control, emergency repair, navigation, beach erosion control, and mitigation of damage caused by previous corps projects. Each category has different design, cost-sharing, and planning requirements.

The corps uses the different categories to play a shell game of funding; consequently some replenishment projects go unrecorded. For example, the agency reported that Wrightsville Beach, North Carolina, received 4.6 million cubic yards of sand at a total cost of $25 million in two separate pumping operations between 1965 and 1984 (USACE 1984, 74). In fact, 6.9 million cubic yards with a price tag of nearly $30 million had been pumped onto the beach in six separate operations during that time (Leonard, Dixon, and Pilkey 1990, 134).

The four unrecorded projects were authorized as navigation projects. The corps is required to dispose of dredging materials in the cheapest manner possible and often sells the dredged sand to local cities to offset the cost of dredging and disposal. The sand is simply pumped onto a beach and spread around with bulldozers. The corps does not consider these replenishment projects even though sand is pumped onto a beach; consequently, they are not recorded as replenishment operations. The navigation authorization is a popular way of funding projects when local cost-sharing requirements cannot be met. Between 10 and 35 percent of all federally funded projects are authorized under the navigation category (Trembanis, Pilkey, and Valverde 1999, 335).

Beach replenishment has occurred in nearly every state with a coastline. Some coastlines, however, have seen more projects; the eastern coast barrier islands have the nation's most replenished beaches (more than 345 million cubic yards have been placed on 147 East Coast beaches; table 10.1). The region also received the most financial support—a total of $1.7 billion, nearly five times more than any other area (Trembanis, Pilkey, and Valverde 1999, 335).

To qualify for funding, projects must prevent flood damage to private and public property. Thus, federal policies limit shore protection projects to densely developed areas with high economic value (NRC 1995, 14). The large disparity in protection efforts among the regions reflects the economic importance of the East Coast's recreational beaches. It also illustrates how subsidies are directed to wealthy areas.

Pumping costs also vary across regions and among funding sources. The New England region had the highest pumping costs at $11.71 per cubic yard. Compared with others states like North Carolina and Florida, pumping projects are more difficult to carry out along the sharp, craggy New England coast.

Projects authorized with federal navigation funds usually had lower pumping costs than other federal projects within a region. For example, pumping costs for navigation projects along the Gulf Coast were approximately half the cost of other federal projects. The lower costs reflect that navigation projects have limited standards and requirements for pumping sand.

Table 10.1 Regional Beach Replenishment Expenditures and Volume, 1956 to 1996

Region	Expenditures ($1,000)	Volume of Sand (cubic yards)	Average Cost per Cubic Yard
East Coast	$1,740,966	344,708,000	$5.05
Gulf Coast	361,842	75,894,000	4.77
Great Lakes	196,277	24,968,000	7.86
New England	140,279	11,979,000	11.71

Source: Program for the Study of Developed Shorelines (2001).

Privately funded beach replenishment tends to be less expensive than publicly funded projects. The average cost from 1950 to 1993 for local and privately funded projects was $4 per cubic yard, compared with the $5 per cubic yard for federal projects (Trembanis, Pilkey, and Valverde 1999, 337).

PAYING THE BILL FOR BEACH REPLENISHMENT

A common criticism of federal shoreline protection is that the beneficiaries of a project contribute a fraction of the cost, whereas the majority of the costs are paid by taxpayers. One way to curb the subsidy appetite of coastal communities is to increase the cost-sharing requirement—those who directly benefit pay a larger share of the costs. Even James Houston, corps chief engineer supports this idea. "The person who lives right on the coast, it seems like maybe they ought to pay more than somebody that lives inland or lives in the middle of the state" (quoted in Gaul and Wood 2000, 14).

For most replenishment projects, the federal government covers 65 percent of the cost; state and local governments are required to cover the remaining 35 percent. On average, the corps meets this federal requirement. The agency's 1996 review showed that the federal government and taxpayers paid for approximately 60 percent of the total cost of all replenishment projects built between 1950 and 1993. The report found that the federal share increased to 66 percent for projects in construction after 1993, but that there were wide variations in federal cost sharing among projects (USACE 1996, ix). This is particularly true for more recent projects; federal contribution after 1993 varied from a low of 13 percent to 100 percent.

Several attempts have been made to reform federal funding for shoreline protection. In 1995 the Clinton administration proposed to increase the cost-share requirement for local sponsors to 75 percent. The proposal also would have increased the benefit-cost ratio requirement to at least two, up from the present requirement of one. The administration's proposal included a sizable slice of pork. In an attempt to gain support from the agency and local beach protection groups, the bill included provisions that increased funding to states and local communities for planning and implementing replenishment projects that would no longer be covered by the corps. It is questionable whether the proposal would have led to reform. It would have increased the local cost-sharing requirement but made more federal funds available to state and local governments.

Changing the benefit-cost ratio requirement is unlikely to have much effect on funding decisions. The agency is well aware that the ratio is a critical determinant in the success of all the agency's projects. Congress funds only projects with favorable ratios, and corps district budgets are based on the cost of congressionally approved projects. The districts are also responsible for conducting the initial benefit-cost analysis that Congress relies upon when approving funding. Consequently there is enormous pressure at the district level to show favorable ratios for costly projects. This is reflected in the agency's record of underestimating costs and over-stating benefits. In 2000 a career staff economist came forward with allegations that senior district officials were manipulating key economic results to improve the benefit-cost ratio for a major shipping channel project. The allegations spurred an investigation that determined that this was a widespread problem throughout the agency (Department of Defense 2000). Though not always as blatant as the most recent scandal, analysis problems are common for coastal projects. The corps tends to estimate the cost for the best-case scenario and does not account for the dynamic variability of projects along a coastline (Pilkey and Dixon 1996, 227).

Increasing the cost-share requirements could substantially change the size, scope, and frequency of projects. Demand for federal funding by coastal communities and other replenishment supporters would likely lessen if they were responsible for a larger portion of a project's cost. Cost-sharing reforms for other federal water projects have had similar effects.

A study sponsored by the National Bureau of Economic Research analyzed cost-sharing changes in the 1986 federal Water Resources Development Act, the primary funding bill for federal water projects. The bill required, for the first time, that local governments cover 30 to 50 percent of these costs. The study found that the law resulted in a 35 percent drop in overall spending, along with a 48 percent drop in federal outlays to the states (DelRossi and Inman 1998, 30).

Prior to 1986, state and local officials routinely asked congressional representatives for a new dam, harbor, or shipping channel. To make local constituents happy by bringing federal support to their districts, members of Congress would insert local projects into the federal water bill. Consequently federal taxpayers would pay for projects with limited national interest. The change in cost-sharing requirements, however, forced local and state governments to become more fiscally responsible. The National Bureau of Economic Research study found that requests were reduced or redirected to smaller projects (DelRossi and Inman 1998, 30). "The message is that if someone gives you something for free, you want a lot of it. If you have to pay for a portion of that something, you want less," comments Robert Inman, the study's coauthor (as quoted in Shell 1999).

WHO BENEFITS FROM BEACH REPLENISHMENT PROJECTS?

Federal replenishment projects are intended to protect shorelines against flooding and erosion. Projects designed solely to create recreational beaches are not eligible for funding. In fact, most artificial beach projects serve both purposes, but the reality is that the demand for federal subsidies is driven more by recreational interests than storm protection. Former congressman Mike Synar of Oklahoma observed that it is the local chambers of commerce that lobby Congress for beach projects, not local emergency preparedness officials (Pilkey and Dixon 1996, 94).

Many seaside communities staunchly defend the federal replenishment program. For example, the National Wildlife Federation and the Taxpayers for Common Sense published a report in 2000 chronicling twenty-five environmentally harmful and financially wasteful corps projects. Number ten on that list was a $70 million plan to pump sand onto Fire Island, a barrier island off the coast of Long Island, New York. The notoriety upset the Fire Island Association, the local homeowner's group, which issued a scathing response.

Fire Island is a narrow, thirty-two-mile sliver of sand located less than an hour from New York City. It is accessible only by ferry, and vehicle traffic is largely restricted. There are more than 3,800 privately owned properties onto the island, many of which are weekend or vacation homes. It is also home to several parks and protected areas, including the Fire Island National Seashore. Beach erosion has become a problem in recent years. On several occasions, storms have threatened to breach the tiny island and wipe out several miles of beachfront property.

The corps and the Fire Island Association devised a pumping project as a temporary solution to the erosion problem. Sand would be pumped onto twelve miles of Fire Island, including six miles of the national seashore. The association is hoping to revive an $800 million federal plan to permanently stabilize barrier island beaches along Long Island (Stoddard 2000). That plan was shelved during the Carter administration due to high costs and uncertain benefits.

Former representative Rick Lazio led the charge on Capitol Hill for the interim project. He is a longtime supporter of federally financed restoration projects and occasionally holds campaign fund-raisers on the island. In fact, he owns a vacation home in Fair Harbor, one of Fire Island's seventeen communities. Some have accused Lazio of supporting the bill because he could benefit financially from the project (McCoy 2000). "Why is the federal government paying for virtually private beaches for Rick Lazio and his beach buddies?" asks Jeff Stein of Taxpayers for Common Sense (as quoted in McCoy 2000). Lazio dismissed criticism by noting his support for the project is no different than his support for federal funding for the public schools his children attend.

One of the main criticisms raised by the National Wildlife Federation and Taxpayers for Common Sense is that the local community and homeowners will pay less than 7 percent of the project's construction costs (Stein et al. 2000, 26). The Fire Island Association ignores the fact that federal taxpayers will be tapped for more than $65 million for a temporary solution to protect private beach homes. The association asserts that Fire Island's beaches and homes provide numerous economic benefits. Although this may be true, it is unclear why the localized benefits warrant overwhelming federal funding.

SAND CASTLE SCIENCE: HERE TODAY, GONE TOMORROW

The corps has had mixed results with beach replenishment. Some beaches are highly stable, lasting twenty to thirty years before major maintenance is needed. Others, however, disappear quickly. For example, in 1982, the engineers constructed a $5 million beach in Ocean City, New Jersey, that disappeared in three months.

The corps is generally optimistic in its predictions of the life span of most artificial beaches—too optimistic, some claim. Predictions of twenty to thirty years are not uncommon. Yet a Duke University's Program for the Study of Developed Shorelines showed that less than 12 percent of artificial beaches on the Atlantic Coast and 10 percent on the Gulf Coast lasted more than five years (Pilkey and Dixon 1996, 87). The study also found that most artificial beaches lasted only one to five years. The short life span has some people wondering if the corps is doing nothing more than building castles in the sand to be swept away by the next storm.

One reason for the high variability of success for beach projects is that the engineers fail to account for local factors that affect stability (Pilkey and Dixon 1996, 87), relying almost exclusively on mathematical models to predict a beach's longevity. These models, however, are a generalized view of the world and are unable to account for important site-specific factors, argues Pilkey.

Mathematical models of beach behavior suffer because science and engineering are at a rudimentary state of understanding surf zone processes and have no way to measure most of them. The models do not take into account the uncertainty of storms and the interaction of different processes going on at the same time. And they make the incorrect assumption that all beaches are the same. (Pilkey and Dixon 1996, 62)

By incorporating local and regional knowledge of beach durability, the Duke researchers used corps data to come up with what they believe are more realistic durability predictions for replenishment projects. Table 10.2 shows a comparison of some of the durability predictions with those estimated by Duke's shoreline development program. In nearly all cases, the corps estimates are more than ten times greater than the ones calculated by Duke researchers.

Table 10.2   Estimated Life Span of Artificial Beaches (Years)

Beach	Corps Life Span Estimate	Duke Life Span Estimate
Seabright, NJ	30	1–4
Ocean City, NJ	11.5	1–3
Sandbridge, VA	6–7	1–3
Topsail Beach, NC	12	2–5
N. Myrtle Beach, SC	36	3–5
Myrtle Beach, SC	36	2–4
Garden City, SC	12	2–4
Folly Beach, SC	24	1–3

Source: Pilkey and Dixon (1996).

Again, the corps has an incentive to overestimate the durability of replenishment projects: Life span estimates directly relate to a project's benefit-cost ratio—longer life spans mean larger benefits. And large, positive benefit-cost ratios are crucial for projects to move forward. The agency is also well aware that Congress is unlikely to stop funding partially completed projects. Congress continues funding a project even if it does not perform as well as originally projected. For example, as in the case of the Carolina Beach project, it continued to approve funding despite massive overruns (Pilkey and Clayton 1987, 7).

THE ENVIRONMENTAL IMPACTS OF BEACH REPLENISHMENT PROJECTS

Beach replenishment is often viewed as more environmentally friendly than other beach stabilization methods. In a lengthy examination of replenishment, the National Research Council noted that "beach nourishment is a viable engineering alternative for shore protection and is the principal technique for beach restoration" (NRC 1995, 28). Although beach replenishment may be a better option for protecting oceanfront property than hardened structures such as sea walls and jetties, the environmental impacts are largely unknown and little studied.

Yet the limited but growing evidence suggests that replenishment causes more harm than good. According to Kevin Moody, a U.S. Fish and Wildlife Service biologist, there are no documented cases in which a plant or animal community has been fully restored after a replenishment project. Water turbidity, habitat loss, and sedimentation are all problems connected with replenishment. Some scientists believe that replenishment is causing siltation in coastal reef areas. For example, sediment loading in coral reefs off the coast of Miami Beach is a recurring problem: The reefs are being buried alive by sand that is washed away from continually replenished beaches (Pilkey and Dixon 1996, 85).

There is also concern that sand pumping has disrupted nesting and breeding habitat for many coastal species such as sea turtles (NRC 1995, 111). The ability of hatchlings to survive is partially determined by the nest habitat. If the replenished sand is darker or has high silt content, it may increase the sand's temperature, which is significant because the sex of the turtle is determined by the nest temperature. Warmer nests could change the population structure if there is more of one sex. Another concern for the turtles is the frequent formation of erosion scarps on replenished beaches. Such scarps or small cliffs block the turtles' path to drier nesting areas on the beaches.

Beach replenishment projects are also accused of encouraging coastal development. Compared with inland communities, many coastal areas have experienced high growth rates. The cause, however, of the growth is not entirely clear. The corps asserts that its shore protection efforts do not cause development (USACE 1996, xii), but critics counter that development is inevitable where the federal government subsidizes construction of artificial beaches.

The Atlantic and Gulf Coast barrier islands are areas where corps beach protection and development seem to be synonymous. Barrier islands are particularly important for the protection of mainland ocean fronts, serving as the first line of defense from ocean storms. Before 1945, development covered approximately 10 percent of the barrier islands along the Atlantic and Gulf Coasts. By the early 1980s, barrier islands were being developed at a rate of 6,000 acres a year (Ackerman 1997, 18). More than 50 percent of the total historical volume of sand pumped onto these coasts coincided with growth. The question remains whether replenishment causes growth or if the corps is simply responding to development patterns. Only one study to date, sponsored in part by the corps, attempts to address this question. It examined growth in forty-two beach communities from Maine to Texas to determine if federally subsidized beach protection projects induce development.

The study found that average annual rate of growth in beach housing units between 1960 and 1992 was 50 percent higher than the average for the entire nation (Cordes and Yezer 1998, 128). Yet these numbers include all beaches, not just the ones where the engineers were active. The study isolated those areas to compare growth between beach communities with and without federal shore protection projects, and found a small difference. The average annual rate of growth in housing units was 4.1 percent in areas with projects, whereas it was 3.8 percent in communities in which the corps was not active (Cordes and Yezer 1997, 4).

The study concluded that government programs that lower the economic losses from storms can induce development; however, the link between coastal development and federally funded replenishment projects was unclear. Many coastal communities have indeed experienced substantial growth following the approval of corps replenishment projects. The study cites that development may have been caused by other economic factors (Cordes and Yezer 1998, 128) and concluded that federal programs such as subsidized flood insurance have a greater influence on coastal development than beach restoration projects, an issue discussed in Gerard (2002).

PRIVATE ALTERNATIVES

Coastal communities often contend that they simply cannot afford the cost of shoreline protection with federal assistance. Yet along the barrier islands of South Carolina, private property owners are demonstrating that protection can occur without federal or state aid. Hilton Head Island was one of the first places to undertake private efforts to protect local beaches. Other coastal islands including Seabrook, Kiawah, Dewees, and Dataw are following the Hilton Head example. In total more than thirty South Carolina beach communities are financing beach protection projects without federal aid (Rinehart and Pompe 1997, 551). The beaches are privately owned on all the islands, providing property owners with an incentive to maximize the value of their property.

One reason so many communities argue for public funding is that most of the nation's beaches are not privately held. The absence of property rights creates incentive problems as well, giving rise to many of the environmental problems in coastal areas. When ownership rights are not defined, users have little incentive to invest their own money in beach protection. Without private ownership, coastal property owners are unable to exclude potential beach-goers; therefore, property owners are unable to realize the full value of their beaches. Consequently landowners are reluctant to invest their own resources into beach protection.

Beach privatization, as demonstrated in South Carolina, helps internalize the cost of maintaining those areas. On Hilton Head, residents paid to have sand brought in, widening the beach by 150 feet; this improvement increased the value of an oceanfront house by an average of $22,718 (Pompe and Rinehart 1994, 145). But federal money for replenishment projects comes with strings: Communities that participate in federal shore protection projects must provide public access to the replenished area. For communities with private beaches, accepting federal money would mean opening their sandy lands at zero price. Also, the corps often wants to construct large dunes that block beach views. Communities such as Seabrook and Dewees are paying for their own restoration so that property owners retain the private use of their beaches and the ocean view (Rinehart and Pompe 1997, 554).

Private or community beach protection projects are funded in a variety of ways. The most common approaches are through annual beach taxes or special assessments that are approved and imposed by local property owners. Not all projects are approved, however. At Seabrook, beach residents rejected a proposal from the local property owner's association to pump 300,000 cubic yards of sand onto a nearby beach (Rinehart and Pompe 1999, 8). The project would have cost each owner $357, but it failed. The majority of residents were not convinced that the project was necessary or worth the expense.

Coastal communities in other states are also choosing to pay for protection measures, but the number is still small when compared with federal replenishment projects. Less than 5 percent of all beach nourishment projects are funded with private or local money. Most are considerably smaller in scale and usually carried out at considerably lower costs than federal or state projects. The projects tend to be less bureaucratic and are better able to respond to varying annual sand losses. As a result, most locally managed projects are quite successful and carried out more efficiently than federal projects (Trembanis, Pilkey, and Valverde 1999, 337).

There are a variety of reasons that some areas choose to pay for their own beach protection. For example, the communities of South Seas Plantation and Jupiter Island, Florida, pay for their own artificially nourished beaches to avoid the public access stipulation that comes with public money. Other communities see self-funding as a way to improve beach management. Virginia Beach, Virginia, replenished its beaches with its own resources, to avoid the corps's inflexible rules and rigid replenishment standards.

A 1972 study conducted by the city and the agency reviewed the performance of replenishment at Virginia Beach and found that small annual nourishments were more effective than larger nourishments spaced several years apart. Larger volumes of sand disappeared more rapidly. In 1995 Virginia Beach asked the corps for help. The agency began pumping large volumes of sand onto the beach in three-year intervals despite the findings of the 1972 report (Pilkey and Dixon 1996, 83). This action illustrates the agency's tendency toward large-scale projects.

The experience on South Carolina's barrier islands, as well as other beaches, clearly demonstrates that beach protection can be effectively carried out without public money and federal intervention and shows the close link between private property rights and environmental protection. Protection efforts on many of these beaches would not have occurred without the ability of beachfront property owners to realize the value of their investment.

Privatization encourages innovation, adaptation to local conditions, development of creative protection, and replenishment methods beyond the agency's one-size-fits-all, large-scale projects.

PAYING THE PRICE OF BEACH PROTECTION

The corps has been shown to engage in some shady practices, jacking up benefit costs to make sure that projects are built. But this is old hat for the agency. It has done this for years and has built many projects, such as dams in the West, that have a horrible benefit-cost ratio. But the corps is not fooling Congress, which in fact is well informed and knows the game better than anyone and could put a stop to inefficient projects. Unfortunately, members and their constituents like the largess they bring home.

For example, federal tax dollars collected from Oregon to Florida pay for beaches in New Jersey—a great deal for beachfront property owners in New Jersey, who get subsidized beach protection that they could obviously pay for on their own. Alternatively, the New Jersey legislature could appropriate state tax revenues for beach protection. The state would have more incentives to be careful with its own money than New Jersey senators appropriating federal taxpayer dollars for local pork barrel projects.

The cost of federal beach replenishment is shared equally by taxpayers even if there is no beach in their state—people in Montana support coastal beaches even if they may never step foot on them. Furthermore, if coastal states engaged in beach replenishment, they would be less likely to follow the corps model. As we see from the Virginia Beach example, coastal states and communities would be more likely to be a model adapted to local beach conditions. Hence, if such replenishment is to occur, coastal states could do it more efficiently and be more attuned to local environmental conditions.

The other question is that of federal subsidies captured by private builders. There is no justification for federal taxpayer money paying for replenishment projects along Miami Beach. Hotels and other property owners who capture the benefits could tax themselves to pay for such projects. Again, several communities in South Carolina demonstrate that local taxes offer an alternative to funding shoreline protection.

Ultimately, the problem is not the corps. The corps is no different from any other federal agency that responds to Congress. The agency is not filled with corrupt people trying to do bad things—it does what Congress tells it to do. Given that the environmental consequences are at best neutral, and perhaps negative, there is even less justification for this activity. It is just one more case of Washington taking from Peter to pay Paul; there is no economic or environmental justification for that transaction.

CONCLUSION

Beach replenishment projects obviously create value for landowners and local residents. Otherwise local governments and groups like the Fire Island Association would not seek and defend federal funding so vehemently. But there are a number of unresolved issues regarding the federal beach replenishment program. The costs, benefits, and environmental consequences are unclear. Regardless, federal support for beach nourishment is difficult to justify especially when some private landowners show a willingness and ability to pay for the protection of their own beaches.

Most advocates and critics agree that some reform is needed. Those directly benefiting from beach replenishment projects should pay a greater share of the cost. The question that remains is whether the federal government should be responsible for shoreline protection, or if those duties are better suited to state and local governments or private property owners. As it stands, the federal program is more costly and larger in scope than privately funded replenishment projects, and certainly is not environmentally superior to local efforts.

Critics of the program advocate a strategy of retreat rather than pumping more sand onto the nation's shorelines. They argue that replenishment is costly and wasteful because the sand is simply washed away. The corps and the National Research Council see replenishment as a viable and cost-effective method of protecting the nation's beaches. They contend that the objection to replenishment should not be based entirely on the fact that artificial beaches are temporary solutions. They also point out that retreating from the shorelines is not always cost effective or practical. In some cases, pumping sand is an effective protection measure.

The problem with the current policy debate is that it focuses too much on whether a project's benefits outweigh the costs. Though some efforts have been made to reform cost-sharing requirements, the policy debate focuses little on who is accruing the costs and benefits of replenishment. Under federal beach protection policy, the beneficiaries of replenishment projects absorb a fraction of the cost. Refocusing the debate on this issue helps move the nation toward meaningful reform of our shoreline protection policies. A vital part of this reform should be rethinking beach ownership. If coastal communities and beachfront property owners are to be expected to pay for shoreline protection, they should be able to exclusively enjoy the fruits of their investments.

The majority of beaches are held in common for public use. Yet adjacent communities and landowners are directly affected by the management of these beaches. The best reform may simply be a move toward privatized beaches in conjunction with the elimination of federally funded sand replenishment projects. This would force property owners, communities, and state and local governments to select the most effective, cost-efficient, and environmentally sensitive methods of beach protection. After all, they are their beaches.

REFERENCES

Ackerman, Jennifer. 1997. Islands at the Edge. *National Geographic*, August.

Cordes, Joseph J., and Anthony M. J. Yezer. 1997. Does Subsidized Beach Protection Change Land Use? *Illinois Real Estate Letter* (Winter): 3–6.

———. 1998. In Harm's Way: Does Federal Spending on Beach Enhancement Protection Induce Excessive Development in Coastal Areas? *Land Economics* 74(1): 128–45.

DelRossi Alison, and Robert Inman. 1998. Changing the Price of Pork: The Impact of Local Cost Sharing on Legislators' Demand for Distributive Goods. NBER Working Paper W6440, March. Online: www.nber.org/papers/w6440 (cited: May 15, 2001).

Department of Defense. 2000. *U.S. Army Inspector General Agency Report Investigation*. Case 00-019. Washington, DC, November.

Gaul, Gilbert M., and Anthony R. Wood. 2000. In Defense of Jersey's Shores: For Army Engineers, the Atlantic Is an Indomitable Enemy. *Philadelphia Inquirer*, March 9.

Gerard, David E. 2002. Federal Flood Policies: 150 Years of Environmental Mischief. Chapter 4 in this volume.

Grunwald, Michael. 2000. Engineers of Power: An Agency of Unchecked Clout. *Washington Post* (first of five articles), September 10.

Heinz Center for Science, Economics and the Environment. 2000. Evaluation of Erosion Hazards. April. A report prepared for the Federal Emergency Management Agency. Washington, DC. Online: www.heinzcenter.org. (cited: May 15, 2001).

Houston, James. 1995. Beach Replenishment. *Shore and Beach* 63: 21–24.

Leonard, Lynn, Katharine Dixon, and Orrin Pilkey. 1990. A Comparison of Beach Replenishment on the U.S. Atlantic, Pacific, and Gulf Coasts. *Journal of Coastal Research* (Summer): 127–40.

McCoy, Kevin. 2000. Lazio's Beach Bailout Hits Home. *New York Daily News*, June 6.

Morris, Marya. 1992. The Rising Tide: Rapid Development Threatens U.S. Coast Areas. *EPA Journal* (September/October): 39–41.

National Research Council. 1995. *Beach Nourishment and Protection*. Washington, DC: National Academy Press.

Pilkey, Orrin H., and Tonya Clayton. 1987. Beach Replenishment: The National Solution? *Coastal Zone*, May.

Pilkey, Orrin H., and Katharine L. Dixon. 1996. *The Corps and the Shore*. Washington, DC: Island Press.

Platt, Rutherford, C. Miller, T. Beatley, J. Melville, and B. Mathenia. 1992. *Coastal Erosion: Has Retreat Sounded?* Boulder: Institute of Behavioral Science, University of Colorado.

Pompe, Jeffrey, and James Rinehart. 1994. Estimating the Effects of Wider Beaches on Coastal Housing Prices. *Ocean and Coastal Management* 22: 141–52.

Program for the Study of Developed Shorelines. 2001. The U.S. Beach Nourishment Experience: New England, East Coast, Barrier Islands, Gulf of Mexico, and Great Lakes Shorelines. Online: www.geo.duke.edu/research/psds/psds_tables.htm (cited: March 26, 2001).

Rinehart, James, and Jeffrey Pompe. 1997. Entrepreneurship and Coastal Resource Management. *Independent Review* 1(4): 543–60.

———. 1999. Preserving Beaches. *PERC Reports*, June.

Shallant, Todd. 1994. *Structures in the Stream.* Austin: University of Texas Press.

Shell, Robbie. 1999. Putting a Price Tag on Government. *Wharton Alumni Magazine*, Spring. Online: www.wharton.edu/alum_mag/issues/spring1999/feature_2.html (cited: May 15, 2001).

Stein, Jeff, Peter Moreno, David Conrad, and Steve Ellis. 2000. *Troubled Waters: Congress, the Corps of Engineers, and Wasteful Water Projects.* A report by Taxpayers for Common Sense and the National Wildlife Federation. Washington, DC, March.

Stoddard, Gerard. 2000. NWF Plays Fast and Loose with Facts About the Shore. White paper. Online: fireislandassn.org/loose_and_fast_4_00.htm (cited: May 15, 2001).

Trembanis, Arthur, Orrin Pilkey, and Hugo Valverde. 1999. Comparison of Beach Nourishment along the U.S. Atlantic, Great Lakes, Gulf of Mexico, and New England Shorelines. *Coastal Management* 27: 329–40.

U.S. Army Corps of Engineers. 1984. *Shore Protection Manual*, vols. 1 and 2. Vicksburg, MS: Coastal Engineering Research Center, U.S. Army Corps of Engineers Waterways Experiment Station.

———. 1996. *Final Report: An Analysis of the U.S. Army Corps of Engineers Shore Protection Program.* IWR Report 96-PS-1. Vicksburg, MS.

Index

About the Political Economy Forum Series

PERC is the nation's oldest and largest institute dedicated to original research that brings market principles to resolving environmental problems. PERC, located in Bozeman, Montana, pioneered the approach known as free market environmentalism. It is based on the following tenets: (1) private property rights encourage stewardship of resources; (2) government policies degrade the environment; (3) market incentives spur individuals to conserve resources and protect environmental quality; and (4) polluters should be liable for the harm they cause others. PERC associates have applied the free market environmentalism approach to a variety of issues, including national parks, resource development, water marketing, integrity of fisheries, private provision of wildlife habitat, public land management, and endangered species protection.

PERC's activities encompass three areas: research and policy analysis, outreach, and environmental education. Its associates conduct research, write books and articles, and lecture on the role of markets and property rights in environmental protection. PERC holds conferences and seminars for journalists, congressional staff members, business executives, and scholars. PERC also holds an annual free market environmentalism seminar for college students and sponsors a fellowship program that brings graduate students to its facilities for three months of research and study on an environmental topic. PERC develops and disseminates environmental education materials for classroom use and provides training for kindergarten through twelfth-grade teachers.

In 1989, PERC organized the first of an annual conference series called the Political Economy Forum aimed at applying the principles of political economy to important policy issues. Each forum brings together scholars in economics, political science, law, history, and other disciplines to discuss and refine academic papers that explore new applications of political economy to policy analysis. The forum papers are then edited and published as a book in PERC's Political Economy Forum Series. PERC believes that forums of this type can integrate "cutting edge" research with crucial policy issues.

From time to time, the series includes books not generated from PERC forums. These books are chosen based on their use of the free market environmentalism approach and their superior scholarship. The contributions to *Government vs. Environment* challenge the notion that the government is the preferred option for managing the environment. Environmental studies traditionally focus on real or alleged failures of the private sector to provide adequate environmental protection or amenities. Such problems are usually presumed to be best solved by government controls. Numerous studies conducted at PERC have addressed the issue of how to improve private-sector performance. This book focuses on the performance of government as a environmental steward. The studies here, which cover a range of government activities over time, should cause us to pause carefully before presuming that politically run agencies will necessarily produce superior results for the environment today and tomorrow.

PERC hopes that scholarship such as this will help advance the environmental policy debate and looks forward to future volumes in this series.

About the Contributors

Matthew Brown is a PERC research associate and adjunct professor of economics at Montana State University. He is a graduate of Florida State University, where he received a bachelor's degree in economics. He also holds a master's degree in economics from The American University and did graduate work in statistics at Montana State University. Brown has conducted research on land management and economics for several of the nation's leading public policy research institutes. His research interests include the effect of economic growth on the environment, the use of markets to preserve natural and cultural resources, and international environmentalism. Brown's research has been featured in domestic and international publications including the *New York Times,* the *Apple Daily* of Hong Kong, and *Regulation.*

Holly Lippke Fretwell is a PERC research associate whose current research emphasis is on federal lands management. She holds a bachelor's degree in political science and a master's degree in resource economics from Montana State University. Fretwell has worked with Northwest Economics Associates in Vancouver, Washington, where she examined timber export regulation in the Pacific Northwest, and has consulted for Plum Creek Timber and the Center for International Trade in Forest Products (CINTRAFOR). She has presented papers promoting the use of markets in public land management and has provided expert testimony on the state of U.S. national parks and the future of the Forest Service. Fretwell is the author of numerous articles that have appeared in professional journals as well as the *Wall Street Journal,* the *Journal for Environmental Economics and Management,* the *Journal of Forestry,* and *Consumer's Research.* She is also the author of PERC's public lands reports.

David E. Gerard received a B.A. in American studies and economics from Grinnell College and a master's in economics from the University of Illinois. At Illinois he was selected as an Environmental and Resource Economics Scholar, and also received the Western Coal and Transportation Association Award for the outstanding student in natural resource economics. After receiving his Ph.D. in economics in 1997, Gerard became a PERC research associate and continued work on mining issues while teaching economics courses at Montana State University. He is a postdoctoral fellow in the Department of Engineering and Public Policy at Carnegie Mellon University.

J. Bishop Grewell is a research associate with PERC. He graduated from Stanford University with a double major in economics and public policy. His research areas include paleontology, wildlife, and international environmental policy. Grewell's work with Terry Anderson on the "greening" of foreign policy has appeared in the *Duke Environmental Law and Policy Forum, Chicago Journal of International Law,* and as a *PERC Policy Series.* He is author of a state legislators' guide, *Turning Wildlife into an Asset.* Grewell has written case studies for the Stanford Graduate School of Business and a biweekly column for the *Bozeman Daily Chronicle.* His opinion pieces have appeared in numerous newspapers around the country. Grewell is working on a book for PERC about eco-entrepreneurs in the agricultural sector.

Clay J. Landry is a research associate with PERC in Bozeman, Montana. He is the author of *Saving Our Streams through Water Markets: A Practical Guide,* a handbook for environmentalists, agency officials, ranchers, farmers, and others who want to use water markets to protect fish and other wildlife. He serves as an associate editor for *Water Resource Impact,* a magazine published by the American Water Resources Association, and is finance and regulation editor for *Global Water Intelligence,* an international water industry newsmagazine published in London. With an extensive background in public policy and applied economics research, Landry has advised both state and local governments and water users on water policy throughout the United States, Australia, Brazil, and the United Kingdom. Landry helped start the Montana Water Trust, a nonprofit organization dedicated to purchasing water for environmental needs.

Donald R. Leal is a PERC senior associate. His pioneering work comparing federal and state management of forests and parks demonstrates how management incentives can be changed to achieve greater fiscal accountability and better stewardship of public lands. Leal is coauthor with Terry Anderson of *Free Market Environmentalism* (1991), which received the 1992 Choice Outstanding Academic Book Award and the 1992 Sir Antony Fisher International Memorial Award. The revised edition of the book was published in 2001. *Enviro-Capitalists: Doing Good While Doing Well*, also coauthored with Anderson, received the 1997 Choice Outstanding Academic Book Award. Leal has written numerous articles that have appeared in the *Wall Street Journal, New York Times*, and *Chicago Tribune*, as well as specialized journals. He received his B.S. in mathematics and M.S. in statistics from California State University at Hayward.

Roger E. Meiners is professor of law and economics at the University of Texas at Arlington and a PERC senior associate. He received his Ph.D. in economics from Virginia Tech and his law degree from the University of Miami, where he was an Olin Fellow at the Law and Economics Center. He has taught at Texas A&M University, Emory University, Clemson University, and the University of Miami, and he was director of the Atlanta office of the Federal Trade Commission. Meiners is coeditor with Peter J. Hill of *Who Owns the Environment* (1998), with Andrew Morriss of *The Common Law and the Environment* (2000), and has written other books and articles on law and economics.

Andrew P. Morriss is Galen J. Roush professor of business law and regulation and associate dean for Academic Affairs at Case Western Reserve University in Cleveland, Ohio, and a senior associate at PERC. He received his law and master's of public affairs degrees from the University of Texas at Austin and his Ph.D. in economics from Massachusetts Institute of Technology. Morriss has written extensively on environmental law and policy, western legal history, and empirical law and economics topics.